Who Do You Think You Are?

Do you think that you are someone who:

- is outgoing, sociable?
- tends to find fault with others?
- is a reliable worker?
- remains calm in tense situations?
- values artistic, aesthetic experiences?
- is reserved?
- is considerate and kind to almost everyone?
- can be somewhat careless?
- is relaxed, handles stress well?
- prefers work that is routine and simple?

But how do others see you?

Read on to find out more.

Who Do You Think You Are?

Explore Your Many-Sided Self with

THE BERKELEY PERSONALITY PROFILE

KEITH HARARY, PhD, AND
EILEEN DONAHUE ROBINSON, PhD

A PLUME BOOK

PLUME
Published by Penguin Group
Penguin Group (USA) Inc., 375 Hudson Street, New York, New York 10014, U.S.A.
Penguin Group (Canada), 10 Alcorn Avenue, Toronto, Ontario, Canada M4V 3B2
(a division of Pearson Penguin Canada Inc.)
Penguin Books Ltd., 80 Strand, London WC2R 0RL, England
Penguin Ireland, 25 St. Stephen's Green, Dublin 2, Ireland (a division of Penguin Books Ltd.)
Penguin Group (Australia), 250 Camberwell Road, Camberwell, Victoria 3124, Australia
(a division of Pearson Australia Group Pty. Ltd.)
Penguin Books India Pvt. Ltd., 11 Community Centre, Panchsheel Park, New Delhi – 110 017, India
Penguin Books (NZ), cnr Airborne and Rosedale Roads, Albany, Auckland 1310, New Zealand
(a division of Pearson New Zealand Ltd.)
Penguin Books (South Africa) (Pty.) Ltd., 24 Sturdee Avenue, Rosebank,
Johannesburg 2196, South Africa

Penguin Books Ltd., Registered Offices: 80 Strand, London WC2R 0RL, England

Published by Plume, a member of Penguin Group (USA) Inc. Previously published in a HarperCollins
edition.

First Plume Printing (revised edition), May 2005
10 9 8 7 6 5 4 3 2 1

Copyright © Keith Harary, PhD, and Eileen Donahue Robinson, PhD, 1994, 2005
All rights reserved

Ⓟ REGISTERED TRADEMARK—MARCA REGISTRADA

LIBRARY OF CONGRESS CATALOGING-IN-PUBLICATION DATA

Harary, Keith.
    Who do you think you are? : explore your many-sided self with the Berkeley Personality
Profile / by Keith Harary and Eileen Donahue Robinson.—2nd ed.
        p. cm.
    Includes bibliographical references and index.
    ISBN 0-452-28599-2 (trade pbk.)
    1. Berkeley Personality Profile. I. Donahue Robinson, Eileen. II. Title
BF698.8.B42H37   2005
155.2'83—dc22
                                                                    2004021073

Printed in the United States of America

Contents

Chapter 7

Chapter 8

Chapter 9

Chapter 10

Epilogue

Perforated Sections:
  General Profile
  Instructions and Tests

Acknowledgments

We wish to express our sincere appreciation to the colleagues and friends on whose insights and research we have drawn in developing the Berkeley Personality Profile. We also particularly wish to express our great appreciation to all those who responded to our ongoing National Personality Survey.

A special note of thanks goes to our perceptive friend and valued colleague, Pamela Weintraub, former editor at large of *Omni* magazine, who recognized the need for a scientifically valid, self-administered approach to personality testing and commissioned the original version of the Berkeley Personality Profile. Many thanks also to our insightful friends and colleagues Keith Ferrell and Patrice Adcroft, former editors of *Omni*, where the original version of the Berkeley Personality Profile and National Personality Survey first appeared in September 1991. We would also like to acknowledge Kathy Keeton and Bob Guccione, whose vision of *Omni* helped inspire us to make the art and science of personality testing accessible to the public. Our thanks also to the editors and staff of *Psychology Today* for their support in bringing additional sections of the Berkeley Personality Profile to public attention and helping us to gather additional data for the National Personality Survey.

Special thanks also go to our astute friend and colleague Oliver P. John, of the Institute for Personality and Social Research and the

Department of Psychology at the University of California at Berkeley, whose scientific expertise, wisdom, and good humor all provided essential elements in the development of the Berkeley Personality Profile. We also wish to express our sincere gratitude to the many other experts whose insights and suggestions upon which we have drawn, including communications researcher Diana Reiss, of Columbia University and the Wildlife Conservation Society; and psychologists Auke Tellegen, of the University of Minnesota; Douglas Jackson, of the University of Western Ontario; Ron Holden, of Queen's University; Robert Hogan, of the University of Tulsa; Mike Honaker, of the American Psychological Association; and David Saunders, formerly of Educational Testing Service.

We are also indebted to those researchers on whose work we have drawn heavily in designing the multifaceted perspective of the Berkeley Personality Profile and in interpreting the meaning and applications of the profile results. They include psychologists David M. Buss, at the University of Texas at Austin; Paul T. Costa Jr., of the National Institute on Aging of the National Institutes of Health; Lewis R. Goldberg, of the University of Oregon; Samuel D. Gosling, of the University of Texas at Austin; Robert M. McCrae, of the National Institute on Aging of the National Institutes of Health; Richard W. Robins, of the University of California at Davis; Brent W. Roberts, of the University of Illinois; and Sanjay Srivastava, of the University of California at Berkeley. Many thanks also to Jonathan Goldberg for suggesting that we include the Points for Reflection, and also to Anne Goldberg, Suzie Holmes, Michael Smith, Nancy MacNeal, Barbara Rubin, and David Lutz for their wisdom and insights. Our special thanks as well to John McBarron at the White Eagle for fostering a haven for creative thinking. We have also been inspired by the theories and writings of George Kelly, Abraham Maslow, Michael Polanyi, Hannah Arendt, and Carl Rogers. To all those who have supported and encouraged our efforts but are not mentioned here, please accept our thanks.

Our special appreciation also goes to our wonderful and thoughtful editor, Gary Brozek, not only for breathing life into this new edition but also for his valuable insights on the expanded dimensions of the Berkeley Personality Profile. Special thanks as well to our former editor and still valued friend, Amy Hertz, who did so much to make the first edition possible. We also extend our sincere appreciation to our dedicated literary agent, William Gladstone, and the entire Waterside Productions team, for their superb support and encouragement.

A particular note of appreciation also goes to our spouses and families: to Darlene Moore, for her invaluable suggestions and meticulous assistance with preparing the new edition manuscript and laying out the Berkeley Personality Profile; to Rob Robinson, for his technical insights, patience, and emotional support; and especially to Colin, Andrew, and Graham Robinson for their humor, inspiration, and enthusiasm about their mommy's new project.

We also extend our appreciation to the Institute of Personality and Social Research at the University of California at Berkeley, and the board of directors and board of scientific advisers of the Institute for Advanced Psychology for their role in supporting our research.

Foreword to the New Edition

When the Berkeley Personality Profile made its debut as a cover story in *Omni* magazine more than a decade ago, a million copies of that record-breaking issue disappeared off the shelves virtually overnight at news-stands across the country. Since then, *Omni* magazine itself has disappeared, living on for a time as an award-winning Internet edition, and now continuing only as a special memory in the minds of her readers, editors, contributors, and collectors who came to love the magazine for its cutting-edge explorations of all areas of science. The Berkeley Personality Profile itself has flourished, later appearing in a series of cover articles in *Psychology Today,* and then as the original edition of this book, which reached hundreds of thousands of readers. Over the years, we have heard from many thousands of our readers, who have been exceptionally generous in sharing with us the results of their individual explorations, using the Berkeley Personality Profile as their guide. Their encouragement and enthusiasm have inspired us to complete this expanded and revised edition, which adds important new dimensions to that process.

The science of personality research has also continued to evolve. The Big Five Model of Personality, upon which the Berkeley Personality Profile is based, has established itself as the premier theoretical model for scientific research in the field. It is also being widely applied in other disciplines, including clinical psychology, human factors engineering, sociology, anthropology, business, economics, and political science. The Big Five Inventory, which serves as the scientific foundation for the Berkeley Personality Profile, has been validated in a variety of languages with millions of research subjects all over the world, drawing on decades of technical investigation carried out at leading universities—including at the University of California at Berkeley, where Oliver P. John and Eileen Donahue Robinson first developed it years ago. Through continuing advances in Internet-based methods, the number of participants who have contributed to this research has swelled into the millions.

At universities around the world, more and more research continues to be conducted concerning the complexities of personality structure and the multifaceted nature of the self, using the framework of the Big Five personality dimensions. In our own continuing effort to expand and refine the Berkeley Personality Profile, we have drawn upon ongoing research in personality stability and change over time, first impressions, behavior genetics, infant temperament/early-appearing personality styles, and studies of the way personality emerges early in life.

This revised and expanded edition of *Who Do You Think You Are?* includes new sections on your Past Self-Image and Future Self-Image, which will give you a chance to think about the ways in which your personality has changed over the course of your life, and how it may continue to change in years to come. It also includes a new section on your Alter Ego, which we hope will stimulate your imagination as you consider the roads not traveled—the person that you could have been if you had followed a different path, and how your Alter Ego may still sometimes emerge in ways that might surprise you. We hope you will continue to find the Berkeley Personality Profile to be a useful tool in your own ongoing process of self-discovery.

—Keith Harary and Eileen Donahue Robinson,
Spring 2004

Introduction

What am I really like? How well do I know myself? How do others see me? These are basic questions about human nature that people have asked themselves for thousands of years. The oracle at Delphi admonished the ancient Greeks to "Know thyself." The tenet "The unexamined life is not worth living" is typically attributed to Socrates, the ancient Greek philosopher. In our century, Sigmund Freud argued that self-insight was necessary to achieve a happier, healthier, less neurotic life, and many psychotherapists today agree: gaining a better understanding of ourselves is the first step toward self-improvement.

But how can we achieve this better sense of self, a comprehensive view of who we are? This enlightening book traces a path to improving our self-understanding. It presents a powerful and multifaceted approach to self-knowledge, an approach based on extensive research in the scientific field of study known as *personality psychology*.

Many intellectual traditions endeavor to answer questions about human nature, including literature, philosophy, history, and sociology. However, personality psychology is distinguished from these other fields because it combines empirical methods of inquiry with an approach that takes the individual person as the basic unit of analysis. The field dates back to the 1930s, when psychologist Gordon Allport published the first textbook on the subject, titled *Personality: A*

Psychological Interpretation. The young field quickly differentiated itself from other disciplines within academic psychology. Clinical and counseling psychologists continued to focus on "abnormal" behavior, deviant character, and maladjustment. Personality psychology, in contrast, studied healthy, well-functioning individuals and focused on issues such as creativity and achievement in both the personal and professional realms.

Two significant achievements of the still-young field of personality psychology have particular relevance to the issue of self-insight. One is the discovery and development of the *Five Factor Model*, which addresses one of the most fundamental problems in the field: the search for a scientifically compelling taxonomy of personality traits—that is, the task of identifying a comprehensive yet finite set of attributes or dimensions by which personality can be described. The Five Factor Model provides an initial solution to this problem by defining five basic dimensions that people use to describe themselves and others in many different cultures and languages.

The other major breakthrough is the description and specification of what has become known as the *multifaceted self-concept*. Philosophers and psychologists have long realized that personality is not fixed; how people see themselves depends on the situation they are in, the person they are interacting with, their fears, ideals, and personal goals. Research over the past fifteen years has led to the development of techniques to describe and measure these different self-perspectives, and now these methods are available to help individuals integrate their inner experience and the outer expression of their personality.

These two fundamental findings—that there are five basic personality dimensions and that there are innumerable possible self-perspectives—have provided the foundation of the Berkeley Personality Profile.

Before the development of this test, the Five Factor Model and the theory of the multifaceted self were applied only in research and some therapeutic contexts. In fact, although the procedures in this book have been used widely in contemporary research, this is the first time they are being made available for self-exploration and self-understanding. In our research at Berkeley, for example, we have conducted several studies in which individuals describe their own personality and behavior. We then compare their self-descriptions with the way they are described by their friends, coworkers, and other independent observers. In these studies, however, individual research participants are not provided with personal feedback; the findings are analyzed and presented only at the level of group averages.

The need to make these ideas and procedures available to interested individuals in the general public was apparent, and it was Keith Harary and Eileen Donahue who took on this important mission. They have succeeded in bringing together a vast amount of past and current research on personality structure and self-concept, research published in articles scattered across a wide range of scientific journals. They have integrated the separate literatures on the Five Factor Model and the multifaceted self, and then applied the resulting system to a wide range of important and personally relevant contexts in which we experience and manifest our personalities.

At the heart of this book is what the authors term the *reflective approach* to personality testing. More than anyone else, they realize that personality is not one thing, but rather must be understood from multiple perspectives. The distinctions they suggest may seem subtle, but they are crucial to a thorough understanding of the individual: the inner self that we experience privately and the outer self that we show to others; changes in the self we strive for and those we dread; the way we see ourselves as spouses and lovers, as friends, as workers, and in our relationships with our parents and children; the various ways we come across to others, to our partners, family members, and coworkers, and the impressions they form about us; and how all these perspectives blend to form the unique individual that each of us is.

In the Berkeley Personality Profile, the reflective approach holds up a multifaceted mirror to allow you to examine yourself from all these different perspectives. The reflective approach also empowers you as the individual who is both the source and the key to self-understanding. You can do all the testing, scoring, and interpretation by yourself. There are no trick questions, and there is no need to send away your responses in order to have them interpreted. The do-it-yourself approach taken here is completely under your personal control. You alone select the relevant others from whom to obtain the "outsiders'" personality perspectives that are an essential component of the reflective approach.

All the personality impressions, scoring, and interpretations are explicitly quantitative. Yet, the authors have not gone overboard and filled the book with cold and impersonal statistics. For most of the profiles, your own responses provide the framework for comparison and interpretation. The authors clearly and concisely help you interpret what the scores, profiles, and differences mean. The Interpretation Guides and Points for Reflection sections provide further empowerment to the self-reflecting individual. Thus the emphasis throughout the book is not on one's unchanging, seemingly fixed personality structure or personality type. Rather, the focus is on the individual's potential, on the range of possible behavior and experience, on the growing and evolving personality as it is lived and expressed throughout the life course.

Harary and Donahue provide you with the itinerary and route maps to embark on a journey through the many fascinating and challenging contexts of your personality. The journey begins with an exploration of the contrast between the inner self as you experience it and the outer self as you express it in your overt behavior. Next, the authors guide you toward an examination of your ideal self and feared self—the way you wish you were and the way you hope you'll never become. Further down the road, they provide an opportunity for you to examine yourself in the most important roles you play in everyday life and to consider the impressions that others who know you in these different roles have formed of you.

Rather than provide ready-made answers, the reflective approach taken in this book helps you ask the right questions—what you should think about and explore to continue to increase your self-insight, thereby making your life happier, more fulfilling, and perhaps less neurotic. Those who have traveled through this book and tried out the many fascinating exercises it contains can truly say that they have followed the ancient mandate of the oracle at Delphi: They have come to know themselves in a way few others ever will.

—*Oliver P. John*
Associate Professor of Psychology
University of California at Berkeley
February 1994

Perspectives on Your Personality

Your personality is the essence of who you are and how you appear to other people. It lends continuity to your identity over time, tying together your early childhood and ongoing life experiences, your unique approach to the people and events around you, and your aspirations and apprehensions about how you may develop in the future. It affects, and is affected by, how others perceive and respond to you. It is reflected in the things you say, the way you feel, and the way you choose to lead your life. It is also reflected in the way others perceive and respond to you, as well as in your personal beliefs, goals and expectations, hopes and fears, and even the way you perceive other people and interpret their behavior. The more you understand about your personality, the better you can understand your actions, your feelings, and your relationships.

In recent years, the science of personality psychology has taken a major leap forward. The reason: competing lines of research at leading universities worldwide are finally converging. After over sixty years of extensive scientific inquiry into diverse aspects of personality—such as personality development, the relationship between culture and personality, and the effects of personality on life experiences—researchers are finally reaching a consensus about the basic psychological ingredients that make us who we are.

In large-scale scientific investigations of personality, five basic dimensions, nicknamed "the Big Five," consistently emerge. The Big Five reflect broad patterns in the way individual personality styles differ with respect to expressiveness and extraversion, interpersonal warmth, approach toward work and other responsibilities, degree of emotional intensity, and engagement in creative and intellectual pursuits. In spite of some technical disagreements about the precise interpretation of some of these dimensions, the significance of the Big Five is now widely recognized among a growing circle of researchers. Big Five proponents contend that this unifying model of personality allows them to organize decades of research discoveries, concerning hundreds of different personality traits, within a single, meaningful, broad-based framework.

Extensive research has also confirmed that the way in which you see yourself, both overall and in specific social settings, has crucial implications for your long-term personal development and mental health. The perceptions others hold of you are equally important because they directly affect the opportunities you are given to develop your skills and talents, to interact with others in a positive environment, and to develop a basic sense of identity, effectiveness, and self-worth. Knowing how others perceive you can also empower you to interact with them more effectively, and even allow you to correct any mistaken impressions they may have of you. Developing the ability to "see yourself as others see you," in other words, can dramatically influence your psychological well-being.

In the spirit of assisting you to develop this vital understanding, we present the Berkeley Personality Profile, a powerful new approach to self-discovery drawn from the latest research in personality assessment. Unlike many other well-known personality tests that can only be administered and interpreted by professional psychologists, the Berkeley Personality Profile is designed to be easily self-administered by anyone. Yet its original approach goes a step beyond such popular self-administered tests as the Lüscher Color Test and the Enneagram by providing a scientifically valid approach to personality assessment that has been tested and proven in cutting-edge research.

Based on extensive scientific investigations conducted at the University of California at Berkeley and other leading universities and institutions, the Berkeley Personality Profile is an easy-to-follow psychological map that will help you chart the unmarked roads of your public and private self. It allows you to use the Big Five model as a tool for understanding your personality in innovative ways that focus not only on how you view yourself but also on how you are viewed by others. We like to call this new approach *reflective* because it relies not on interpretation by a professional test analyzer but on your own insights and those of your friends, loved ones, and associates.

Like a mirror, the Berkeley Personality Profile will help you see yourself as others see you, comparing your perceptions of your own behavior with the ways in which you are perceived by those in your immediate world. It will also give you valuable insights into the relationship between your actual self-image and your notions of the person you would ideally like to be, as well as the person you most fear becoming. In addition, the Berkeley Personality Profile will help you explore the connection between your private view of yourself and the ways in which you experience and project your personality in a variety of social settings. In this new and expanded edition, the Berkeley Personality Profile will also give you the chance to explore your past and your future self-image and how these distant perspectives on your personality affect the way you see yourself today. It will also take you deep into your alter ego to explore the kind of person that you might have been, or could become, if you allowed certain submerged dimensions of your personality to rise up to the surface. Finally, this innovative test will help you explore your relationship with an especially important person in your life—a spouse, lover, or special friend—to examine how your mutual perceptions affect this significant relationship.

Personality Profiles vs. Personality Types

What the Berkeley Personality Profile won't do, however, is box you into an unrealistic category or assign you to a personality *type*. Several type-casting approaches to personality, such as the Enneagram and the Myers-Briggs Type Indicator, or MBTI, have become so fashionable that some observers have dubbed these approaches "the new astrology." Just as the zodiac assigns you to one of twelve astrological signs on the basis of your birthday, the MBTI assigns you to one of sixteen personality type categories based on your answers to a questionnaire. In a similar fashion, the Enneagram categorizes you as one of only nine possible types. Once they have categorized you, such approaches assume that you are like other people of the same type in many ways, such as your interests and aptitude for particular careers and basic way of relating to other people.

Critics contend, however, that such type-oriented approaches to personality are simplistic and often inaccurate, in the end perhaps diminishing our vision of who we are. Almost any system that divides people into types can seem to hold a certain wisdom—if only because we cannot help but take a certain comfort in believing that the vast complexities of human nature can be summarized in such a simplistic fashion.

More and more psychologists are coming to believe that normal human behavior transcends any notion of label or type and is far more complex and flexible than type-oriented models suggest. In fact, personality theorist Carl Jung, from whose work the MBTI types were derived, believed that assigning individual people to type categories was a regrettable miscarriage of his theory, constituting no more than a "childish parlor game."[1]

Contemporary personality assessment and research models the elements of human nature in a more flexible and realistic way. This is why each section of the Berkeley Personality Profile provides you with separate scores on the Big Five dimensions of personality—five distinct pieces of information that are uniquely descriptive of your personality as seen from a particular perspective. We'll show you how to transfer your scores from each section of the test to a special *personality profile* that synthesizes all the information into a single visual representation without sacrificing any of the richness or complexity inherent in each score. By placing the Big Five dimensions side by side, the profile allows you to compare your score on Expressive Style with your scores on Interpersonal Style, Work Style, Emotional Style, and Intellectual Style, all at a glance.

How does this approach avoid the pitfalls of personality typecasting? To answer that question for yourself, consider what would happen if you tried to typecast each of the fifty United States as being either an eastern or western state, relative to the Mississippi River. Although Illinois and Massachusetts are both east of the Mississippi, Illinois and Missouri actually share more in common because both are midwestern states—that is, because they both fall somewhere near the middle of the East–West continuum that stretches from the Atlantic seaboard to the Pacific Coast. A state isn't simply eastern or western, it can fall anywhere in between.

Personality profiles work in the same fashion. For any particular dimension, such as the Expressive Style dimension, which stretches from extreme introversion at one end to extreme extraversion at the other, a personality profile would describe your score in degrees, along a continuum, rather than as an absolute. You're not simply introverted *or* extraverted—you exhibit a certain degree of both introverted and extraverted behavior. The average degree or level of introversion or extraversion that you express is every bit as important as whether you fall closer to the introversion or the extraversion side of the scale.

This dimensional approach toward personality is the one most commonly used by personality researchers, and the approach used in the major personality inventories used by professional psychologists, including the California Psychological Inventory (CPI), the Multidimensional Personality Questionnaire (MPQ), the NEO Personality Inventory (NEO-PI), and others. You might find it a little more complex than the typecasting models with which you may be familiar, but we think you'll also find that it provides a much more accurate and in-depth picture of who you really are.

The History of the Berkeley Personality Profile

In late 1989, the editors of *Omni* magazine contacted Keith Harary to see if an original personality test could be developed that would be scientifically valid, straightforward enough to be taken and scored by anyone, and flexible enough so that people could interpret their own scores within the context of their individual lives. As Dr. Harary began to scrutinize the well-respected personality tests available in the field, he realized that many paper-and-pencil tests provide results that are standardized and statistically valid, but most stop short of allowing the people taking the test to become active participants in the process of evaluating the meaning of their own results in the dynamic context of their daily lives. This realization led Dr. Harary to develop the "reflective" approach to personality assessment, which uses a simple, statistically reliable paper-and-pencil format to bring together multiple perspectives on an individual's life, allowing the test taker to "see himself as others see him."

It also led him to the University of California at Berkeley, where he met and collaborated with personality psychologists Eileen Donahue Robinson and Oliver P. John, at the university's Institute of Personality and Social Research. Their close collaboration, combining Dr. Harary's reflective approach and basic test format with a scientifically validated personality test that Dr. John and Dr. Robinson had developed over several years of intensive empirical research, led to the development of the Berkeley Personality Profile. Dr. Harary and his editors decided to call the test the Berkeley Personality Profile from its first appearance in print because the research contribution that Dr. John and Dr. Robinson made was so significant that it helped transform the original concept into a validated scientific instrument.

The original portion of the Berkeley Personality Profile appeared in a full-cover feature article by Dr. Harary in *Omni* magazine.[2] The readership response was so dramatic that one million copies of that record-breaking issue sold out at newsstands all over the country virtually overnight. Later sections of the Berkeley Personality Profile also appeared in articles written by Dr. Robinson and Dr. Harary in a three-part series published by *Psychology Today*.[3] The expanded edition of the Berkeley Personality Profile that appears in this book, however, goes far beyond those earlier articles. Each self-perspective is treated here in considerably more depth and detail than ever before, by providing more extensive interpretations as well as new, self-focused questions specifically pinpointed to help you explore how your personality affects, and is affected by, your relationships, your daily activities, the significant events in your life, and even your distinctive ways of thinking about yourself. In this new and revised edition, we have expanded the Berkeley Personality Profile even further, adding additional perspectives on your personality that will provide exciting new insights into the way you see yourself and your relationships with those around you.

The empirical cornerstone of the Berkeley Personality Profile is the test upon which it is built, called the Big Five Inventory, or BFI. The thirty-five questions you'll be using in the test were selected from the BFI, a research-oriented instrument constructed by Oliver P. John and Eileen Donahue Robinson, at the University of California at Berkeley, as a quick but comprehensive way of measuring the Big Five factors of personality. The BFI was developed using empirical techniques like those used to develop the NEO-PI and the MPQ.

Professor John and his team at Berkeley began with trait adjectives from the Adjective Check List, or ACL, a test developed by psychologist Harrison Gough and widely used in research since 1949. They carefully selected the adjectives that clearly defined the Big Five dimensions, expressive style, interpersonal style, work style, emotional style, and intellectual style, based on statistical analyses of the responses of large samples of people who had taken the ACL over the years. Next, they converted the trait adjectives to short questions that are more specific and easier to respond to than the adjectives alone. They then administered the new test questions to thousands of additional research participants from all over the country, many of whom also took other tests measuring the Big Five. Based on statistical analyses of the participants' responses, the research team refined the set of test questions, over and over again, until they finally identified those that provide optimal measurement of the Big Five personality dimensions.[4]

We selected the BFI as the foundation for the Berkeley Personality Profile for its uniqueness both in size and in simplicity. Although it reliably and validly measures all five distinct dimensions of personality, its shortened version is a trim thirty-five questions in length, compared to the more than two hundred fifty items that appear on other personality inventories. The questions we selected for the BFI were specifically designed so that people could answer them relatively quickly and easily. Most importantly, the test was designed so that it would be easy for almost anyone to take and score without any special training.

The Berkeley Personality Profile builds upon the BFI in a way that takes advantage of its empirical strengths and yet gives it a flexibility never before seen in a self-administered, empirically oriented personality test. It does so by providing a detailed portrait of your personality that covers the Big Five dimensions in a wide variety of specific social settings, and from many different perspectives, rather than providing only a generalized impression of your personality, as most personality inventories do. And, while you will have the opportunity to compare your personality to the normative information collected from our research samples, this is not the only standard of comparison open to you. In fact, we believe you will find that the unique reflective approach taken by the Berkeley Personality Profile offers you a standard of comparison that is far more personally relevant than any normative sample available.

The reflective approach turns to those within your immediate social and cultural milieu as a standard for comparison; in effect, it self-adjusts for the unique perspective of your particular social group. For example, the relative standard for aggressiveness among downtown Manhattan residents, who must respond assertively to the demands of their fast-paced environment, is likely to be different from the standard among rural residents living along the Columbia River Gorge outside Portland, Oregon. Using the reflective approach of the Berkeley Personality Profile, the relative aggressiveness of your Interpersonal Style will be rated by people from your own social, environmental, and cultural background. Consequently, only if your level of aggressiveness is markedly greater than the norm for your environment are you likely to be considered unusually aggressive within the context of this test. The same holds true for every other personality trait measured by the Berkeley Personality Profile.

In addition, regardless of the standards of the broader milieu within which we find ourselves, most of us also express different sides of our personalities to varying degrees with different people. Whether we live in Boston or Honolulu, or identify closely with particular ethnic, age-related, occupational, or other groups, we are likely to express different aspects of our personalities at work, at home, with our friends, with our acquaintances, and with our loved ones. By examining the different ways in which you express your personality in a variety of circumstances, the Berkeley Personality Profile provides an opportunity for you to explore the relevance of any shifting expressions of your personality that may emerge in one situation but not in another, and for any temporary personality ups and downs that you, as the individual interpreting the test, will be able to recognize and account for in your own life.

The Berkeley Personality Profile offers a unique interpersonal measure of your personality, basing its assessment on real-world judgments of your behavior by those who know you well and interact with you on a regular basis. As you interpret your results, you may come to better understand not only who you are but also the nature of your personal relationships in all their diverse forms.

What's So Big About the Big Five?

As someone who has spent a lifetime with other people, you probably already know a lot about personality. You know that people differ from each other in many important ways, and that some characteristics are especially well suited for those in certain life situations. A good spouse, for example, needs to be caring and communicative, while an effective manager needs to be decisive, and a successful research scientist needs both curiosity and patience. This kind of knowledge, gained through practical experience rather than formal learning, is called "implicit knowledge." Research on the way people use traits to think about and describe themselves and others suggests that you probably already have some implicit knowledge of the Big Five.

Consider, for example, the personality traits *talkative*, *energetic*, and *sociable*. These three traits obviously have quite different meanings. Nevertheless, those who see themselves, and are seen by others, as being talkative are usually *also* seen as being energetic and sociable. Each trait is distinctive, but the three characteristics often go together. In the last few decades, research teams all over the world have been studying how people from all walks of life use such traits to describe their own and others' personalities. When they analyzed the results, they made a startling discovery. Even though different researchers started with completely different sets of traits, and studied people from diverse cultural, ethnic, educational, and socioeconomic backgrounds, the same five basic dimensions of personality kept emerging in comprehensive studies of personality. For perhaps the first time in the history of the field, personality psychologists found something a majority could agree upon: most of the traits that people use to describe personality can be drawn together into five broad dimensions. Because each dimension represents a thread of shared meaning that ties together a very large number of more specific traits, they are often called the Big Five personality dimensions.

Each of the Big Five dimensions actually captures an entire continuum of individual differences, such that the behavior characteristic of people at one end of the dimension is the opposite of the behavior of those at the other extreme. The first of the Big Five dimensions, for example, refers to a person's *Expressive Style*, which may range from being quiet, restrained, and introverted to being energetic, enthusiastic, and extraverted—or anywhere in between. The second dimension, *Interpersonal Style*, ranges from being aloof, inconsiderate, or even cruel at one extreme to being warm, generous, and even self-sacrificing at the other. The third dimension, *Work Style*, concerns the extent to which an individual focuses on tasks and meets responsibilities, ranging from preferring to procrastinate and take it easy to working hard with intense dedication to commitments. The fourth dimension, *Emotional Style*, concerns an individual's temperament and typical way of dealing with stress, ranging from being calm, relaxed, and even-tempered to being moody and emotionally intense. Finally, *Intellectual Style* refers to the extent to which a person favors familiar and traditional ideas and experiences or prefers to question the norm, taking an original, creative, or analytic approach toward life. Some researchers use the roman numerals I to V to label the Big Five, while others prefer the names Extraversion (or Surgency), Agreeableness, Conscientiousness (or Will to Achieve), Neuroticism (or its opposite end, Emotional Stability), and Openness (or Culture). Still others use the initials E, A, C, N, and O. No matter which labels are used, however, there is widespread agreement about the general meaning of each of the Big Five personality dimensions and the broad cluster of personality traits that falls within each dimension. We chose the terminology that we use in the Berkeley Personality Profile because it clearly expresses the full continuum of individual differences on each dimension, while other systems describe only one end of each dimension—although the full range of individual differences is always implied by other naming systems as well. For convenience, we have provided a quick Big Five reference table in the back of the colored, perforated scorecard section of the book.

Subsequent research has shown that the Big Five extend well beyond the traits that people use to describe themselves in casual conversation. Researchers found the same five dimensions in psychologists' most sophisticated tests, many of which were designed to measure complex theoretical constructs far removed from everyday ideas about personality. Even more striking, crosscultural research has confirmed the existence of the same five dimensions among speakers of numerous foreign languages, including German, Dutch, Spanish, Russian, Hebrew, Japanese, Korean, Chinese, and Tagalog.

In the last several years, in fact, more and more research findings point to the central role that the Big Five personality dimensions play in directing the course of an individual's life. Babies are born with distinctly different temperaments, in large measure because of the genes they inherit from their parents. From the first few days of life, visible signs of a baby's unique Expressive Style, Interpersonal Style, and Emotional Style can already be easily observed. Even though Work Style and Intellectual Style cannot be observed in a baby's behavior until he or she is a little older, the raw genetic material from which these characteristics develop is already in place, as shown by studies comparing the personalities of siblings, particularly twins, and other family members. Identical twins, for example, who are genetically identical in every way, develop strikingly similar Big Five personality characteristics even when they grow up in radically different family environments, separated by adoption at birth.

Of course, a newborn's personality is hardly carved in stone. Even identical twins' personalities, though similar, nevertheless differ in important ways. This is because nutritional factors, the type and amount of intellectual stimulation that is made available at crucial times, the degree of security experienced in the family environment, and other personal experiences all can influence development with respect to the Big Five.

Personality may have an even bigger impact upon life experience, however, than life experience has upon personality. Dominant traits that are observable early in life have a powerful influence on the way that a child experiences his or her personal and interpersonal world. For example, we know a young boy who was born with very strong predispositions toward both Emotional Style and Expressive Style. Colin's volatile Emotional Style was first evidenced by frequent bouts of uncontrollable screaming that began on the day he was born. Now five years old, he has come to understand his hardwired negative emotions and works very hard to keep them from interfering with his daily activities. Fortunately, Colin's enthusiastic and gregarious Expressive Style provides a decided advantage. From earliest infancy, he was animated, outgoing, and always in motion. He discovered he could *run* on the same day he first learned to walk, and never looked back. Every evening, when his parents collapsed on the sofa after dinner, the tireless toddler took the spotlight in what came to be called the "Colin Variety Hour," prancing and singing and showing off in every conceivable way. As he grew, he found more sophisticated ways of burning off energy and engaging others, although he occasionally reprised his early antics to entertain his baby brother, Graham (whose fun-loving Expressive Style and amiable Interpersonal Style make him the perfect audience). Whereas Colin's intense negative emotions might otherwise be turned outward, driving him away from other people and disrupting his relationships, Colin's dynamic Expressive Style drives him irresistibly *toward* others and fuels his enthusiastic approach toward life.

Research shows that people's personality characteristics with respect to the Big Five dimensions powerfully influence the way they behave and the choices they make. In this way, personality has wide-ranging effects on health and exercise habits, relationships, and career paths.

Given this converging evidence for the Big Five, many leading personality researchers have now adopted the *Five-Factor Model* of personality, which states that the Big Five dimensions that people notice and describe in their everyday observations coincide with the five basic dimensions along which human personalities really do differ. In effect, the Five-Factor Model suggests that everyday people's implicit knowledge about personality as expressed in their familiar language is roughly on target—or at least that their practical insights into human behavior prime them to notice the personality characteristics that matter in real life.[5] This is why we think you'll find it both fascinating and natural to explore your own personality in relation to the Big Five in the Berkeley Personality Profile.

The Big Five in the Context of Your Life: Personality, Lifestyle, and Health

Because the five dimensions measured by the Berkeley Personality Profile draw on the extensive body of research associated with the Five-Factor Model of personality, knowing your scores on the five personality styles can actually help you understand and control recurrent patterns in your own life experience. Your personality might be leading you repeatedly to make the same types of lifestyle choices, seek out the same types of personal relationships, drift into the same types of work situations, and experience the same types of worries, delights, or frustrations.

Shyness, for example, is one component of Expressive Style that has been shown to have important effects on people's life trajectories. Those who are shy often find that the nervousness they feel in social situations holds them back, and makes social risk taking an inordinate challenge. In one study, boys who were identified as being very shy when they were children were compared to boys who were not shy—and both groups were followed up many years later to observe the long-term effects of shyness. Those who had been shy as children still seemed reluctant to try out new social roles as adults. As a result, they were a full three to four years older than the nonshy comparison group by the time they married, had children, and began stable, long-term careers. Perhaps because of this delay, or perhaps because of the difficulty they experienced in asserting themselves, these men also tended, on the average, to achieve less success in their careers compared to the achievements of the nonshy comparison group.

A parallel study of women who were identified as shy or nonshy as children uncovered a different pattern. Many of the women in this particular study followed what was then considered to be a "traditional" female role. They married, raised children, and worked little if at all outside the home. Within the family-centered context of their lives, shyness created no particular problem because it did not interfere with their ability to interact intimately, affectionately, and effectively with their friends and family, around whom they did not feel shy.[6]

What are the consequences of having an Expressive Style that is decidedly not shy? Your Expressive Style not only affects the decisions you make in your life, such as whether or not to become involved in an unfamiliar social situation, but also the smallest details of what you think and do when you are interacting with other people. In one study of conversational styles, for example, it became apparent that those on the extraverted, or outgoing, side of the Expressive Style dimension actively try to establish common ground between themselves and the person to whom they are talking, while those on the opposite, or more introverted, side of the Expressive Style dimension tend to act more like an impartial interviewer, asking questions and encouraging the other person to talk, but revealing relatively little about themselves.[7]

Each of the other Big Five personality dimensions influences the course of people's lives in similar ways. Your motivation for achievement, which is one component of Work Style, was probably a central factor in the type of occupation you chose. One study, for example, compared college students with high and low levels of achievement, and followed up on them fourteen years later, at midcareer, to evaluate the types of jobs they held. Those who had high achievement motivation in college were, at midcareer, about four times as likely to be holding down jobs that required initiating actions and being responsible for decisions, compared to those who had low achievement motivation in college.[8]

Emotional Style has been widely associated with health-related problems and symptoms. People with intense emotional styles, particularly those who experience a great deal of tension and anxiety, report more frequent and severe physical symptoms, such as colds, flus, and aches and pains. This might be a direct result of the intense negative emotions they experience on a day-to-day basis. Strong negative emotions such as fear, anxiety, and anger are associated with strong physiological responses in the body—they can make your heart race, make you breathe harder, perspire more, and tense your muscles. This might, in turn, make you feel achy, jittery, and unable to sleep. Having an intense Emotional Style can sometimes lead to sharp, angina-like chest pains, even among those whose hearts are perfectly healthy. Fortunately, these highly emotional individuals are *not* more prone to serious or life-threatening illnesses than most other people; they live just as long, on the average, as everyone else. They do, however, spend much more time worrying about their health than most other people do.

On the other hand, research does suggest that those with an overtly hostile, antagonistic Interpersonal Style are somewhat more likely to develop heart disease than those with a more pleasant manner. Ironically, while an intensely negative Emotional Style may make you feel sick, having an outwardly hostile Interpersonal Style may be the real killer.[9]

Intellectual Style, which reflects the extent to which you are geared toward new experiences and ideas, is likely to be related to how you structure your time and what you do in the course of a day. When asked to list spontaneously "what they're up to" at any given time, people with a highly open Intellectual Style report being engaged in more so-called personal projects at a time. They are also more likely to say that their projects are consistent with their personal values, and are more likely to be enjoying their projects, compared to those with more narrowly focused or conventional Intellectual Styles.[10]

The Big Five personality dimensions, and the characteristics related to those dimensions, are now being used so widely in personality research that we could not begin to summarize in this book all the previous research linking the Big Five to important life consequences. Instead, we encourage you to begin exploring the role that the Big Five personality dimensions play in your own life. The test materials and profile sheets in the chapters that follow will help you to understand the interplay of all five personality dimensions from several perspectives—your hidden Inner Self, the Outer Self you show to others, the Ideal Self you are striving to become, the Feared Self you may actively be working to avoid, the Partner Self you reveal to your romantic partner or best friend, and the Reflected Self you show to your professional colleagues, your family, and your other friends. Additional perspectives include your image of your Past Self as you were at one or more significant points in your life, and your image of your Future Self as you expect to become at some significant points yet to come. You'll also have a special opportunity to explore the secrets of your Alter Ego, and the ways in which even the unexplored dimensions of your personality can still exert their influence.

Along the way, we'll tell you about our own research findings that link people's scores on the various parts of the Berkeley Personality Profile to significant situations and relationships in their lives. At the end of each chapter, we will also provide a series of specially focused Points for Reflection that will help you explore the ways in which your own scores on the Big Five dimensions are related to your personal actions, your life experiences, and your intimate relationships. We'll begin this process of self-discovery by exploring the secrets of your innermost self.

Notes

1. For further information, see C. G. Jung, *Psychological Types* (Princeton, NJ: Princeton University Press, 1971), xiv.

2. For further information, see K. Harary, "The *Omni*-Berkeley Personality Profile," *Omni* (September 1991): 48–59.

3. For further information, see K. Harary and E. Donahue, "The PT/Berkeley Personality Profile, Part 1: Exploring Your Possible Selves," *Psychology Today* (May/June 1992): 68–76; E. Donahue and K. Harary, "The PT/Berkeley Personality Profile, Part 2: Social Selves," *Psychology Today* (July/August 1992): 68–76; E. Donahue and K. Harary, "The PT/Berkeley Personality Profile, Part 3: Transpersonal Selves," *Psychology Today* (September/October 1992): 70–75.

4. As a result of ongoing research, the set of test questions has been further refined and slightly revised since the original version of the Berkeley Personality Profile first appeared. The longer version of the BFI is recommended for research purposes. For details on the development of the test, see the technical report by O. P. John and E. M. Donahue, *The Big Five Inventory, Technical Report of the 44-Item Version* (Berkeley: Institute of Personality and Social Research, University of California, 1994).

5. For an overview, see R. R. McCrae and O. P. John, "An Introduction to the Five-Factor Model and Its Applications," *Journal of Personality* 60 (1992): 175–219.

6. For details, see A. Caspi, G. H. Elder Jr., and D. J. Bem, "Moving away from the World: Life-Course Patterns of Shy Children," *Developmental Psychology* 24

(1988): 824–31; and A. Caspi, D. J. Bem, and G. H. Elder Jr., "Continuities and Consequences of Interactional Styles Across the Life Course," *Journal of Personality* 57 (1989): 375–406.

7. For details, see A. Thorne, "The Press of Personality: A Study of Conversations Between Introverts and Extraverts," *Journal of Personality and Social Psychology* 53 (1987): 718–26.

8. For details, see D. C. McClelland, "N Achievement and Entrepreneurship: A Longitudinal Study," *Journal of Personality and Social Psychology* 1 (1965): 389–92.

9. For a review of research on the Big Five and health psychology, see T. W. Smith and P. G. Williams, "Personality and Health: Advantages and Limitations of the Five-Factor Model," *Journal of Personality* 60 (1992): 395–424.

10. For details, see B. R. Little, L. Lecci, and B. Watkinson, "Personality and Personal Projects: Linking Big Five and PAC Units of Analysis," *Journal of Personality* 60 (1992): 501–25.

Your Private Self and Public Image

Novelists, philosophers, and psychologists have often compared the intricate layers of the human personality to an onion. The outermost layer, your *Outer Self*, is the part of your personality that most people see. As you peel away the outer layer, you find the more intimate aspects of your personality that may be known exclusively by your partner, family members, and a few close friends. Finally, you reach the innermost core of your personality, your *Inner Self*, which you alone can know completely. While others can easily observe your outward behavior, and listen to how you publicly explain yourself, only you may be truly aware of your innermost feelings, fears, aspirations, and motives, including those that are only partially conscious. The sole person with direct access to your Inner Self is you, because only you know what it *feels like* to be you.

All of us form personal beliefs about ourselves, and beliefs about the way we come across to other people, that exert a powerful influence on our sense of well-being and our behavior. Your Inner Self-Image, or most private view of yourself, represents your individual values and guides your judgment of how you should act in any given situation. Your Outer Self-Image, or overall sense of how other people see you, allows you to adapt your actions to navigate the constraints imposed by the way you believe your actions will be interpreted by others. It thereby helps you to develop realistic strategies for meeting your personal priorities in your relationships.

Charting Your Inner and Outer Self-Images

The development of both the Inner and Outer Self-Image is an ongoing, lifelong process. Your Inner Self-Image gradually changes as your private, career, and family life influence the responsibilities others expect you to fulfill, the opportunities that become available to you, and the extent to which you are able to meet your responsibilities and make the most of your opportunities. It is influenced by who you believe you are deep inside and how you would most like to be seen as a person. It may also be heavily influenced by the aspects of your personality that are on your mind most often. Some people, for example, tend to ruminate and allow themselves to become overly self-critical, overlooking their own best qualities that are readily apparent to others.

Your Outer Self-Image evolves in response to other people's feedback about your personality, and your interpretations of how they see you. If you believe others tend to perceive you in an unfairly negative way, for example, this belief will influence your Outer Self-Image. If you believe others tend to be overly generous in their estimation of you, this belief will also influence your vision of your Outer Self.

In this chapter, we invite you to begin the Berkeley Personality Profile by exploring the relationship between your Inner and Outer Self-Images. By comparing and contrasting these two essential perspectives on your personality, you can gain valuable insights into the impact that both points of view have on the way you come across in your everyday life. To help you apply this knowledge to effect positive changes in your life, a series of Points for Reflection follows at the end of the chapter.

In chapter 3, you will have the opportunity to complete a brief follow-up to your exploration of your Inner and Outer Self-Images: a personality test in which you will describe your overall or *Unified Self-Image*, embodying the most honest and valid aspects of your Inner and Outer Selves combined. In future chapters, you'll also have a chance to find out what others who know you really think about your personality.

We think it is important, however, for you first to put yourself in other people's shoes and consider the possible bases for their perceptions.

You may complete any individual section of the Berkeley Personality Profile and interpret it entirely on its own. Combining the results of all eight sections, however, will allow you to achieve a much broader and more penetrating examination of your personality as a whole. Therefore, although it is not essential that you do so, we recommend that you complete chapters 2 and 3 before moving on. The Unified Self-Image Profile that you will develop as a result will serve as a basic standard of comparison for interpreting most of the other tests in this book.

A word of caution: The Berkeley Personality Profile is not intended as a means of assessing the state of your mental health and does not provide any form of psychotherapy. We urge those who have a history of emotional and other psychological problems to check with a qualified professional psychologist before proceeding. If any of the issues that are raised for you as you explore the Berkeley Personality Profile are at all troubling to you, we recommend that you discuss these issues with a licensed professional therapist or counselor before proceeding further.

How to Take and Score the Test

Turn to the pullout test materials provided in the back of this book. Cut out the vertical, multicolored scorecards numbered 1 and 2. The test instructions are in the black-and-white section, and the two color-coded sections each contain one full test. Pull out the perforated sections (you may wish to leave in one of the color-coded test sections in case you want to take the test again at a later date or give the extra test to your partner. Extra blank scorecards are also provided in case you need them). Cut out the vertical, multicolored scorecards numbered 1 and 2. Place Scorecard 1 alongside the thirty-five statements in the Berkeley Personality Profile, making certain the colored rows on the test questions match up with the colored rows on the scorecard. Because the scorecards are two-sided, be certain that you are using the correct side for each section of the test.

To begin, stop and consider your Inner Self-Image, or the way you see yourself deep inside, for a few moments. For each of the thirty-five statements, rate as honestly as possible the extent to which you agree or disagree that the statement is true of your Inner Self, following the instructions provided on the test.

After completing Scorecard 1, set it aside and take a five- or ten-minute break. Then use Scorecard 2 to respond to the same thirty-five statements for your Outer Self. Think about your Outer Self (how you think others see you) for a few moments, then rate as honestly as possible the extent to which you agree or disagree that each of the thirty-five statements describes your Outer Self. For the most accurate assessment of your personality, do not change any of your responses once you have completed the scorecard, and *do not* look back to Scorecard 1 while you are filling out Scorecard 2.

After you have completed both scorecards, turn to the General Profile Instructions (found in the black-and-white perforated section), which provide general guidelines for filling out the nine profiles you'll be completing in the Berkeley Personality Profile. Then follow the Individual Scoring Instructions to compute your scores, and graph them on the color-coded Inner/Outer Self-Image Profile, provided along with each test in the perforated sections. This profile will show your Inner and Outer Self-Image scores together in one convenient color-coded chart. It will allow you to see at a glance where your Inner and Outer Self-Images differ dramatically, and where they are quite similar. To guide you through the scoring process, we have provided a completed example of an Inner/Outer Self-Image Profile, contributed by one of the respondents to our *Psychology Today* survey, included with the test instructions.

Inner/Outer Self-Image Interpretation Guide

On your Inner/Outer Self-Image Profile, each of the five color-coded personality dimensions exhibits a continuum of scores, with the opposite ends of the continuum representing opposite ways of approaching certain kinds of interests and activities, as explained in chapter 1. In each case, very high scores (from about 29 to 35) and very low scores (from 7 to about 14) both indicate the predominance of a particular style of behavior, with the behavior of high scorers being opposite to the behavior of low scorers. People who score in the middle range of the scale (between about 19 and 22) tend to engage in both styles of behavior about equally.

Throughout the book, the cutoff scores used to separate the scoring categories in the interpretation guides are approximate. If your score falls near the border between two categories, you may wish to consider the interpretation provided for both categories as potentially informative about your personality. The scoring categories were guided by our research on the normative responses of people who have taken each portion of the Berkeley Personality Profile, but at the same time are designed to make sense to readers taking and scoring the test at home. We chose this approach because, while you may compare your scores to the typical scores of our research participants, the *primary* purpose of the Berkeley Personality Profile is to help you make individualized comparisons between a variety of different perspectives on your personality.[1]

To learn more about your scores, begin with your Inner/Outer *Difference* Scores, which you wrote in the *third row* of boxes on your Inner/Outer Self-Image Profile. Below, you'll find a separate section for each of the Big Five personality dimensions. *First,* look up your color-coded Inner/Outer Difference Score for each dimension in the appropriate section below—orange for Emotional Style, green for Interpersonal Style, and so forth. *Second,* look up your separate Inner and Outer Self-Image Scores (from the first and second rows of your profile) in the subparagraphs below the appropriate section for your Inner/Outer Difference Score. To simplify this process, be sure that for each color-coded dimension you made a star next to either your Inner Self-Image Score or your Outer Self-Image Score, whichever was larger, as described in the instructions.

You may wish to circle the portions of the interpretation guide that correspond to your score in each section, so that it will be easy to review your test results at a glance later on. As you read the test interpretations, it is essential to keep in mind that they are based on the way you described yourself in the Inner and Outer Self-Image portion of the test. If you find that the interpretation for one of the personality dimensions is off just slightly, it may be because you interpreted the test questions a little differently than people generally do. If you feel, however, that any of the interpretations do not suit you at all, check for possible mistakes in marking your responses or computing your scores. You should also check to be certain that you are looking up the scores from the correct rows of the profile in each portion of the interpretation guide.

Inner/Outer Difference Scores—Expressive Style (Orange)

- **Inner/Outer Difference Scores between 0 and 2**: You feel that other people generally know and understand your style of expressing yourself in activities and social interactions. *More specifically:*

  If both your Inner and Outer Self-Image Scores fall on the low side of the scale (below about 18): You feel that you are generally a private person who keeps to yourself and that other people understand and accept this aspect of your personality.

  If one or both of your Inner and Outer Self-Image Scores falls around the middle of the scale (between 19 and 22): You probably assert yourself and express your feelings and opinions only when you think it is necessary and appropriate for you to do so. You generally feel that others understand that when you do take a stand in public, it concerns a matter that is truly important to you.

  If both your Inner and Outer Self-Image Scores fall on the high side of the scale (above about 23): You probably feel a good deal of energy and enthusiasm when you are around other people. You therefore feel comfortable asserting yourself in a wide variety of social situations. You generally feel that others take your no-nonsense expressions of your suggestions, ideas, and opinions at face value.

- **Inner/Outer Difference Scores between 3 and 6:** You feel that there is a small to moderate discrepancy between the way you see yourself and the way others see you with respect to your Expressive Style. *More specifically:*

  If you marked a star next to your Inner Self-Image Score on the profile: You feel that others tend to think of you as somewhat more private, shy, or reclusive than you feel you really are deep down inside. You may, for example, feel that others sometimes forget to invite you to parties or social gatherings because they underestimate your interest in those sorts of events.

If you marked a star next to your Outer Self-Image Score on the profile: You feel that deep down inside you are a little more shy than other people realize. You think others see you as more active, energetic, or outgoing than you feel you really are. This may happen because you involve yourself in a lot of public and social situations, leading others to think such situations are easy for you, when in fact you sometimes have to try hard to work up the level of enthusiasm others expect of you.

- ***Inner/Outer Difference Scores of 7 or greater:*** You feel there is a considerable gap between the way others perceive your social behavior and your actual desire to express and assert yourself in social situations. *More specifically:*

If you marked a star next to your Inner Self-Image Score on the profile: You feel that others tend to think of you as considerably more introverted and withdrawn than you believe yourself to be. You may feel, for example, that although you often speak your mind and attempt to assert yourself, others may fail to listen to you or take you seriously simply because they continue to *think* of you as an unassertive person.

If you marked a star next to your Outer Self-Image Score on the profile: You feel that deep inside you are much more quiet, retiring, or private than others realize. This might be the case, for example, if you direct a lot of energy into friendships and social gatherings but don't always have enough energy and enthusiasm left over for other, more solitary areas of your life that are nevertheless also important to you. In this case, others might think of you as a perpetually happy, energetic, and outgoing individual simply because you always make an effort to show your best side whenever you are at parties or social gatherings.

Inner/Outer Difference Scores—Interpersonal Style (Green)

- *Inner/Outer Difference Scores between 0 and 2:* You feel that others generally know and understand your style of dealing with the needs and feelings of other people. *More specifically:*

  If both your Inner and Outer Self-Image Scores fall on the low side of the scale (below about 18): You feel it is important to give your own needs top priority. You believe others realize that putting your own needs first is sometimes necessary because you would be unable to help them if you did not help yourself. In addition, some people score in this range because, over time, they have developed "compassion fatigue" from giving too much of themselves all the time. Others score in this range because they have become cynical of other people's constant cries for support and unwillingness to help themselves.

  If one or both of your Inner and Outer Self-Image Scores falls around the middle of the scale (between 19 and 22): You feel that you balance your own needs with the needs of others. You realize that sometimes you need to look after yourself so that you will have the strength and resources available to come to the aid of other people, while at other times it is important to set all of your personal concerns aside to help a friend or family member in a crisis situation.

  If both your Inner and Outer Self-Image Scores fall on the high side of the scale (above about 23): You generally put compassion for others ahead of your personal concerns. You may find it difficult to put your needs ahead of others' needs even when that is the "logical" thing to do. You believe most people who know you recognize your caring and forgiving nature as one of your best features.

- *Inner/Outer Difference Scores between 3 and 6:* You feel there is a small to moderate discrepancy between the way you see yourself and the way others see you, concerning the way you respond to the needs and feelings of other people. *More specifically:*

If you marked a star next to your Inner Self-Image Score on the profile: You feel you are more caring, compassionate, and helpful than others might realize. Some people in positions of authority, for example, find they have to maintain a tough image so that other people don't take advantage of them, even though they are really quite kindhearted and accepting once you get beyond that tough exterior.

If you marked a star next to your Outer Self-Image Score on the profile: You feel that others see you as more caring, compassionate, or selfless than you believe yourself to be. You may feel, for example, that many of the things you do to help others are also beneficial or enjoyable for you in some way, which other people may not realize.

- *Inner/Outer Difference Scores of 7 or greater:* You feel there is a considerable gap between your own and others' image of your response to the needs and feelings of other people. *More specifically:*

If you marked a star next to your Inner Self-Image Score on the profile: You feel that you make much more of an effort to be helpful and sympathetic than you are given credit for by other people. You may feel, for example, that you really are kind and giving whenever someone is honestly in need and would benefit from your generosity. At the same time, you may think that other people see you as a little harsh because, as a matter of principle, you prefer not to help those who have done nothing to earn your trust or assistance.

If you marked a star next to your Outer Self-Image Score on the profile: Deep down inside you feel that you are considerably less giving and compassionate than other people see you as being. Some people may score in this range because, due to a temporary state of depression, they downgrade their positive qualities and try to convince themselves that people who think well of them must be mistaken. Most people who score in this range do so, however, because they are modest and honestly feel that their acts of kindness are really nothing special, but are simply the sorts of things that anyone in their position would do.

Inner/Outer Difference Scores—Work Style (Yellow)

- **Inner/Outer Difference Scores between 0 and 2:** You feel that other people generally know and understand your approach toward work and other responsibilities. *More specifically:*

  If both your Inner and Outer Self-Image Scores fall on the low side of the scale (below about 18): You feel you are informal about deadlines and organizational matters, and may find that you are easily distracted. You also feel, however, that you are open and honest about your approach toward such matters, so that other people understand your Work Style or at least know what to expect when working on a project or committee with you.

  If one or both of your Inner and Outer Self-Image Scores falls around the middle of the scale (between 19 and 22): You probably feel that you are more effective and efficient in some work or achievement situations than others. At your best, you may be systematic, dedicated, and even a perfectionist, while at other times you may be careless, haphazard, or absentminded. In addition, you feel that others who know you understand these aspects of your Work Style.

  If both your Inner and Outer Self-Image Scores fall on the high side of the scale (above about 23): You feel that you are reasonably self-disciplined and serious about the commitments and responsibilities you take on at work. In addition, you feel confident that others know they can depend on you to do your job effectively, to make deadlines and meetings on time, and to come through for them in a crunch.

- **Inner/Outer Difference Scores between 3 and 6:** You feel there is a small to moderate discrepancy between the way you see yourself and the way others see you with respect to your approach toward work and other responsibilities. *More specifically:*

  If you marked a star next to your Inner Self-Image Score on the profile: You feel you are a little more serious about work and commitments than others give you credit for being. You may, for exam-

ple, feel that you try to do your best at work but that your efforts
sometimes go unnoticed because you work closely with others who
share in the credit that is due you.

*If you marked a star next to your Outer Self-Image Score on the
profile:* You feel you are a little less serious about deadlines and responsibilities than you let other people know. Some people score in
this range, for example, because they try to work quickly and efficiently so that they will have time left over to relax and enjoy life. If
they are successful, they may feel they are "getting away with something" because others overestimate the time and effort they invest in
their work.

- **Inner/Outer Difference Scores of 7 or greater:** You feel there is a
  considerable gap between your own and others' perceptions of your
  approach toward work and other responsibilities. *More specifically:*

  *If you marked a star next to your Inner Self-Image Score on the
  profile:* You feel that you are much more dedicated and responsible
  than other people realize. You may, for example, feel that you really
  apply yourself at work but that your efforts go unnoticed because of
  an unappreciative boss, because others underestimate how difficult
  your job really is, or because someone else takes credit for your hard
  work.

  *If you marked a star next to your Outer Self-Image Score on the
  profile:* You feel that you are much less serious and responsible at
  heart than other people know. You may, for example, feel that many
  of your accomplishments are due in part to luck or privilege, or that
  your work comes easily for you, so that others often give you more
  credit than you feel you deserve.

Inner/Outer Difference Scores—Emotional Style (Red)

- **Inner/Outer Difference Scores between 0 and 2:** You feel that other
  people generally know and understand your style of dealing with
  problems and anxieties. *More specifically:*

If both your Inner and Outer Self-Image Scores fall on the low side of the scale (below about 18): You feel that you are in solid control of your emotions and are typically calm, cool, and collected in stressful situations. You also feel that other people recognize this quality in you.

If one or both of your Inner and Outer Self-Image Scores falls around the middle of the scale (between 19 and 22): You feel that your emotional reactions are generally moderate. Irritations may worry you or ruffle your feathers a bit, but you rarely feel terribly nervous, upset, or unsettled. In addition, you feel that others have an accurate view of this aspect of your character.

If both your Inner and Outer Self-Image Scores fall on the high side of the scale (above about 23): You like to get your problems off your chest from time to time and deal with stress by outwardly expressing your anxieties and frustrations. You feel that others who know you are also aware of this side of your emotional nature.

- *Inner/Outer Difference Scores between 3 and 6:* You feel there is a small to moderate discrepancy between your style of dealing with problems and anxieties as you see it and how it is seen by other people. *More specifically:*

If you marked a star next to your Inner Self-Image Score on the profile: You feel that you are somewhat more emotionally reactive than other people realize. At times, for example, you may feel worried or upset on the inside but make a real effort not to let others know the full extent of your emotions.

If you marked a star next to your Outer Self-Image Score on the profile: You feel that others see you as more emotionally reactive than you see yourself. You may, for example, feel that others often misinterpret the things you say or do, leading them to believe you are feeling more frustrated or anxious than you actually feel.

- *Inner/Outer Difference Scores of 7 or greater:* You feel there is a considerable discrepancy between your style of dealing with problems and anxieties as you see it, and the way this side of your character is seen by others. *More specifically:*

If you marked a star next to your Inner Self-Image Score on the profile: You feel that you are much more emotionally reactive than other people realize. You may, for example, have a temper that you have learned to control over the years. Alternatively, you may often feel worried or unsure of yourself at work or in family or social situations, but also feel that you are generally successful in hiding your concerns from others.

If you marked a star next to your Outer Self-Image Score on the profile: You feel that other people see you as much more emotionally reactive than you envision yourself as being. You may, for example, feel that others worry needlessly about you because they misinterpret your behavior as an indication that you are frustrated, worried, or upset when you actually are not. Some people also score in this range because they make a conscious and deliberate attempt to make others think that they are much more temperamental than they really are—motivated by the belief that if others fear their reactions, they will be left alone in peace.

Inner/Outer Difference Scores—Intellectual Style (Blue)

- *Inner/Outer Difference Scores between 0 and 2:* You feel that other people generally know and understand your approach to new ideas and experiences. *More specifically:*

  If both your Inner and Outer Self-Image Scores fall on the low side of the scale (below about 18): You see yourself, and feel you show yourself to others, as being a person who is moderate or cautious in your approach toward new ideas and experiences. You appreciate the beauty of simplicity and prefer to stick with tried-and-true traditional ways until a new way of doing things is actually proven to be worth embracing.

  If one or both of your Inner and Outer Self-Image Scores falls around the middle of the scale (between 19 and 22): You see yourself as a person who sees value both in traditional ideas and experiences and in trying out new approaches. In addition, you feel that others see you accurately as a balanced person in this respect.

If both your Inner and Outer Self-Image Scores fall on the high side of the scale (above about 23): You see yourself as being, and feel you show yourself to others as, a person who welcomes new ideas and approaches to life, enthusiastically embracing abstract pursuits such as aesthetics, philosophy, and analytic reasoning.

- **Inner/Outer Difference Scores between 3 and 6:** You feel there is a small to moderate discrepancy between the way you see yourself and the way others see you with respect to your approach toward new ideas and experiences. *More specifically:*

If you marked a star next to your Inner Self-Image Score on the profile: You feel you are a little more open-minded than other people realize when it comes to trying out new things or dealing with abstract ideas and principles such as philosophy, aesthetics, and mathematics. You may, for example, have a somewhat routine job or lead a rather traditional lifestyle but nevertheless enjoy a private interest in the latest scientific discoveries, current debates about social policy, or contemporary art forms and music.

If you marked a star next to your Outer Self-Image Score on the profile: You feel that you are somewhat more traditional than other people realize. You may, for example, lead a hectic, modern lifestyle in which you are generally happy but wish from time to time that you could live a simpler life or return to a less complicated time.

- **Inner/Outer Difference Scores of 7 or greater:** You feel there is a considerable gap between the way you see yourself and the way others see you with respect to your approach toward new ideas and experiences. *More specifically:*

If you marked a star next to your Inner Self-Image Score on the profile: You feel that you are considerably more interested in abstract ideas, artistic and imaginative pursuits, or state-of-the-art technology than other people realize. You may feel, for example, that your more creative side is underutilized in your current job or somewhat undervalued by your friends and family.

If you marked a star next to your Outer Self-Image Score on the profile: You feel you are considerably more cautious than other people realize when it comes to embracing abstract ideas or accepting new technologies that might dramatically alter your lifestyle. You may, for example, have a rather exciting job that keeps you on the cutting edge of your field but nevertheless prefer to relax in a more traditional atmosphere at home.

Negotiating Your Private Self and Public Image

Did you notice that one part of the test—either the Inner Self-Image or the Outer Self-Image—was easier for you to complete than the other? If you found it easy and natural to think about your Inner Self, chances are you have a high level of what psychologists call *private self-consciousness*. Research has shown that people who are high in private self-consciousness tend to monitor their personal feelings and private experiences carefully, and are consequently less suggestible than other people. They make decisions and direct their behavior in accordance with their own internal feelings and attitudes, and are less likely to conform to peer pressure or coercion.

On the other hand, if you found it was easy and natural to think about your Outer Self, you probably have a high level of *public self-consciousness*. Research shows that people who are high in public self-consciousness tend to pay more attention to the outward indications of their personality, such as their expressive gestures, personal quirks and mannerisms, and physical appearance. Not surprisingly, they are much better than those low in public self-consciousness at knowing what type of impression they are making on other people at any given time.

If you found it quite natural to describe both your Inner Self and your Outer Self, you may be high in *both* private and public self-consciousness, which means that you probably spend a great deal of time thinking about both your Inner Self-Image and your Outer Self-Image. If so, you may have characteristics associated with both ways of thinking about yourself; for example, you may direct your behavior in accord with your own internal feelings, and yet may also be keenly aware of the impression your behavior creates in others' eyes. Of course, some individuals have a low level of both private and public self-consciousness. They prefer to think about their Inner and Outer Self-Images only when one of the two is challenged.[2]

When we gave this portion of the test to the readers of *Omni* magazine, virtually all of those who responded to our survey saw important differences between their Inner and Outer Self-Images. About 95 percent of the 1,300 people who responded reported that their Inner and Outer Self-Images differed, by at least 3 points, on one or more of the Big Five personality dimensions. In fact, three-quarters of those surveyed reported that their Inner and Outer Self-Images differed substantially on two or more dimensions, while fully half reported Inner/Outer differences on three or more personality styles.

If you would like to know how the specific pattern of differences you perceived between your Inner and Outer Self-Images corresponds to the differences our *Omni* readers saw in themselves, compare your results to the findings in Table 2.1.

The table shows, for example, that 10 percent of those surveyed scored their Inner Self higher on Expressive Style than their Outer Self, by a difference of 3 points or more, indicating that they felt they were considerably more assertive and outgoing than other people saw them. Meanwhile, 40 percent scored their Outer Self at least 3 points higher on Expressive Style than their Inner Self, indicating that they believed others saw them as more outgoing and assertive than they privately believed themselves to be. Half (50 percent) of our respondents scored their Inner and Outer Selves about the same on Expressive Style (within 2 points), indicating that they believed others saw them appropriately in this regard. The most common and least common differences found for the remaining Big Five dimensions are presented in Table 2.1. Your Outer Self-Image, of course, reflects how you *believe* others see you. While your hunches may be essentially correct, it is also possible that your perceptions are biased in some way. It may be, for example, that others have a much more positive—or negative—impression of you than you realize. When we compared our *Omni* readers' Outer Self-Image scores to the scores given to them by their family, friends, and coworkers, the news

Table 2.1: Common Inner/Outer Differences[3]

Expressive Style (Orange)
Inner Self more
outgoing, assertive
10 percent

Inner and Outer equally
outgoing, assertive
50 percent

Outer Self more
outgoing, assertive
40 percent

Interpersonal Style (Green)
Inner Self more
warm and caring
25 percent

Inner and Outer equally
warm and caring
50 percent

Outer Self more
warm and caring
25 percent

Work Style (Yellow)
Inner Self more
responsible
20 percent

Inner and Outer equally
responsible
55 percent

Outer Self more
responsible
25 percent

Emotional Style (Red)
Inner Self more
tense, emotional
40 percent

Inner and Outer equally
tense, emotional
40 percent

Outer Self more
tense, emotional
20 percent

Intellectual Style (Blue)
Inner Self more
open, imaginative
30 percent

Inner and Outer equally
open, imaginative
60 percent

Outer Self more
open, imaginative
10 percent

was good for *most* of the people who participated in our study. For the majority, others who knew them described them as more extraverted, more interpersonally giving, and more responsible than they described themselves to be. Not everyone, however, received such glowing reviews from those who knew them.

One key to interpersonal success appears to be modesty: Those who claimed to have a few flaws of which others might not be aware were, in fact, usually viewed by others as especially warm, caring, and responsible individuals. Less modest individuals, who consistently claimed their Inner Self was better than others acknowledged it to be, tended to be viewed by those who knew them as somewhat self-centered and irresponsible.

Self-Presentation

What causes the differences that people see between their Inner and Outer Self-Images? Your Outer Self is affected in part by how you *want to believe* others see you, and in part by the feedback that you receive during your interactions with others. Your Outer Self is also affected, however, by *self-presentation*, your deliberate attempts to create a particular impression in other people's eyes.

As you think about your Outer Self and the ways in which it differs from your Inner Self, you may discover that you use self-presentation for a variety of reasons. Sometimes people employ *strategic self-presentation*, attempting to create a particular impression specifically to increase their power or status in a relationship. While this may at first sound self-promoting and disingenuous, skillful, strategic self-presentation can be quite essential for people in certain occupations. Doctors, ministers, and politicians, for example, may deliberately present only the most professional and respectable sides of their personalities, withholding their private doubts, fears, or opinions in order to create and maintain a certain public image they feel is necessary to do their jobs effectively.[4]

You may also know people who, for example, use self-presentation to create an unusually rosy Outer Self out of a concern for others, because they do not wish to worry others needlessly with their private affairs. Others hide behind a veneer of self-presentation out of defensiveness, because they fear that others will not like or approve of them if they open up, or because they fear that opening up to others will be too emotionally painful.

How much self-presentation is normal, healthy, or adaptive? That depends on your own individual personality, life circumstances, and relationships. Although you are always presenting some particular side of your personality whenever you talk to or interact with another person, people differ in the extent to which they present a side of themselves that is one-sided, disingenuous, or somehow incomplete.

There is no such thing as an ideal level of self-presentation that each of us should strive for. Rather, you must determine how much self-presentation is ideal *for you*—and *when* you should employ it. If you feel a lack of intimacy in your life, believe that no one knows or understands the "real you," or wonder whether others could fully accept you as you are, you may be engaging in too much self-presentation. In this case, you may want to make a real effort to show a more genuine or more complete view of your personality—at first to one or two people whom you trust, and gradually to more of the people in your life. This approach, over time, will draw your Inner and Outer Selves closer together. Conversely, if you feel that people take advantage of the weaknesses and anxieties that you openly express, or sometimes fail to take you seriously because they know your softer side too well, then you may need to monitor your behavior more closely and engage in more strategic self-presentation than you normally do in these problem situations.

Culture, Prejudice, and the Outer Self

Self-presentation involves aspects of your Outer Self-Image over which you have some deliberate control. But other aspects of your Outer Self are not so easily managed. The way others interpret your behavior may be influenced strongly by subtle cultural factors. For example, two children behaving in essentially the same way might be perceived as rude or undisciplined in Japanese society, but precocious in the United States—or vice versa.

In addition, others may hold stereotypes and prejudices about people of your race, age, gender, and cultural or professional background, or about those who dress or talk the way you do, or who share other physical characteristics in common with you. These stereotypes and prejudices might drastically influence the way others interpret your behavior. If people were to patronize you and treat you as though you were emotionally weak and childlike because of your physical stature, for example, this could become a part of your Outer Self-Image—a part of how you *believe* others see you—even if you knew inside that they were wrong. The values and expectations of your society and subculture influence the way in which others perceive and respond to you, which in turn impacts the development of your Outer Self-Image.

Points for Reflection

It is natural, after completing this exercise, to feel that you might like to change your Outer Self-Image in one or two areas. You may also feel that there are aspects of your Inner Self-Image that you would like to work on. The Points for Reflection that follow are designed to help you clarify these feelings and explore some of your options as you apply the results of this first section of the Berkeley Personality Profile to your everyday life.

Before you reflect on the questions that follow, take a moment to review your Inner/Outer Self-Image Profile. We suggest that you focus on those personality dimensions for which your Inner and Outer Self-Images differed most strongly, because people generally find these discrepancies to be especially thought-provoking. You may also wish to review the five sections of the interpretation guide that specifically describe your scores.

1. Do you feel your Inner Self-Image or your Outer Self-Image is closer to the "real you"? Do you feel that either image might potentially involve some elements of self-deception, self-flattery, or self-criticism, or are you satisfied that your self-assessment from each perspective is more or less realistic?

2. Focus on those areas in which your Inner Self-Image differs from your Outer Self-Image by 3 points or more, and ask yourself whether these differences are in any way deliberate. Take a moment to think about the possible reasons you may have for hiding a side of your personality from others.

Do you feel that certain matters are intensely private and should not be shared with anyone who is not an intimate friend or loved one? Do you feel that, for better or worse, the special circumstances of your occupation, living situation, or other factors preclude true openness beyond a certain level? Do you sometimes fear that others would not appreciate the subtler aspects of your inner nature, or may simply reject you if you openly reveal yourself? If you do harbor

such feelings, ask yourself if they are completely realistic, and if
there are ways in which you might be able to restructure your relationships in a way that allows you to be more open.

3. If there are large differences between your Inner and Outer Self-
Images, consider the consequences you experience in your life as a
result of not expressing or acting in accord with your Inner Self-
Image. These consequences may be positive or negative. Some of
them may be entirely unintentional, perhaps isolating you in unexpected ways from other people. Conversely, there may also be situations in which you wish you were less revealing of your Inner Self,
because you feel that you allow yourself to become too vulnerable in
these situations.

4. Although there may be many situations in which you deliberately
hide your Inner Self, there may also be situations in which you feel
that people do not perceive the "real you" despite your best efforts
to communicate. In these situations, others' perceptions of you may
be influenced by their generalized *attitudes*, such as their personal
prejudices about people from particular ethnic, religious, or racial
groups, or about people who talk, act, or dress in a particular way.
Other people might also form preconceived notions about you because you remind them of someone they know, such as a parent, sibling, coworker, or former lover.

Consider the ways in which your Outer Self-Image is influenced by
others' prejudices and preconceptions. Consider, also, the ways in
which these biases may go so far as to influence the innermost image
you hold of yourself—either by leading you to internalize those biases or to define your Self-Image as a *reaction against* the stereotypes you are forced to confront. Are there ways you could deal
more effectively with others who treat you as a stereotype, without
either internalizing their preconceptions or defining your self-image
as a reaction to their perceptions?

5. Now consider the ways in which the *actions* of other people may
also contribute to the misconceptions they may have about you. Is
there someone in your life, for example, who constantly interrupts

you, never listens to your ideas, or never gives you the opportunity to prove yourself? Or is there someone who puts you on a pedestal, always trying to please or impress you, rather than really getting to know you? Are there steps you can take to capture their attention long enough so that they may come to know you better? Would it be appropriate and beneficial for you to take these steps at this point in your relationship?

6. Although you may sometimes suffer from other people's mistaken ideas about your personality, there are also ways in which your own actions can contribute to their perceptions. You may, for example, find yourself compelled to take an ethical stand as a matter of principle, but your behavior could be interpreted by others as a predisposition toward controversy or an unwillingness to get along in groups. Or you may allow the pressures you are feeling in one area of your life, such as your work life, to influence your behavior toward the people in another area of your life, such as your family life.

Consider the ways in which your actions may contribute to the perceptions you believe other people hold about your personality. Would it be sensible and appropriate to communicate clearly the feelings and intentions that are motivating these actions, so that others might come to understand you at a deeper level? Or is it possible that your Outer Self-Image really represents the more honest and accurate portrayal of your personality, while your Inner Self-Image is somewhat idealized, dramatized, or out of date?

Notes

1. For those who have a professional interest in the design of the Berkeley Personality Profile, the scoring categories for the Inner/Outer Difference Scores were selected so that for each of the Big Five personality styles, the two categories representing strong Inner/Outer differences (7 points or greater) would each encompass a maximum of 15 percent of our *Omni* respondents, while the category representing no difference between the Inner and Outer Self-Images would include about 40 percent to 60 percent of respondents. The actual percentage of respondents in each scoring category varies across the Big Five personality styles. Further details are available from the authors on request.

2. For more on private and public self-consciousness, see A. H. Buss, *Self-Consciousness and Social Anxiety* (San Francisco: Freeman, 1980); M. F. Scheier and C. S. Carver, "Two Sides of the Self: One for You and One for Me," in J. Suls and A. G. Greenwald, eds., *Psychological Perspectives on the Self,* vol. 2 (Hillsdale, NJ: Erlbaum, 1983), 123–57. For a dissenting opinion, see R. A. Wicklund and P. M. Gollwitzer, "The Fallacy of the Private-Public Self-Focus Distinction," *Journal of Personality* 55 (1987): 491–523.

3. To be considered substantially different, an individual's Inner and Outer Self-Image scores must have differed by 3 points or more on a particular Big Five dimension. For simplicity, percentages were rounded to the nearest multiple of 5.

4. For more on strategic self-presentation, see E. E. Jones and T. S. Pittman, "Toward a General Theory of Strategic Self-Presentation," in J. Suls, ed., *Psychological Perspectives on the Self,* vol. 1 (Hillsdale, NJ: Erlbaum, 1982), 231–62.

Chapter 3

The Unified Self

Your Inner Self-Image portrays a singularly personal view of your personality that takes into account how you feel about yourself in different situations, as well as your underlying motives and intentions—even when you don't clearly express them in your behavior. Your Outer Self-Image reflects a kind of average accounting of your observations about the ways in which people have responded to your behavior throughout your life. While your innermost view of your personality has its own validity, your Outer Self-Image may include true elements that you have inwardly chosen to neglect or failed to take seriously in forming your Inner Self-Image.

Some theorists argue that your beliefs about how others see you form the very core of your self-concept. Philosopher George Herbert Mead, for example, believed that children develop their sense of self by observing how other people treat them, speak to them, and respond to their behavior. According to Mead, children develop a generalized sense of how others perceive them based on the way others act toward them, in time internalizing and adopting these notions to form their self-image.

Other theorists contend that your Inner Self-Image is a better measure of the "real you." Psychologist Carl Rogers, for example, emphasized the importance of "organismic experience," or the subtle physiological responses that reflect how you really feel about yourself and about the people and situations around you. Others emphasize the important role that spiritual experience plays in the formation of a person's identity. Because these are private events to which only you have access, one might argue that only your Inner Self-Image could accurately reflect this aspect of yourself.

Which perspective represents the "real you"? We believe the answer lies somewhere in between: that your true personality represents a unified image that emerges at the crossroads of your Inner and Outer Self-Images. The Points for Reflection in chapter 2 offered you a chance to contemplate separately the validity of your Inner and Outer Self-Images for each of the Big Five personality dimensions. The goal of the present chapter is to help you reach a unified resolution of who you are with respect to each dimension.

In completing the Unified Self-Image section of the Berkeley Personality Profile, we recommend that you focus on making your most honest assessment of your true personality. Try not to be overly self-critical. At the same time, resist the temptation to casually dismiss the impressions you feel others have of you. If you wish, you may find it helpful to compare your Inner Self-Image and Outer Self-Image scorecards and review the individual test questions to which you responded differently.

How to Take and Score the Test

After you feel you have reconciled the differences between your Inner and Outer Self-Images, use this fresh perspective to complete your Unified Self-Image Scorecard (Scorecard 3 on the flip side of Scorecard 2). Then turn to the Unified Self-Image Profile (provided in the perforated sections) to score your test and profile your results, and look up your Unified Self-Image Score for each personality style in the interpretation guide. There is no need to rush as you complete the various scorecards and profiles. Rather, you should proceed at a pace that feels right for you.

Unified Self-Image Interpretation Guide

Keep in mind that you know yourself better than we do. The interpretations that follow are based strictly on the way you *described yourself* on the Unified Self-Image portion of the test. If you feel the interpretation for a particular personality dimension does not fit you well, it may simply be because you interpreted the test questions in that color-coded category somewhat differently than people usually do. You may also have been feeling slightly depressed or out of sorts on the day you completed this portion of the test; if so, you may wish to consider retaking the test on another day. If the interpretations below seem dramatically different than the way you see yourself, however, you may wish to double-check the way you marked your responses and computed your scores.[1]

Unified Self-Image Scores—Expressive Style (Orange)

Expressive Style, the first of the Big Five personality factors, is a broad dimension that encompasses a series of closely related personality characteristics. Three of the most important aspects of Expressive Style are sociability, positive emotionality, and activity or energy level.

- *If your score falls between 7 and 15:* Your Expressive Style score indicates that you tend to keep to yourself in social situations. You may value your privacy highly, you may be shy, or you may simply feel it is inappropriate to share your views and opinions unless someone has specifically asked for them. You may think it unwise to be overly optimistic for fear of looking foolish or being disappointed. Many people who score themselves in this range on Expressive Style are feeling a temporary lack of energy and enthusiasm, while others are simply more interested in mental than physical pursuits.

- *If your score falls between 16 and 21:* Your Expressive Style score indicates that you do not feel uncomfortable around others but prefer not to be in the limelight at parties and social gatherings. You may be quiet or reserved around strangers, warming up only after someone else has made the first move. Even when you're feeling good about something, you may prefer to savor your emotions rather than just letting go. Many people who score themselves in this range on Expressive Style are careful in the way they budget their energy resources for everyday activities.

- *If your score falls between 22 and 29:* Your Expressive Style score indicates that you enjoy being an active person—perhaps at parties and social gatherings, or perhaps through participating in sports and other physically demanding pursuits. You are probably direct with others and generally not shy about expressing enthusiasm or saying what is on your mind. Many people who score themselves in this range on Expressive Style feel energetic a good deal of the time but find that their energy resources are not necessarily boundless.

- *If your score falls between 30 and 35:* Your Expressive Style score indicates that you are animated and outgoing in social situations and probably not shy about becoming the center of attention. Even when others might feel confined by social traditions or taboos, you may find it easy to strike up a conversation with a total stranger. You may be adventurous, or even daring, in your expressions of positive emotions. Many people who score themselves in this range on Expressive Style feel that they have almost boundless energy but wish they had more time to live life to the fullest.

Unified Self-Image Scores—Interpersonal Style (Green)

Interpersonal Style, the second of the Big Five personality factors, concerns the level of intimacy you maintain in your personal relationships. Interpersonal Style encompasses both your orientation toward others, or how you feel about them, and the way you actually act toward other people. You might ask yourself, for example, if you usually feel trusting toward others and tend to accept people for who they are, or if you tend to be more critical or impersonal in your approach. Do you tend to be giving, cooperative, and easy to get along with, or are you sometimes argumentative or selfish?

- *If your score falls between 7 and 18:* Your Interpersonal Style score indicates that you find it difficult to trust others and may spend considerable time and effort securing your own needs before you go out of your way to assist other people. Different people take on this interpersonal style for different reasons. Some would like to trust others but fear getting hurt or being exploited. Others find it difficult to trust others until that trust is earned.

- *If your score falls between 19 and 21:* Your Interpersonal Style score indicates that you generally cooperate with other people but can also be selfish, impersonal, or perhaps aggressive at times in your relationships. You may occasionally find yourself pursuing your own desires at another person's expense, and later wonder why you were not more understanding or compassionate. Sometimes people act this way *not* because they are cold and uncaring, but instead because they are under a lot of pressure to attend to their own needs. You may, for example, sometimes feel that you simply can't find the time and energy to meet everyone else's needs until you have first solved your own more immediate problems.

- *If your score falls between 22 and 29:* Your Interpersonal Style score indicates that you genuinely care about other people. You probably find it relatively easy to trust people and accept them for who they are, which helps you to get along well in your personal relationships. Most people who score themselves in this range on Interpersonal Style are willing to cooperate with others in order to meet the needs of an entire social group. They are able to work for the benefit of the group without compromising their individuality or sacrificing their personal needs.

- *If your score falls between 30 and 35:* Your Interpersonal Style score indicates that you are extremely concerned with the welfare of other people. You may, for example, be so sympathetic to others that it is terribly distressing for you to see anyone else feeling hurt or unhappy. Sometimes this means working exceptionally hard to help other people in any way you can, or even sacrificing your own desires in order to make another person happy. People sometimes score themselves in this range because they are dedicated to certain social and ethical principles. By giving of themselves to help others, they are simply living up to their own standards of how human beings ought to treat one another—with love, compassion, and respect.

Unified Self-Image Scores—Work Style (Yellow)

Work Style, the third of the Big Five personality dimensions, includes much more than the way you behave and approach challenges when you are at work. Instead, Work Style refers to your general values and attitudes about dedication to activities at work, at home, and even in your leisure activities. Work Style includes, for example, your feelings about working hard to accomplish your goals, about being efficient and setting out carefully devised plans, and about being focused on your work, social, and family responsibilities.

- *If your score falls between 7 and 18:* Your Work Style score indicates that you prefer not to be tied down by plans, schedules, or responsibilities. You may procrastinate or simply find that you are easily distracted and sometimes have difficulty following tasks through to completion. Some people who score themselves in this range feel that they are lazy or lack direction in life. Others who score themselves in this range, however, are ready and willing to work hard when it is required but feel that work is a means to an end rather than being enjoyable in and of itself.

- *If your score falls between 19 and 21:* Your Work Style score indicates that you sometimes have difficulty accepting responsibility or following plans through to completion. Or you may simply feel overly constricted when your day's activities are too neatly planned out in advance. You probably work hard for the things you really want but may sometimes find it difficult not to procrastinate. You may hesitate when you are unsure about your goals, when you're distracted by something more interesting, or out of an underlying fear of failure. Alternatively, some people who score themselves in this range rarely procrastinate but instead take on too many responsibilities simultaneously. They often feel disorganized or inefficient as a result.

- *If your score falls between 22 and 29:* Your Work Style score indicates that you are generally achievement oriented and tend to finish a job once you have started it. You probably take your commitments and responsibilities quite seriously but also probably try *not* to let concerns such as these dominate your life. You may, for example, be selective in the projects you take on, so that you can complete them carefully, thoroughly, and efficiently and still take time out when you feel you have earned a break. Or, if you do tend to take on many projects at one time, you probably find that although you feel yourself slipping behind every once in a while, you nevertheless accomplish most of what you set out to do.

- *If your score falls between 30 and 35:* Your Work Style score indicates that you value commitments and responsibilities highly and rarely let anything interfere with your plans to accomplish a goal. You take your promises—to yourself and others—very seriously. You work as hard as you need to in order to avoid disappointing those who depend on you, such as friends, family members, and coworkers. Some people who score themselves in this range on Work Style accomplish their goals by working tirelessly until everything is completed. Others do so by being selective in the projects they take on. Still others do so by being systematic, focused, and efficient so that they are able to fulfill many different commitments in a relatively short period of time.

Unified Self-Image Scores—Emotional Style (Red)

Emotional Style is the fourth of the Big Five factors of personality. Your Emotional Style includes the extent to which you experience and express difficult emotions such as tension, frustration, or self-doubt, as opposed to feeling and acting calm and self-confident even under extreme stress.

- *If your score falls between 7 and 14:* Your Emotional Style score indicates that you are calm, cool, and collected. You are probably not easily frustrated and do not carry a grudge. You are also likely to feel confident and self-assured in almost all situations. Although you may be leading a lifestyle in which only a few minor tensions arise from day to day, it is more likely that you lead a normal, hectic life but simply do not allow stressful events to bother you. You may, therefore, be the type of person that other people turn to in emergency situations.

- *If your score falls between 15 and 21:* Your Emotional Style score indicates that you are essentially stable, but not without your more emotional side. You may, for example, *experience* moderate to strong reactions to stresses and negative events but carefully control the way in which you *express* those emotions when you are around other people. Alternatively, you may experience negative emotions such as frustration or anxiety relatively infrequently, so when you feel it is justified, you do not hesitate to express these sentiments as a means of letting others know how you really feel.

- *If your score falls between 22 and 27:* Your Emotional Style score indicates that you experience rather strong emotions, although you may or may not express them openly. Some people who score themselves in this range on Emotional Style tend to be nervous or tense. Others experience occasional self-doubts or may, at times, be a little oversensitive. Although you may feel moody, temperamental, or even irritable under stress, you are probably able to keep these feelings in check most of the time.

- *If your score falls between 28 and 35:* Your Emotional Style score indicates that you experience and probably express very strong and passionate emotions. Some people who score themselves in this range on Emotional Style have a quick temper and may be prone to impassioned outbursts. Others who score themselves in this range tend to feel insecure or unsure of themselves rather than upset at the situation or the people around them. Still others score themselves in this range because they are acutely susceptible to environmental stress and find themselves feeling on edge a good deal of the time.

Unified Self-Image Scores—Intellectual Style (Blue)

Intellectual Style, the fifth of the Big Five personality factors, concerns the extent to which you tend to embrace fresh ideas, novel activities, and innovative approaches to art, philosophy, or science. Some people actively seek out original ideas, if only to explore them or try them on for size, while others prefer to take a more conservative approach toward radical fads and concepts.

- *If your score falls between 7 and 18:* Your Intellectual Style score indicates that you prefer the simple things in life, perhaps simply feeling more at home with traditional views and values than with newfangled ideas and approaches toward art, culture, and everyday life. You probably take a hands-on conventional or tried-and-true approach to life rather than living as a dreamer with your head in the clouds. You also probably try to take life as it comes rather than constantly searching for some hidden meaning behind the immediately obvious.

- *If your score falls between 19 and 21:* Your Intellectual Style score indicates that you generally like the simple things in life but are willing to entertain some less conventional ideas and values when these seem appropriate. You may occasionally find yourself giving in to tradition and later wondering why you weren't willing to take a more progressive approach toward new ideas and possibilities. Sometimes people who score themselves in this range on Intellectual Style would like to challenge the system—at least a little—but also value the sense of comfort and stability that comes with tried-and-true traditions and lifestyles.

- *If your score falls between 22 and 29:* Your Intellectual Style score indicates that you are open to new approaches toward art, culture, and philosophy, though not given to flights of fancy. You are probably willing to accept new solutions to age-old problems, for example, but only after their value has been demonstrated. You see yourself as someone who likes to be challenged by new ideas as long as nobody tries to pull the rug out from under you. You consider yourself a progressive thinker, but not a radical, and may enjoy finding simple solutions to complicated problems.

- *If your score falls between 30 and 35:* Your Intellectual Style score indicates that you prefer to break new ground and challenge tradition at every opportunity rather than giving in to convention or to other people's expectations of how you *should* behave. You think of yourself as a sharp and open-minded person, someone with broad-ranging and sophisticated interests who is willing to explore all sides of even the most complicated and controversial issues. In addition, you probably have an active imagination and a restless curiosity about the world around you.

What Role Does Personality Play in Your Life?

The myriad facets of your personality are continually interacting in response to subtle shifts in your immediate surroundings. Together, your personality and your environment form a complex system that makes it quite difficult for anyone to predict precisely what you will do in any situation or at any given moment. This unpredictable quality is one of the wonders of human personality and is part of what makes you unique. The other side of your singular charm, however, is the coherence or familiar pattern in your personal style that makes you seem "comfortable" to your family, friends, and close acquaintances.

When you stepped back and took an overall view of your personality in the Unified Self-Image portion of the Berkeley Personality Profile, you probably noticed some of these regularities—including patterns in the types of activities you prefer, in the values that guide your feelings and decisions, in the way you apply yourself toward meeting your goals, and so forth. Chances are that these are precisely the patterns that have played, and will continue to play, an essential role in determining the details of your life story—from major life achievements to minor traumas, from crisis and loss to coping and resolution, from the intricately woven subplots to the cast of supporting characters that form the panorama of your life. Your personality might be leading you to face the same types of challenges, enter relationships with individuals who always treat you in the same way, commit yourself to the same types of obligations, and wind up feeling the same worries, delights, or frustrations repeatedly throughout the course of your life.

But your personality has not already determined the ultimate course of your life story. At each turning point in your life, there are usually several options open to you that are compatible with your individual style. By following your head, your heart, or your familiar habits, you choose one possibility over the others that are available to you.

When you follow your head and your heart, you're using your past experience to actively seek out those situations and environments that you believe will allow you to flourish and find fulfillment. When you follow your habits, behaving in ways that feel safe simply because they are familiar, you may stumble into situations with predictable, perhaps negative, consequences. At such times, you should stop to think about whether your habitual patterns are really healthy, and whether they promote your long-term growth as an individual. Understanding the consistent factors in your personal style that are highlighted in the Unified Self-Image portion of the Berkeley Personality Profile should help you to understand, and, when necessary, control, the recurrent patterns in your own life experience.

In our own research, we examined the Big Five personality profiles and the lifestyle choices made by the 1,300 readers of *Omni* magazine who responded to our survey. We found many striking links between personality and lifestyle, many of which may also hold true for you.

The majority of people we studied kept fairly healthy lifestyles, including regular exercise, not smoking, and drinking alcohol infrequently if at all. Nevertheless, specific differences in health-related habits were clearly associated with differences in personality styles.

Those with particularly extraverted, enthusiastic Expressive Styles tended to exercise more, and worry less about their health, than those with more reserved Expressive Styles. They also, however, more frequently drank both coffee and alcohol. If you have an extraverted, enthusiastic Expressive Style, you may wish to consider how this may be affecting your health, and whether there is a way for you to take advantage of the benefits of your high energy level while resisting the temptations that may be associated with your sociability. If you have a quiet, reserved Expressive Style, and find that you exercise less frequently than you would like, you may simply have to push yourself a little harder to overcome your disinclination and meet your goals.

Emotional Style, however, was by far the personality dimension that turned out to be most relevant to understanding people's health-related habits and concerns. Having a strong and passionate Emotional Style can have both positive and negative consequences, but it is its darker side—the negativity, worrying, and undue anxiety suffered by some people with intense Emotional Styles—that can sometimes lead to health-related problems.

After statistically controlling for age and other factors, we found that, compared to those who were more relaxed and easygoing, people with intense Emotional Styles were less likely to exercise, more likely to smoke and take sleeping pills, and more likely to report aches and pains and worry about their health. This may be because strong negative emotions are associated with certain physiological responses in the body, such as increases in perspiration, respiration, heart rate, and even muscle tension, which in turn lead to feeling achy, jittery, and unable to sleep.

If you have an intense Emotional Style, however, you needn't necessarily worry about your long-term prognosis. Many researchers have found that although many people who are intensely emotional are keenly aware of aches, pains, and other health-related symptoms, they do not suffer from life-threatening health problems, such as cancer and heart attacks, any more frequently than those with more relaxed emotional styles.

Your Intellectual Style has likely influenced your goals and activities. If you had the opportunity to go to college and made a conscious decision to do so, for example, your Intellectual Style may have been instrumental in your choice. After statistically controlling for age and other factors, we found that those whose Intellectual Style indicated a preference for unconventional ideas and experiences were almost twice as likely to have obtained college degrees as those whose Intellectual Style indicated a preference for traditional values and lifestyles.

Your Work Style may be closely associated with your life situation. We found that older people, especially those with spouses and children who depend on them, saw themselves and were seen by people who knew them as more hardworking, focused, and responsible than younger people in more carefree life situations. And, apparently, old work habits die hard; those who were retired were rated as the most work oriented and responsible of any group in our study.

Points for Reflection

After completing this exercise, you may find yourself considering the ways in which your personality has influenced the kinds of experiences you have had in your life and the ways you have responded to these experiences, as well as the overall course your life has taken. You may even feel that you would like to change some specific aspects of your personality.

The Points for Reflection that follow are designed to help you clarify these feelings and explore some of your options as you apply the results of this second section of the Berkeley Personality Profile to your everyday life. They also focus, specifically, on three important processes through which features of your personality and your environment *interact* to give coherence, predictability, and stability to your experiences throughout the course of your life.[2]

Before you reflect on the questions that follow, take a moment to review your Unified Self-Image Profile. You may also wish to refer to the five sections of the interpretation guide that correspond specifically to your scores.

1. When you interpret and respond to a situation differently than another person in the same situation, psychologists describe your behavior as a *reactive interaction* between your personality and the circumstances in

which you find yourself. One person stopped by a volunteer requesting donations for a homeless shelter, for example, might be inspired to contribute his or her own time as well as money to the cause, while the next person approached might suspect a swindle and report the same volunteer to the police as a suspected con artist.

Consider the ways in which your overall personality would lead you to react to the following situations. How might your reactions be similar to those you would expect from most other people, and how might they be very different? Take at least five minutes to imagine yourself in each of these situations before moving on to the next one:

A) You just discovered that you've won the state lottery and will receive a sum of $5 million per year for the rest of your life.

B) You just discovered that you have an incurable disease and have less than one year to live.

C) You just discovered that your romantic partner, with whom you share a mutual commitment to monogamy, has been having a sexual affair.

D) You just discovered that someone in your work environment has been lying to your professional colleagues about a project on which you have been working together. When you bring the matter to your colleagues' attention, they urge you to hide the truth to protect the public image of your field or profession.

2. Your personality may lead you (consciously or not) to get yourself into the same types of situations repeatedly. Psychologists refer to this behavior and its consequences as a *proactive interaction*. Parents who move to a new school district because their child is associating with peers who always get into trouble, for example, may find that their child will continue to seek out and become friends with troublemakers, no matter where they move.

Think of some familiar circumstances in your own life—both positive and negative—in which you seem to find yourself again and again. Something in your personality or your habitual way of behaving may be leading you into those situations. Are there ways in which you set yourself up for failure or disappointment by repeating certain destructive patterns? If so, can you somehow recognize the telltale signs in advance and alter your behavior to steer clear of those situations in the future?

Are there other areas in your life in which you almost always feel happy and successful? You shouldn't necessarily attribute your good fortune to luck in these areas of your life; in truth, something about your personality most likely helps you to find your way into those environments that allow you to thrive. Can you identify what you're doing right in these situations and apply this knowledge to help you become "luckier" in other areas of your life as well?

3. When your personality leads you repeatedly to elicit a certain type of response from other people, psychologists refer to this behavior and its consequences as an *evocative interaction*. Happy, optimistic people who smile all the time, for example, probably find that others, including strangers, frequently smile back at them. This may, in turn, lead them to conclude that the world is a positive place and that human beings are basically decent. Grumpy, suspicious people, on the other hand, may consistently evoke negative responses from others, which in turn may lead them to have a very different view of the world and human nature. Similarly, if you tend to act foolishly, people will frequently treat you as though you are a fool; if you tend to act cool and aloof and walk around town with a posture that shows it, strangers aren't likely to stop you on the street and ask directions; and if your behavior and facial expressions suggest empathy, others are likely to tell you their problems.

What are the ways in which you actively elicit certain kinds of responses to your personality from other people? Are you entirely happy with this situation, or are there certain kinds of responses that you would prefer not to elicit from others in the future? What steps can you take to elicit more favorable responses to your personality from those around you?

4. Do you hold certain negative opinions about your personality that seem to be true only because you have never tried to expand your

horizons? If you consider yourself a shy person, for example, have you ever taken the risk of speaking in front of a large group in an effort to overcome your shyness? In a very real sense, you are only as wise as your firsthand experiences have taught you to be. Once you've learned that you were duped by a dishonest used-car dealer, for example, you are unlikely to repeat the same mistake. In a more positive sense, once you've learned that you are capable of feeling truly fulfilled in your work life, romantic life, and personal friendships, you are unlikely to settle for less satisfying situations. Recognizing your own positive potential can dramatically alter your personality for the better. Consider the ways in which you might reach out and expand your horizons to achieve more of your latent positive potential.

5. Look around at your overall life circumstances and consider your own part in creating the situation in which you currently find yourself. Are you entirely happy with your present lifestyle? If you are not, do you tend to blame outside circumstances and other people for the things that make you unhappy? Do you believe, for example, that an unhappy childhood inevitably set you up for failure as an adult, or that other "bad luck" events entirely beyond your control somehow permanently altered your personality? Is it possible that, instead of being entirely at the mercy of these events, you have *maintained* their ill effects in your life by continuing to dwell upon them when you could have been taking positive steps to move forward?

Consider the ways in which you have consciously chosen to respond to important life events and circumstances, such as the loss of a job or the birth of a child. How have your actions and emotions influenced—for better or worse—the course of subsequent events? Are there ways in which you can choose to respond differently in the future in order to bring about the positive changes you desire?

The Bitter and the Sweet

As you have focused on honestly describing your Inner, Outer, and Unified Self-Images, you have probably also come to recognize—at least in the back of your mind—that there are certain personality characteristics that you would ideally like to have but do not necessarily feel you have yet achieved. There are also, no doubt, other personality characteristics that you would like to avoid developing as you progress along the path of your personal evolution. By focusing more directly on your "possible selves," both ideal and feared, you can gain important additional insights into your own personality and behavior. In the following chapter, you'll do just that by exploring your Ideal and Feared Self-Images.

Notes

1. For those who have a professional interest in the design of the Berkeley Personality Profile, the scoring categories in this section of the test were designed so that the middle two categories would be divided at the midpoint of the dimension, which corresponds to a score of 21 for each of the Big Five personality styles. The two extreme categories for each dimension were set so that the scores for 5 percent to 10 percent of our research participants would fall in the extreme category on the *less* common side of each dimension (that is, the highest scoring category for Emotional Style, and the lowest scoring category for all other personality styles), while the scores for 20 percent to 25 percent of participants would fall in the extreme category on the *more* common side of each dimension (that is, the lowest scoring category for Emotional Style, and the highest scoring category for all other personality styles).

2. For more detailed information on personality-environment interactions, see A. Caspi and D. J. Bem, "Personality Continuity and Change Across the Life Course," in L. A. Pervin, ed., *Handbook of Personality Theory and Research* (New York: Guilford, 1990), 549–75.

Achieving Your Ideals and Facing Your Fears

One of the essential characteristics that distinguishes human beings from the rest of the animal kingdom is our irrepressible desire for personal fulfillment and achievement. Consider, for example, the remarkable bravery and sacrifice of the New York City firemen and other rescuers who gave their lives while rushing to rescue those trapped in the collapsing World Trade Center during the September 11 terrorist attack, and the uncommon courage displayed by demonstrators who stood before the oncoming tanks in the notorious Tiananmen Square massacre. Although it often goes unnoticed, the selfless determination of those who labor interminable hours at minimum wage to help put a son or daughter through college, who volunteer in crisis centers and soup kitchens to help the less fortunate, and who devote themselves to countless other worthy causes in the hope of improving conditions all over the planet is no less significant.

Where do people find the energy and ambition to overcome incredible odds and innumerable obstacles to reach a distant goal? How do they manage to commit themselves to continue striving even after they've reached a goal, to try to surpass their own past performance in the pursuit of true excellence?

The secret of their outstanding motivation may be imagination. Many psychologists, including such famed personality theorists and clinicians as Carl Rogers and Karen Horney, and many noted contemporary personality researchers such as Hazel Markus at the University of Michigan and E. Tory Higgins at New York University, believe that people strive toward personal growth by creating an inner vision of the person they would ideally like to be and endeavoring to live up to that image. Like the Inner and Outer Self-Image you have already explored in preceding chapters, your *Ideal Self-Image* serves a vital psychological purpose.

Your Ideal Self-Image helps you to define in detail the personal goals you would like to pursue so that you can develop realistic strategies for achieving them. It allows you to contemplate how you will feel if you are successful in reaching your objectives, and to imagine how accomplishing them might change your lifestyle, your behavior, and even your personality. By consciously visualizing yourself as an "Academy Award–winning actor," an "effective leader," a "top-notch salesperson," or whatever you personally would most like to become, and comparing this fantasy to your current self-image, you can mentally rehearse the changes in behavior and perspective that are crucial to realizing your goal. Imagining your Ideal Self also makes your distant dreams seem more real and attainable, making it easier for you to believe in yourself, which is the first step to success.

But few of us think exclusively of success. Some researchers are beginning to believe that, as sources of motivation, our innermost fears may rival the power of our highest aspirations. Just as your Ideal Self-Image represents the person you would most like to become if everything goes your way in life, your *Feared Self-Image* represents your view of the person you could potentially become in a "worst-case scenario." During difficult economic times, for example, many people develop an Ideal Self-Image of the carefree and generous person they could become if they never had to worry about financial problems again. At the same time, they may be harboring a Feared Self-Image of the selfish and insecure person they might become if they were to lose their job, their health insurance, and their home.

Although your *possible selves* may appear quite improbable at times, they play pivotal psychological roles because they are both personally meaningful and potentially real. They help you visualize and contemplate all the positive and negative options that are open to you in your life so that you can feel better prepared psychologically to respond to whatever may come your way. They also liberate you from the actual constraints of your current life circumstances and from the sometimes weighty expectations of others. In the wide-open spaces of your imagination, you are completely free to decide what is best for *you*, and to plan the steps you should be taking now to help improve your future. Because no one else knows the intimate details of your innermost fears and fantasies, you need never allow others to dictate the Ideal Self-Image you should be striving to fulfill, or the Feared Self-Image you must ultimately avoid.[1]

Different people want wildly dissimilar things out of life. Some people dream of becoming international celebrities. Others would be equally content to live anonymously, enjoying the peace and quiet of a provincial existence. Some people desire fast-paced careers, while others prefer less demanding jobs they leave behind at the end of the day to enjoy their favorite leisure activities.

Just as people are motivated by singular goals and ideals, they are motivated to avoid distinctive personal fears. An individual involved in a competitive occupation might fear losing his or her edge. Another person in the identical position might fear working too hard and forgetting how to enjoy the finer moments in life. One student entering college might fear becoming socially isolated and withdrawn due to scholastic pressures. Another might fear becoming involved in so many social activities that little time remains for schoolwork, family, and special friendships. The particular fears you develop are likely to be directly related to your life experience, resembling the troubles that you or someone with whom you identify in some way has suffered in the past.

Your Feared Self-Image can influence, positively or negatively, the way you act, the way you feel, and the things that motivate you. If you fear that easing up at work might prevent you from getting a promotion, you might call that aspect of your Feared Self-Image to mind in order to recharge your batteries whenever you feel yourself losing motivation, thereby using your fear to maintain your productivity. If you fear that company-wide cutbacks could cause you to lose your job regardless of how hard you work, your fear might actually make it more difficult for you to be productive. In order to make your fears work positively for you, you need to feel that you have the power to determine your own destiny by taking positive steps to avoid the things you dread.

How can you put both your Ideal Self-Image and Feared Self-Image to work for you? The first step is understanding the content of your ideals and fears in detail. Often, you may be only partly aware of the hopes that are enticing you at some gut level to prefer one option over another, and the fears that are causing you to exclude other options before you even consider them. If those hopes and fears are unreasonable or unrealistic, they may be leading you to act in ways that are less than optimal or even self-defeating. By becoming more consciously aware of these hopes and fears, and distinguishing any unrealistic anxieties and phobias from more reasonable apprehensions that must be taken seriously, you can claim the power to determine your most effective course of action.

Many of the typical dreams and nightmares that periodically cross your mind probably concern your general life situation or material possessions. For example, your predominant ambitions might include "being rich" and "living happily ever after," while your prevalent fears might include "being a failure" and "leading a meaningless life." Sometimes, however, the strong emotion you feel in association with your ideals and fears may be linked not so much to changes in your life situation but to changes in your *personality*. Many people fear success, for example, but few fully understand why. Others dream of becoming physically fit but don't understand why they desire it so desperately. By exploring how your personality and relationships might change if your hopes or fears come true, the Berkeley Personality Profile can help you to understand the powerful emotions that are inexplicably tied to your possible selves. If you fear success, for example, you might find this fear to be rooted in the notion that success could cause you to become cold and impatient, or to distance yourself from those you love. If you desperately desire to be thin, you might feel this way because you believe that being thin would make you more self-confident.

One key to making your possible selves work for you is developing realistic Ideal and Feared Self-Images that are specifically suited to your latent potential, your skills and talents, your current life situation, and your personality. As you complete this section of the Berkeley Personality Profile, we will help you to think consciously about and, we hope, to understand better your *specific, personality-relevant* hopes and fears. We will not focus on such external concepts as the possibility that you might someday get rich or find yourself destitute, but rather will concentrate on your innermost wishes and worries about how you will develop as a human being in the future. Most important, we will examine the ways in which these wishes and worries influence your underlying motives, your actions, and your lifestyle.

Later, in the Points for Reflection, we will help you to identify potential problem situations in which you may be reacting more to remote probabilities than to realistic possibilities. By learning to recognize such situations, you may be able to avoid responding in ways that are ineffective and inappropriate, and may instead direct your attention and energy along a more productive path.

How to Take and Score the Test

For your results in this section of the test to be meaningful, it is critical that when rating your Ideal and Feared Self-Images, you think of the best and worst sides of your personality that you honestly believe *would be possible for you to develop*. Do not rate a generic idea of the best and worst possible personality that *anyone* might develop, but rather the best and worst personality that you can imagine yourself developing if your own future should take a turn for the better or for the worse.

Turn to the test materials in the perforated sections at the end of the book. You'll find Scorecard 4 on the flip side of Scorecard 1, which you completed earlier. If you have not already done so, you should also cut out Scorecard 5. Then place Scorecard 4 alongside the thirty-five statements in the Berkeley Personality Profile, making certain the colored rows on the test questions match up with the colored rows on the scorecard.

To begin, stop and consider your Ideal Self-Image, or the personality you would most like to manifest *and feel you can potentially develop*, if everything goes well in your life. For each of the thirty-five statements, rate as honestly as possible the extent to which you agree or disagree that the statement is true of your Ideal Self-Image.

After completing Scorecard 4, set it aside and take a five- to ten-minute break. Then use Scorecard 5 to respond to the same thirty-five statements for your Feared Self. Think about your Feared Self, or the worst-case scenario of the personality *you fear you could potentially develop* should your life not take the course you desire. Then rate, as honestly as possible, the extent to which you agree or disagree that each of the thirty-five statements describes your Feared Self. For the most accurate assessment of your personality, do not change any of your responses once you have completed the scorecard, and *do not* look back to any previous scorecards while you are filling out Score-cards 4 and 5.

After you have completed both scorecards, turn to the Possible Self-Image Profile in the perforated section and follow the instructions to compute and graph your scores. Your Possible Self-Image Profile shows your Ideal and Feared Self-Image Scores, together with your Unified Self-Image Scores from chapter 3, in one convenient, color-coded chart. It allows you to see at a glance the dimensions for which your Ideal and Feared Self-Images differ dramatically from your Unified Self-Image, and those for which all three might be remarkably similar.

On your Possible Self-Image Profile, each of the five color-coded personality dimensions ranges across a continuum of scores, with the opposite ends of the continuum representing directly opposite ways of approaching certain kinds of interests and activities. You have three scores on each dimension: Unified Self-Image, Ideal Self-Image, and Feared Self-Image. These scores can be spread anywhere along the scale. For the Expressive Style dimension, for example, a given individual might have an Ideal Self-Image Score that is very high, accompanied by a Unified Self-Image Score that is somewhat low and a Feared Self-Image Score that is extremely low. Such scores would indicate that she would ideally like to be very sociable, active, and enthusiastic, currently feels that she is actually rather quiet and reserved in most situations, and fears that, if things go poorly in her life, she could become even more shy and withdrawn in social situations in the future. Another person might have Expressive Style scores in the middle range for all three self-perspectives, indicating that he is moderately sociable and yet rather private at times, that he feels that this is the ideal level of Expressive Style for him, and that he has no particular concern that anything could ever happen in his life that would dramatically change his Expressive Style for the worse.

To understand the relationship between your own Possible Self-Image Scores for each of the Big Five dimensions, look up the scores you marked on your profile in the interpretation guide that follows.

Possible Selves Interpretation Guide

Begin by looking up your Unified/Ideal Difference Scores and your Unified/Feared Difference Scores from the *fourth* and *fifth* row of boxes on your Possible Self-Image Profile. Be sure that you made a *star* on the profile next to either your Ideal Self-Image Score or your Unified Self-Image Score, whichever was larger, in each color-coded column. Also, be sure that you made *two stars* in each color-coded column to indicate which was larger, your Feared Self-Image Score or your Unified Self-Image Score.

Below, you'll find a separate section for each of the Big Five personality dimensions. First, look up your color-coded *Unified/Ideal Difference Score*, and second, your *Unified/Feared Difference Score* for each style in the appropriate section—orange for Emotional Style, green for Interpersonal Style, and so forth. You may wish to circle the portion of the interpretation guide that corresponds to your scores in each section so that it will be easy for you to review your test results at a glance later on.

We caution you, once again, to remember that you know yourself better than we do. This interpretation of your Unified, Ideal, and Feared Self-Images is based strictly on the way you *described yourself* in this section of the Berkeley Personality Profile. If you feel that this interpretation does not really fit your personality, it may be because you interpreted the test questions a little differently than people usually do, or you may have been feeling a little depressed or out of sorts on the day you completed the questionnaire. If the interpretation provided below seems very different from the way you see yourself, you may wish to double-check each stage in the computation of your scores. You should also check to be certain that you are looking up the scores from the correct row of the profile in each portion of the interpretation guide.

It is also critical to keep in mind that each of the Big Five personality dimensions refers to a personal *style* and that high-numbered scores are not necessarily "better" or "worse" than low-numbered scores. The score that is best suited to *you* for each dimension depends on your preferences about the kind of individual you would ideally like to be, as well as your fears about those characteristics that would be incompatible with your most cherished values and sense of self.

Unified/Ideal Difference Scores—Expressive Style (Orange)

To learn more about your scores, begin by looking up your Expressive Style Unified/Ideal Difference Score in the *fourth* row of boxes on your profile.

- *If your score falls between 0 and 3:* You currently feel quite satisfied with your Expressive Style. You feel that you appropriately balance your private and social life, and probably feel that you have neither too few nor too many friends. You seldom feel a lack of energy or assertiveness, but neither do you feel an excess of energy perpetually inducing you to act before you have a chance to consider your options carefully. In addition, you probably temper your expressions of enthusiasm with a more reserved attitude in situations requiring discretion.

- *If your score falls between 4 and 7 and you marked a star next to your Ideal Self-Image Score:* You are generally satisfied with the way you express yourself but would like to be able to do so more easily, or to approach opportunities and activities with greater enthusiasm than you typically do. You may see yourself as a little less sociable, and perhaps less comfortable around strangers, than you would ideally like to be. Or you may be happy with the way you interact in social situations but wish you felt a bit more optimistic or energetic in your everyday life.

- *If your score falls between 4 and 7 and you marked a star next to your Unified Self-Image Score:* You are generally happy with the way you express yourself but would like to change at least one aspect of your Expressive Style. You may feel, for example, that you are somewhat more forward or assertive than you would ideally like to be, or that you have a tendency to become a little too loud when you are excited. Or you may enjoy your outward expressions most of the time but wish you felt more calm and could find it easier to settle down at the end of a long, hard day.

- *If your score falls between 8 and 28 and you marked a star next to your Ideal Self-Image Score:* You would like to make some significant lifestyle changes with respect to your Expressive Style. You might, for example, like to release yourself from the inhibiting influence of social rules and restrictions, thereby becoming more playful, spirited, and spontaneous. You may also wish you were more willing to take charge and assume a leadership role in your relationships with others, and would probably like to feel a bit more upbeat and energetic than you typically do.

  If your score is extremely high (17 or greater): You may be contemplating dramatic changes in your Expressive Style, or may already have given up hope of ever drawing your actual personality any closer to your lofty ideals. You may, however, be overidealizing the life of the fun-loving partygoer or adventurer, while at the same time you may be underestimating the value of your own more soft-spoken or low-key approach to life.

- *If your score falls between 8 and 28 and you marked a star next to your Unified Self-Image Score:* You feel that some significant behavioral and other life changes could improve your Expressive Style. You may feel, for example, that you can be pushy and domineering at times, and wish it were easier for you to take the time to appreciate the needs and opinions of others. You might also wish you could slow down a bit and savor the moment—spending more time doing the things you really enjoy and cutting down on other activities that are less important to you.

If your score is extremely high (17 or greater): You may feel that dramatic changes in your personality and lifestyle are necessary so that you may become quieter and more unassuming than you are at this time. You may also feel discouraged and unable to keep your tendency to dominate others under control, or incapable of keeping your opinions to yourself. You may, however, be overidealizing the lifestyle of those whose routines seem more predictable and settled down than your own, while at the same time underestimating the value of your own more outgoing, adventurous, and enthusiastic approach to life.

Unified/Feared Difference Scores—Expressive Style (Orange)

Now look up your Expressive Style Unified/Feared Difference Score from the fifth row of boxes on your profile.

- *If your score falls between 0 and 3:* You are not concerned that your mode of social interaction, your energy level, or the way you experience and express positive emotions could take a turn for the worse. To understand the implications of the close similarity between your Unified and Feared Self-Images, look up your Unified/*Ideal* Difference Score for Expressive Style from the *fourth* row of boxes on your profile.

  If your Unified/Ideal Difference Score for Expressive Style is also quite small (between 0 and 3): You feel that your Expressive Style is so central to your nature or so ingrained in your patterns of behavior that even major life changes are unlikely to influence this aspect of your personality.

  If your Unified/Ideal Difference Score for Expressive Style is moderate to large (4 or greater): You feel that your current levels of energy, assertiveness, and sociability have already hit what is, for you, rock bottom. Although you may feel somewhat discouraged about this at present, it is important to remember that you do have the power and potential to change your Expressive Style so that it more closely resembles your Ideal Self-Image.

- *If your score falls between 4 and 7 and you marked two stars next to your Feared Self-Image Score:* You have no fear of becoming less active, assertive, or sociable than you presently are; instead, you fear that some aspect of your Expressive Style could become too strong or intense, leading to negative social or personal consequences. You may, for example, fear becoming too caught up in social occasions or events to the point that you allow them to interfere with other areas of your life. Or you may fear overwhelming others with your own opinions and suggestions or boring them with endless chatter.

- *If your score falls between 4 and 7 and you marked two stars next to your Unified Self-Image Score:* You show definite concern about maintaining some aspect of your Expressive Style. You may, for example, fear allowing yourself to be dominated by others or withdrawing from the social occasions or events that you currently enjoy. Or you may fear becoming tired and worn out, losing some of your energy or enthusiasm for life.

- *If your score falls between 8 and 28 and you marked two stars next to your Feared Self-Image Score:* You have strong concerns about being able to keep certain aspects of your Expressive Style in check, for fear that being too forward, too assertive, or too enthusiastic could lead to trouble in your career and interpersonal relationships and thereby disrupt your life. You may fear becoming too uninhibited in the way you express your opinions and desires to other people, or allowing yourself to expend too much energy in an unfocused or unproductive manner.

If your score is extremely high (17 or greater): Your fears are extreme and may be unrealistic; you should not allow these fears to prevent you from taking the reasonable personal risks that are essential to developing close relationships with others.

- ***If your score falls between 8 and 28 and you marked two stars next to your Unified Self-Image Score:*** You have strong concerns about maintaining your current level of enthusiasm, expressiveness, or assertiveness. You may, for example, be apprehensive that a significant life change, such as a prolonged illness, could interfere with your way of relating to others—causing you to become too docile, hesitant, or passive in the way you express your feelings, opinions, and ideas to other people. You may also fear becoming too guarded and reclusive, and being unable to muster the energy it takes to get all you really want out of life.

If your score is extremely high (17 or greater): Your fears are extreme and may be unrealistic; you should try not to let these fears prevent you from experiencing life to the fullest, which includes getting in touch with the quieter, more restrained side of your personality.

Unified/Ideal Difference Scores—Interpersonal Style (Green)

Now look at your Interpersonal Style Unified/Ideal Difference Score, in the fourth row of boxes on your profile:

- ***If your score falls between 0 and 3:*** You feel that your Interpersonal Style or approach toward others truly is the style that suits you best. You are probably happy, for example, with the level of intimacy—the degree of closeness or distance—you maintain in your relationships with other people. You probably do not feel that others take advantage of you because you are too nice to them. Instead, you feel that your Interpersonal Style allows you to deal well with others, without compromising your own needs in any significant fashion.

- ***If your score falls between 4 and 7 and you marked a star next to your Ideal Self-Image Score:*** You are satisfied with your Interpersonal Style as a whole but would like to make some specific improvements in your interpersonal relationships. You may wish, at times, that you could be a bit more patient or understanding. Or you may sometimes feel that you are a bit more selfish than you would ideally like to be. In addition, some people who score themselves in this range feel that they have difficulty openly sharing their love with others or allowing themselves to be loved in return.

- *If your score falls between 4 and 7 and you marked a star next to your Unified Self-Image Score:* You have been burned a few times, or at least singed, in your interpersonal relationships. You may feel that you trust others too easily and that you would be less likely to get hurt if you were somewhat more protective of your own needs. Or you may find that when you focus your energy on helping others, they focus on themselves as well, only to forget that you would also appreciate receiving their support in return. People often score themselves in this range not because they want to stop caring for others, but simply because they wish they could better communicate their own needs and thereby *receive* more care and support in their interpersonal relationships.

- *If your score falls between 8 and 28 and you marked a star next to your Ideal Self-Image Score:* You are dissatisfied with your current style of interacting in personal relationships and would like to make some significant changes in your attitudes and behavior toward others. You may wish that you could trust other people more easily and show your affection for them without the fear of getting hurt. You may also feel it should be easier for you to accept the affection that others show for you without withdrawing from them. Sharing your feelings more openly with others, and allowing them to share their feelings with you, would help to make your personal relationships warmer and more intimate. It is important to note, however, that some people who score in this range are dissatisfied in some relationships but very satisfied in others. You may feel, for example, that your truly intimate relationships are very healthy but that some of your other relationships—perhaps with certain relatives or coworkers—would be stronger if you were a bit more patient and considerate, or more willing to listen.

If your score is extremely high (17 or greater): You described your Ideal Self-Image as very warm, caring, and compassionate but described your Unified Self-Image as rather cool and aloof, or perhaps stubborn and difficult. It is possible that you are selling yourself short in your capacity to get along with others. The value you expressed for interpersonal relationships in your description of your Ideal Self-Image shows that you do, in fact, really care about other people—which is the first step toward strengthening your interpersonal relationships.

- *If your score falls between 8 and 28 and you marked a star next to your Unified Self-Image Score:* You feel that you give in too easily to other people's needs or demands, allowing yourself to be hurt too deeply and too often. Although you care about others, you may wish that you more often also took the time to care about yourself. You may feel that by focusing so much on helping other people, and giving too much of yourself, you sometimes forget to look out for your own needs—and that other people tend to forget about your needs as well. You therefore may wish it could be easier for you to voice what *you* want once in a while. Alternatively, some people who score themselves in this range feel that most of their ongoing interpersonal relationships are healthy but find that they tend to rush into romances or other close, intimate relationships too quickly, allowing themselves to be hurt when the affection they express for others is not always returned.

If your score is extremely high (17 or greater): You may be overidealizing the benefit of keeping a safe distance in your dealings with others in order to avoid being hurt. Although you described your Unified Self-Image as being quite warm, caring, and compassionate, you described your Ideal Self-Image as just the opposite: cool and aloof, and perhaps even cynical and suspicious of others' motives. This difference between your Unified and Ideal Self-Image also suggests that perhaps you are being too hard on yourself. Maybe you were recently hurt in an interpersonal relationship in which you showed kindness and caring to another that was neither appreciated nor returned. You may therefore be feeling the need—at least for now—to be more cautious with others. You should not, however, underestimate the value of your warm and caring side.

Unified/Feared Difference Scores—Interpersonal Style (Green)

Your Interpersonal Style Unified/Feared Difference Score can be found in the fifth row of boxes on your profile.

- *If your score falls between 0 and 3:* You do not concern yourself with fears about possible hardships interfering with the depth or quality of your personal relationships. You may, for example, feel confident that your friends would continue to support you in times of trouble, even if you were somewhat less patient and considerate toward them than usual. To understand the implications of the close similarity between your Unified and Feared Self-Images, look up your Unified/*Ideal* Difference Score for Interpersonal Style from the *fourth* row of boxes on your profile.

  If your Unified/Ideal Difference Score for Interpersonal Style is also quite small (between 0 and 3): You feel that your particular way of thinking about and relating to other people's needs is so central to your personality that even a drastic life change would be unlikely to alter the way in which you balance your own interests with the interests of others.

  If your Unified/Ideal Difference Score for Interpersonal Style is moderate to large (4 or greater): You feel that your attitudes toward, and relationships with, other people are already about as strained as they could ever become. Although you may feel discouraged about this at present, it is important to remember that you do have the potential to draw both your feelings and your actions more closely in line with the pattern you have sketched out for your Ideal Self-Image.

- *If your score falls between 4 and 7 and you marked two stars next to your Feared Self-Image Score:* You generally do not worry about changes in the quality of your personal relationships. From time to time, however, you may be concerned that if you show too much caring or consideration for other people, then they will perceive you as too soft and perhaps take advantage of your goodwill. Alternatively, you may fear becoming too attached to one particular person in your life right now but feel that most of your relationships are genuinely strong and healthy.

- *If your score falls between 4 and 7 and you marked two stars next to your Unified Self-Image Score:* You generally do not worry about possible personal hardships interfering with the quality of your relationships. Your test responses, however, indicate a concern that at least one aspect of your Interpersonal Style could suffer in the future. You may, for example, fear losing trust in other people or becoming so self-interested that you feel unworthy of the trust others place in you. Alternatively, you may not be concerned about harming others deliberately but may instead be concerned that you might forget about the needs of others, or be unable to find time to help them, if you come under too much pressure to look after yourself. Alternatively, you may be feeling that a relationship with an individual who is especially important to you is currently at risk but that the rest of your interpersonal relationships are on solid ground.

- *If your score falls between 8 and 28 and you marked two stars next to your Feared Self-Image Score:* You have concerns about possible changes in your Interpersonal Style. You may, for example, worry that if you expend too much time and energy looking after the needs of others, they will eventually take you for granted and fail to appreciate the things you do for them. Many people who score in this range also have severe reservations about becoming involved in intimate friendships and romantic relationships. These feelings generally arise from a sense of vulnerability, sometimes created by painful memories of past relationships, and other times resulting from the uncertainty that accompanies a lack of experience in intimate relationships.

If your score is extremely high (17 or greater): Your fears are extreme and may be rooted more in the past than the present. If you find that such fears are interfering with your ability to become involved with others, try to remember that you should evaluate each relationship in your present life on its own terms, rather than punishing those who are presently in your life for the sins committed by others who have hurt you in the past.

- *If your score falls between 8 and 28 and you marked two stars next to your Unified Self-Image Score:* You have definite concerns that you could potentially lose touch with your caring and compassionate side in the face of some change or hardship in your life. You may, for example, fear becoming so wrapped up in your own needs and problems that you no longer have time to listen to others or support them when they are down. You may fear developing "compassion fatigue," or losing faith that your efforts to help others can even begin to solve the problems in the world. Or you may fear that the temptation of money, fame, or success could lead you to pursue your own personal interests aggressively, at the expense of other people.

  If your score is extremely high (17 or greater): You may wish to consider whether such fears are warranted in your case; your scores indicate that you currently value interpersonal relationships quite highly, so it seems unlikely that you would ever let anything distance you from others for very long.

Unified/Ideal Difference Scores—Work Style (Yellow)

Look up your Work Style Unified/Ideal Difference Score, from the fourth row of boxes on your profile.

- *If your score falls between 0 and 3:* You feel that your approach toward work, plans, and responsibilities is truly the style that suits you best. You are probably happy, for example, with the number and type of responsibilities that you agree to handle, and the way in which you apply yourself toward accomplishing your goals. When you plan activities, you probably do so in a way that does not feel rigid or overly confining for you. You probably enjoy most projects you take on, relishing the work itself rather than feeling that it is only a means to an end.

- *If your score falls between 4 and 7 and you marked a star next to your Ideal Self-Image Score:* You are generally satisfied with your Work Style but would like to make some specific changes in your approach toward work, plans, and responsibilities. You may feel, for example, that you procrastinate a little more than you should. Or you may have no trouble at all applying yourself to a task but sometimes find it difficult to finish projects promptly because you are not as organized or efficient as you would like to be. Alternatively, you may simply feel that you are juggling too many obligations at once, causing problems in one area of your life, such as work, family, housekeeping, or self-improvement.

- *If your score is between 4 and 7 and you marked a star next to your Unified Self-Image Score:* You are generally satisfied with your Work Style but wish you could feel slightly more relaxed in your approach toward plans, responsibilities, and the endless details with which you find yourself dealing. You may, for example, feel too wrapped up in your work and wish you could slow down and take time out once in a while. Perhaps you wish that not quite so many people were depending on you, or you would like to be able to delegate more of your responsibilities to others. Or you may simply feel that you're a little too much of a perfectionist at times and that you worry too much about meticulous details that might not matter in the long run.

- *If your score is between 8 and 28 and you marked a star next to your Ideal Self-Image Score:* You would like to change your Work Style to help you accomplish more or to feel more capable of meeting all of your commitments. You may, for example, have trouble prioritizing your activities. You may wish that you could finish those undertakings that are important to you without worrying so much about lesser projects. Alternatively, some people who score in this range find that they manage to finish what they set out to do, but only at the last minute and in a somewhat haphazard way; people in this situation often wish they could give more careful attention to detail.

If your score is extremely high (17 or greater): You described your Unified Self-Image as somewhat careless or irresponsible, and your

Ideal Self-Image as very capable, responsible, and perfectionistic. This difference suggests that you may, for example, feel that a great number of people are depending on you for many things but that you too often let them down. However, you may not be giving yourself enough credit for the things you *do* accomplish and for all the times that you have been a person that others could depend upon. You may wish to consider the possibility that your problem may be that you hold yourself responsible for matters that are completely beyond your control.

- *If your score is between 8 and 28 and you marked a star next to your Unified Self-Image Score:* You are feeling choked or constricted by social, financial, career, or family responsibilities. You may wish that fewer people were depending on you and that you could loosen up and escape your responsibilities for a while without feeling guilty. Perhaps you wish you could be less of a perfectionist, take on fewer projects, and slow down a bit. Many people who score themselves in this range feel that there are too many demands being placed upon their time and wish that they could delegate more of their responsibilities to someone else.

  If your score is extremely high (17 or greater): You may wish to consider the possibility that you are overidealizing the carefree life that is devoid of responsibilities. You may simply be feeling overwhelmed for the moment and may possibly be forgetting the reasons why you took on so many responsibilities in the first place—because it is rewarding to accomplish your goals and know that others can depend on you.

Unified/Feared Difference Scores—Work Style (Yellow)

Your Work Style Unified/Feared Difference Score can be found in the fifth row of boxes on your profile.

- *If your score falls between 0 and 3:* You are not particularly concerned that your Work Style might change for the worse. You are probably not worried, for example, that you will become more and more bogged down by schedules, plans, and responsibilities in the future. At the same time, you probably are not concerned about slowing down, becoming irresponsible, or finding that the tasks you can accomplish easily today will somehow become more difficult for you to accomplish in the future. To understand the implications of the close similarity between your Unified and Feared Self-Image, look up your Unified/*Ideal* Difference Score for Work Style from the *fourth* row of boxes on your profile.

If your Unified/Ideal Difference Score for Work Style is also quite small (between 0 and 3): You feel that your current approach toward work and responsibilities is so deeply ingrained in your character that nothing in your future is likely to change it in any significant way.

If your Unified/Ideal Difference Score for Work Style is moderate to large (4 or greater): You feel that your current approach toward work and responsibilities is unlikely to change for the worse but that it nevertheless has room for improvement. This improvement may require pulling yourself out of an unfocused or unproductive cycle or, alternatively, letting go of an obsession with perfection. In either case, you do not fear that the impulses creating this difficulty will spin any further out of control than they already are.

- *If your score falls between 4 and 7 and you marked two stars next to your Feared Self-Image Score:* You are not overly concerned about potential changes in your Work Style but have considered the possibility that becoming more serious about your work would constitute more of a hindrance than a help for you. You may, for example, recognize the potential in yourself to become too wrapped up in your career or other responsibilities. You may fear that such concerns could dominate your life if you allowed them to do so. Alternatively, you may fear becoming too much of a perfectionist or a bit too meticulous, and hope that you will be able to keep the big picture in perspective in the future.

- *If your score falls between 4 and 7 and you marked two stars next to your Unified Self-Image Score:* You do not worry excessively about potential changes in your Work Style, although you have probably wondered whether you will be able to maintain your current level of effectiveness and productivity in the future. You may, for example, sometimes fear that you will not always have the drive or motivation to keep up with all the projects and responsibilities that you currently juggle. Alternatively, you may feel that if you become overwhelmed or take on too many obligations at once, you may become inefficient or disorganized, and the quality of your work or your commitment to those who depend on you will suffer as a result.

- *If your score falls between 8 and 28 and you marked two stars next to your Feared Self-Image Score:* You have strong concerns that stepping up your orientation toward work and responsibilities could have definite negative outcomes in your life. You are probably afraid of being tied down by too many schedules, plans, and commitments because such ties might make your life too predictable. You may also fear that giving in to society's work-oriented demands could rob you of certain childlike qualities that you currently cherish in your personality. Some people who score themselves in this range shy away from responsibilities because they are unsure about whether they are capable of succeeding, while others score in this range simply because they prefer a carefree life with few responsibilities.

  If your score is extremely high (17 or greater): Your fears may be out of proportion to reality, suggesting that you should explore the underlying source of your aversion to responsibilities more carefully and think twice before allowing these feelings to influence the course of your behavior.

- *If your score falls between 8 and 28 and you marked two stars next to your Unified Self-Image Score:* You have concerns that your orientation toward your responsibilities, and ability to honor your commitments, could deteriorate for some reason. You may, for example, fear that something could happen to interfere with the comfortable predictability of your life, which currently helps you function effectively. Such unpredictability could distract you from being focused on the myriad details of your work and social life that you must keep organized, and perhaps even force you to relinquish the commitments that you currently juggle.

If your score is extremely high (17 or greater): You may wish to consider whether your fears are exaggerated. If others are available to assist you with some of your responsibilities, for example, you may be pleasantly surprised at the effectiveness of delegation. You may find that delegating some of your responsibilities makes it unnecessary to overextend yourself in the first place, so that you need not worry about keeping up your hectic and demanding pace.

Unified/Ideal Difference Scores—Emotional Style (Red)

Look up your Emotional Style Unified/Ideal Difference Score, from the fourth row of boxes on your profile.

- *If your score falls between 0 and 3:* You feel that the way you experience and express your emotions is truly the style that suits you best. You probably feel that your emotional reactions to people and events are neither too extreme nor too subdued, but instead that you generally respond in a way that is appropriate to the situation at hand. In addition, you probably do not feel that fearfulness or a lack of self-confidence holds you back or prevents you from doing the things you would like to do in your life.

- *If your score falls between 4 and 7 and you marked a star next to your Ideal Self-Image Score:* You would like to heighten your emotional experiences in some way. You may feel that your emotional responses to people or events are too subdued at times. You may, for example, wish that you could experience and express worry and frustration more easily, thereby better communicating your needs and desires to others. Alternatively, you might be someone who performs most effectively under stress or when meeting a tight deadline. You may feel that you currently are not confronted with the kinds of challenges you need to feel engaged and able to perform at your best.

- *If your score falls between 4 and 7 and you marked a star next to your Unified Self-Image Score:* You would like to develop better control over some aspect of your Emotional Style so that you could feel more stable, tranquil, and at ease. You may, for example, feel that you are too irritable and become upset too easily, or that you are more nervous or high-strung than you would ideally like to be. Alternatively, some people who score in this range feel in control of both anxiety and frustration but sometimes find that they do not have all the self-confidence or self-assurance they would ideally like to have.

- *If your score falls between 8 and 28 and you marked a star next to your Ideal Self-Image Score:* You feel extremely cut off from emotional experiences, especially when negative emotions such as fear, frustration, or tension are involved. You may, for example, feel that the emotional passions you once felt have lately been blunted for some reason. Emotional blunting is sometimes a temporary reaction to sadness or grief. Alternatively, you might be feeling unemotional because your life is not currently stimulating enough to keep you feeling emotionally involved in your world.

  If your score is extremely high (17 or greater): Your test score highlights a dramatic difference between the calm and stable emotional responses you currently experience and the dramatic passions that you long to feel. You may wish to consider whether your idealization of intense emotions that are larger than life is rooted more in romantic fiction than in reality, failing to reflect the severe friction that such a temperament can create in real life.

- *If your score falls between 8 and 28 and you marked a star next to your Unified Self-Image Score:* You would like to distance yourself from strong negative emotions, especially anxiety, tension, or self-doubt. You may, for example, feel that you allow yourself to become frustrated too easily and are tired of doing battle with your temper. Or you may be feeling burned out or overworked and wish you could relax in a totally stress-free environment. You may also wish that you could conquer any self-doubts that may be holding you back from striking out in new directions.

If your score is extremely high (17 or greater): You may be over-idealizing the extent to which tranquillity, stability, and self-certainty would improve your life, while also underestimating the excitement and intensity that certain feelings of uncertainty can add to your daily existence.

Unified/Feared Difference Scores—Emotional Style (Red)

Your Unified/Feared Difference Score for Emotional Style can be found in the fifth row of boxes on your profile.

- *If your score falls between 0 and 3:* You are not concerned about losing control of your temper, nor do you feel that any anxiety or self-doubt that you currently keep in check is likely to overwhelm you in the future. At the same time, you are not afraid of losing touch with your feelings and becoming unable to experience or express such difficult emotions as fear, apprehension, or self-doubt. To understand the implications of the close similarity between your Unified and Feared Self-Image, look up your Unified/Ideal Difference Score for Emotional Style from the *fourth* row of boxes on your profile.

  If your Unified/Ideal Difference Score for Emotional Style is also quite low (between 0 and 3): You are satisfied with your current mode of experiencing and expressing your negative emotions. You feel that this aspect of your personality is so central to your personality that it is unlikely to change in any significant way, regardless of whether your life takes a turn for the better or the worse in the future.

If your Unified/Ideal Difference Score for Emotional Style is moderate to large (4 or greater): Your dissatisfaction with your experience of negative emotions—due either to feeling overly sensitive or too insensitive to worries, frustrations, and self-doubt—is tempered by the belief that your emotional experiences are already about as difficult as they could realistically become for you.

- *If your score falls between 4 and 7 and you marked two stars next to your Feared Self-Image Score:* You expressed slight concern that your negative emotions could potentially become too intense for your liking. You may, for example, fear losing control of your temper and lashing out at someone who is making you run out of patience. Or you may be thinking of making major changes or seeking new challenges in your life, and worry that stress or self-doubt might make you moody, irritable, or short-tempered.

- *If your score falls between 4 and 7 and you marked two stars next to your Unified Self-Image Score:* You expressed a few specific concerns about experiencing some drain on your emotional reserves that might leave you out of touch with your feelings. You may, for example, fear that living in an increasingly violent society could desensitize you to many basic human emotions, and leave you feeling only disillusionment. Or you may fear that enjoying too much success in your career or too much stability in your family life could lead you to feel too comfortable and self-secure, to take the good things in life for granted.

- *If your score falls between 8 and 28 and you marked two stars next to your Feared Self-Image Score:* You have fears about either becoming too emotional or losing your self-confidence and sense of security. You may fear that if your life becomes any more difficult, you may lose control over your temper and your anxieties. Or you may envision your ability to cope being stretched to the limit by intense or prolonged stress at work or at home, leaving you feeling frazzled and burned out and interfering with your ability to enjoy life. Alternatively, you may fear that the uncertainty that would accompany any dramatic change in your life, for better or for worse, could compromise your sense of confidence and self-esteem.

If your score is extremely high (17 or greater): You may be allowing unrealistic fears about your emotions to interfere with your ability to deal with frustration, loss, or anxiety in an honest and healthy fashion. If you currently keep excessively tight control over such negative feelings, you may wish to try expressing your emotions more openly in a safe environment with people you trust. You may discover that the consequences of expressing negative emotions are not as severe as you expected.

- *If your score falls between 8 and 28 and you marked two stars next to your Unified Self-Image Score:* You have strong concerns about becoming less emotional. You may, for example, fear that you will become so accustomed to holding back your anger that you will eventually lose touch with this emotion—becoming incapable of standing up for yourself. Or you may feel that your daily existence is becoming less and less challenging. Without a certain amount of stress in your life, you may fear that you will become too placid and lose interest in the challenges that currently motivate you and make you feel alive. Alternatively, you may value your strong emotions because they make you feel connected to other people. You may fear that, if your emotions become less passionate, your relationships will also become less fulfilling.

If your score is extremely high (17 or greater): You may wish to consider whether your fears about losing touch with your emotions are exaggerated. Your Unified/Feared Difference Score indicates that your emotional nature currently plays a central role in your identity. No matter how placid or dull your life situation might become, you will most likely continue to seek out challenges and stimulating situations that bring this aspect of your personality to life.

Unified/Ideal Difference Scores—Intellectual Style (Blue)

Your Unified/Ideal Difference Score for Intellectual Style can be found in the fourth row of boxes on your profile.

- *If your score falls between 0 and 3:* You feel that your Intellectual Style or approach toward art, philosophy, and new ideas is truly the style that suits you best. You probably do not feel overly confined by your ties to tradition or mainstream culture. At the same time, you probably do not feel personally threatened in the face of intellectual or societal change.

- *If your score falls between 4 and 7 and you marked a star next to your Ideal Self-Image Score:* You would like to expand your intellectual and aesthetic horizons in some way. You may wish you were more sophisticated in your approach toward art, music, or literature, less conventional in some of your social or political views, or simply less confined by the boundaries of tradition. Some people who score themselves in this range on Intellectual Style would like to broaden their interests but simply feel too caught up in the demands of everyday existence to allow themselves the luxury of such an intellectual and aesthetic indulgence.

- *If your score falls between 4 and 7 and you marked a star next to your Unified Self-Image Score:* You often feel that life has become too complicated and confusing. You may wish that you could revert to an earlier time and immerse yourself in traditional values and ideology. You may resent being constantly prodded to change in order to keep up with the demands of our fast-track and often fad-oriented society. In all the mayhem of our modern culture, you may be longing for a little peace and stability in your life.

- *If your score falls between 8 and 28 and you marked a star next to your Ideal Self-Image Score:* You see yourself as too simple or provincial and may feel painfully isolated or cut off from the new ideas you long to explore. In addition, you may be feeling overly confined by traditional values and expectations, and wish that it was easier for you to reject the pressures you feel to conform. You may, for example, dream about being more comfortable in expressing your creative side to others, or perhaps becoming part of a bohemian or avant-garde lifestyle, at least for a while.

If your score is extremely high (17 or greater): You may be placing unrealistic demands on yourself to seek out and embrace new ideas in too many fields at one time, such as art, music, literature, philosophy, sociology, science, and politics. You may wish to consider a more accessible creative outlet, perhaps through taking a closer look at the hidden wonder of the simple things around you that you usually take for granted.

- *If your score falls between 8 and 28 and you marked a star next to your Unified Self-Image Score:* You see yourself as open-minded and willing to embrace change but are beginning to tire of the fast track of intellectual and social innovation dictated by the demands of our culture. Although you generally value your intellect and your flexibility in the face of change, you may currently be wondering whether it would be simpler to trade in your fanciful ideas for a nice home-cooked meal of stability, security, and traditional values.

  If your score is extremely high (17 or greater): You may be overidealizing the simple life at the moment and underestimating just how much you would miss your creative and intellectual outlets if you were to surrender to the seductive lure of security and predictability.

Unified/Feared Difference Scores—Intellectual Style (Blue)

Your Unified/Feared Difference Score for Intellectual Style can be found in the fifth row of boxes on your profile.

- *If your score falls between 0 and 3:* You are not especially concerned about experiencing any transformations in your views, values, and approach toward culture and tradition. You feel highly secure in your approach. You are not concerned that anyone or anything you may confront in the future will be strong enough to cause you to alter your overall response to new ideas in science, the arts, philosophy, social issues, and politics. To understand the implications of the close similarity between your Unified and Feared Self-Image, look up your Unified/*Ideal* Difference Score for Intellectual Style from the *fourth* row of boxes on your profile.

If your Unified/Ideal Difference Score is also quite low (between 0 and 3): You feel that your current Intellectual Style is so central to your sense of identity that nothing that might happen in your life is likely to interfere with it. If some aspect of your life, such as your job or your relationship with your spouse, ceased to be intellectually stimulating for you, you would most likely take some definitive action to rejuvenate that part of your existence. Alternatively, if you thought that some aspect of your life was changing too rapidly, you would probably also take action to restore a sense of equilibrium.

If your Unified/Ideal Difference Score is moderate to high (4 or greater): You are dissatisfied with your current creative and intellectual pursuits or with your present inclination toward new and unfamiliar experiences. While this discrepancy between your current self-image and your ideals could be discouraging, you are at least not paralyzed by the fear of becoming even more cut off from new ideas and experiences than you are at the moment.

- *If your score falls between 4 and 7 and you marked two stars next to your Feared Self-Image Score:* You worry relatively little about changes in your personal ideology or in your artistic, philosophical, or scientific sensibilities that could cause you to adopt a more narrow perspective on your experiences. You may, however, be troubled by the nagging thought that you will someday have to give up a cherished idea or tradition in order to make way for personal and cultural growth.

- *If your score falls between 4 and 7 and you marked two stars next to your Unified Self-Image Score:* You generally tend not to worry about changes in your personal ideology or in your artistic, philosophical, or scientific sensibilities. You may, however, fear becoming too set in your ways, at least with respect to one specific aspect of your life. You may fear you might stubbornly resist change, even when it becomes necessary for personal growth or scientific and cultural progress. Or you may be open to the *idea* of change but fear that you may back down when faced with the real implications of taking definitive action.

- ***If your score falls between 8 and 28 and you marked two stars next to your Feared Self-Image Score:*** You value your special ability to see the wisdom and the richness in traditional ways and lifestyles, and fear that something in the future, perhaps the hectic pace of change, could cause you to lose touch with your cultural and intellectual roots. You may feel that to change is to make yourself vulnerable. You may also fear that others will consider you foolish or fanciful if you do not remain loyal to the traditional and accepted ways of your own social or cultural group.

  If your score is extremely high (17 or greater): You may be underestimating the richness of *privately* pondering new approaches and ideas, even if you feel you are presently in a situation in which you must keep your ideas to yourself.

- ***If your score falls between 8 and 28 and you marked two stars next to your Unified Self-Image Score:*** You worry about becoming too set in your ways and unwilling to expand your horizons. You may fear that as your life becomes more and more complicated, you will be unable or unwilling to keep up with the rapid pace of change demanded by modern social, political, and scientific advances. Alternatively, you may fear becoming so tied down by the mundane concerns of everyday life that you will become too conventional—or even boring—and miss out on the artistic and intellectual challenges you currently enjoy.

  If your score is extremely high (17 or greater): Your fears may be unrealistically extreme, given your basic character. Your Unified Self-Image Score indicates that you sincerely value your open-mindedness, flexibility, and capacity for change. It seems unlikely that anything could actually cause you to reject these treasured qualities in yourself.

What Do Others Who Are Like
You Want and Fear in Life?

Our research indicates that what you want out of life depends in large measure on what you currently have—that is, the personality you want to develop depends in part on your current personality. This shouldn't be surprising if you consider it in everyday terms: economically disadvantaged people typically want greater financial security; wealthy people with complicated lives often long for simplicity; and lonely people usually want greater intimacy in their relationships. According to celebrated psychologist Abraham Maslow, individuals who feel that their basic material and interpersonal needs have been met typically strive toward a higher sense of personal fulfillment. Maslow considered this striving toward an ideal level of "self-actualization" to be an essential sign of psychological well-being.[2]

In studying the responses of those who replied to the first of three personality surveys we published in *Psychology Today*, we found many examples of people wanting what they did not have—people with shy Expressive Styles who wanted to be more outgoing, people with moody Emotional Styles who wanted to be more stable, and so forth. But we also found many people who *simultaneously* desired and feared a particular personality change. This pattern seemed to be linked to their current Unified Self-Image, like the one you computed in chapter 3. The pattern occurred most often among people who scored their Unified Self-Image as being low (scores between about 7 and 18) on the Expressive Style, Interpersonal Style, or Work Style dimension.

For example, people who scored low on Expressive Style, indicating that they saw themselves as quiet, shy, and retiring, almost universally (98 percent) expressed an interest in becoming more outgoing and expressive. Despite this desire, however, approximately one-fourth of these individuals simultaneously *feared* experiencing a personality change in that direction. By contrast, middle and high scorers on Expressive Style (scores between 19 and 35) were less conflicted. They typically wanted to maintain or increase their current level of social involvement and feared just the reverse—becoming more isolated and withdrawn.

Similarly, for Interpersonal Style, middle and high scorers (between 19 and 35) typically wanted to maintain or increase their current level of caring about cooperating with others and feared the possibility of losing their sense of kindness and compassion at some point in the future. About 90 percent of those who scored themselves low (between 7 and 18) on this dimension, indicating that they saw themselves as somewhat self-centered, likewise wanted to become more thoughtful and compassionate. Yet one-third were ambivalent about actually enacting this change, fearing the possible consequences of being more open and giving in their personal relationships.

How do people motivate themselves to achieve by focusing on their Work Style hopes and fears? Those scoring in the low range on Work Style (between 7 and 18), indicating an aversion to commitments and responsibilities, seem to be motivated primarily by their ideals: 100 percent of the low scorers in our study wanted to become more hardworking and responsible than they were, although one-fourth clung to their fear of the possible negative consequences of becoming *too* wrapped up in schedules, plans, and responsibilities. High scorers (between 24 and 35) who were already very serious about their commitments, however, appeared to be motivated primarily by their fears. Although they were mixed with respect to whether they felt they should ideally step up their work orientation or remain at their present level, they almost universally expressed a driving fear that some future situation might interfere with their ability to maintain their current level of dedication to work and other responsibilities.

With regard to Emotional Style, most people reported that they would ideally like to be *less* susceptible to negative emotions, such as fear, frustration, and self-doubt. By examining their fears, however, it became clear that many people who *do* have intense emotional reactions feel that—despite the difficulties their feelings sometimes cause for them—they nevertheless gain something positive from their strong emotions and fear losing touch with them. Specifically, among those who scored in the high range on Emotional Style (between 24 and 35), only 60 percent fear becoming more emotional than they already are, and many actually fear becoming *less* emotional. By contrast, those who typically do *not* have intense emotional reactions tend to have strong fears about developing them; fully 90 percent of both middle and low scorers on Emotional Style fear becoming more emotionally intense than they currently are.

Likewise, we found that our respondents' hopes and fears concerning their Intellectual Style also differed as a function of their current score on this dimension. Among those who scored low (between 7 and 18), indicating that they currently enjoy traditional interests and activities, most ideally wanted to be a little more open to new experiences and creative outlets but were split with regard to their fears of becoming either too open-minded or increasingly closed. Intellectual Style, however, appeared to be a central aspect of high scorers' (between 24 and 35) sense of self: they almost universally wanted to maintain or increase their current high level of involvement in intellectual and creative pursuits and almost universally feared somehow losing those interests.

Possible Selves in the Context of Your Life

A great deal of theory and research has been devoted to the study of people's current and ideal Self-Images. Much of this work has focused on explicit comparisons like those you have just made between your Unified Self-Image and Ideal Self-Image. In particular, important psychological consequences have been linked to *self/ideal discrepancies*, or the nature and size of the difference people see between their current and ideal self-image. In counseling clients, psychologist Carl Rogers discovered that those with small self/ideal discrepancies, who saw their current self as relatively similar to their ideal self, tended to have high self-esteem. Clients with large self/ideal discrepancies, by contrast, tended to suffer from low self-esteem. In short, those whose ideals shared little in common with their current self-image were discouraged, often felt worthless for not living up to those ideals, and generally felt powerless to change. Rogers found, however, that during the course of therapy—as his patients gained a greater sense of control over their lives—their current and ideal self-images tended to become more and more similar.[3]

More recently, however, researchers have discovered that having a large self/ideal discrepancy isn't always bad, or at least doesn't always mean the same thing for everyone who experiences it. Specifically, E. Tory Higgins at New York University has found that the *source* of your self/ideal discrepancy is likely to influence the way it affects your motivation and your emotions.

The consequences of having an Ideal Self-Image that doesn't match up with your Unified Self-Image are partly determined by whether you are striving toward an ideal because it represents what you want for yourself or because it represents what you believe a significant person in your life wants for you. In both cases, says Higgins, an *unusually large self/ideal discrepancy* is likely to lead you to experience negative emotions like dejection.[4] If you have selected your own ideals for yourself and believe that you have failed to live up to them, you may feel disappointment, dissatisfaction, and sometimes frustration. If you believe your ideals are what others want for you, you are more likely to experience shame or embarrassment. The key question is whether you believe that you are not living up to your own ideals or are letting other people down.

In addition, Higgins has found that some people strive toward ideals that are based not so much on what they personally believe is best for them but rather on what they believe they ought to do according to some broad-based societal standard or moral code. A large discrepancy between an individual's actual self-image and one of these "ought selves" is likely to lead to a variety of negative emotions that have more to do with fear or agitation than dejection. If you feel that you're failing to live up to your own moral code, you're likely to experience guilt, uneasiness, and self-contempt. If you feel that you're failing to live up to someone else's moral code, you are likely to fear some kind of punishment or retaliation, or to feel threatened or resentful toward those whom you believe are judging you by these standards.

Possible Selves in Action: The Case of Sheila W.

Before we developed the Berkeley Personality Profile, most of the research concerning possible selves examined the Ideal Self-Image and Feared Self-Image separately. It became clear to us as we studied those who responded to our Possible Selves survey in *Psychology Today*, however, that people's ideals and fears often work in tandem to jointly determine their emotions, their motivations, and their behavior.

One striking case came to our attention by way of a long letter one of our respondents attached to her survey. We have included her story here because we hope an exploration of the interplay between her hopes and fears will help you better understand how your own hopes and fears might *interact* to have powerful consequences in your life.

Sheila W. (not her real name) was forty-three years old, a mother of three, twice divorced, and working as a restaurant manager at the time of our survey. She had completed a bachelor's degree at the age of forty and was just about to begin her graduate studies. Here is how she recounted her life story:

> *I grew up in a world where knowledge and education were unimportant and, in particular, women were considered ignorant. To this day, my educational success is viewed with disdain in spite of the fact that I am the first person in my family to receive a college degree and will be the first to go to graduate school. Other siblings are following in my footsteps.*
>
> *My dream has always been to go to school. I was so discouraged by those around me, I married at fourteen, had a child at fifteen, and spent sixteen long years working in a factory, all the while dreaming of going to school and reading every book I could find.*
>
> *Was there something in my personality that allowed me to persevere? If so, can I share this with others, particularly the young? All my life, in my cultural environment I was on the outside looking in. I have never fit in. At forty-three, this is a positive; at fourteen it was misery.*

By combining the reflections Sheila made in her letter with her Possible Self-Image Profile, the personality factors that allowed her to achieve all that she accomplished in the face of so much discouragement from others become clear. The themes she mentioned in her letter—perseverance, education, and the desire to pass something on to the next

Shelia W.
Possible Self-Image Profile

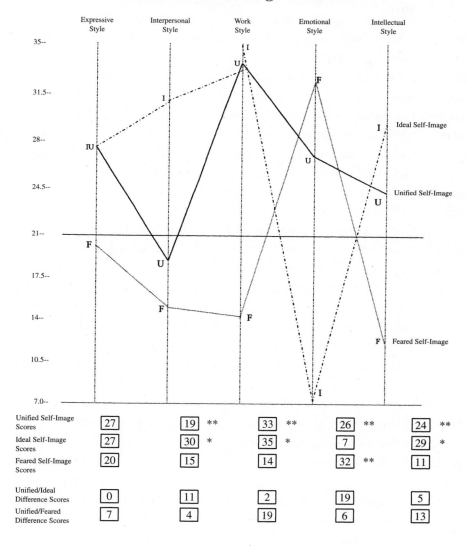

	Expressive Style	Interpersonal Style	Work Style	Emotional Style	Intellectual Style	
Unified Self-Image Scores	27	19 **	33 **	26 **	24 **	
Ideal Self-Image Scores	27	30 *	35 *	7	29 *	
Feared Self-Image Scores	20	15	14	32 **	11	
Unified/Ideal Difference Scores	0	11	2	19	5	
Unified/Feared Difference Scores	7	4	19	6	13	

generation—suggest that the dimensions of Work Style, Intellectual Style, and Interpersonal Style will hold the keys to her story.

Turning first to her Work Style scores, it becomes clear that hard work and perseverance are central to Sheila's identity. Her Unified Self-Image

Score and Ideal Self-Image Score both are extremely high (33 and 35), indicating that she feels exceptionally committed to her responsibilities, feels productive and effective in meeting all the challenges she takes on each day, and feels that she is extremely close to her Ideal Self-Image for the Work Style dimension. Because she could hardly dream of being any closer to her ideal than she already is, it seems likely that something else—such as a fear of *losing* her drive and dedication—is the force that continues to motivate her to work hard and persevere. Her extremely large Unified/Feared Difference Score (19 points) indicates that she has strong fears of being unable to keep up with all the responsibilities she currently juggles. Considering what might happen if she allowed these fears to materialize may well be what motivates her to work so hard and continue to give 100 percent every day. By putting this fear to a positive use, she is able to make the most of it in her life.

Turning next to her Intellectual Style scores, we find a similar pattern: high scores on both the Unified and Ideal Self-Image (24 and 29), indicating progressive attitudes and an openness to new ideas; and a low score for the Feared Self-Image (11), indicating that she fears becoming too conservative and set in her ways. This gives her, once again, a very small Unified/Ideal Difference Score (5 points), but a Unified/Feared Difference Score that is quite large (13 points). Given that she has educated herself and broadened her horizons much farther than anyone ever allowed her to believe was possible, it appears that, for Sheila W., having very similar Unified and Ideal Self-Images combined with a markedly discrepant Feared Self-Image has been a very effective motivator.

And what of her interest in sharing what she has learned with others, "particularly the young"? Her configuration of scores on Interpersonal Style is very different. In this case, she has a very high Ideal Self-Image Score of 30, indicating that she would ideally like to be very generous, cooperative, and helpful toward others. Her Unified Self-Image Score for Interpersonal Style is a rather low 19, approaching her Feared Self-Image Score of 15. This indicates that she sees herself as difficult and self-focused at times, although not as difficult as she fears she could become if her life situation takes a turn for the worse. Looking at the entire pattern, her large Unified/Ideal Difference Score of 11 points appears to be motivating her drive to help others. Her very small Unified/Feared discrepancy of only 4 points probably has little effect on her behavior but may be limiting her sense of efficacy in this area. This is remarkably consistent with the content of her letter, in which she indicates that she has been a good role model for other family members who are now attending college (that is, she feels she has made some progress), but asks for *our* help in figuring out how to share her secret of perseverance and success.

Points for Reflection

How has the relationship between your Ideal, Feared, and Unified Self-Images influenced your own life experience? The Points for Reflection that follow are designed to help you explore this question as you apply the results of this section of the Berkeley Personality Profile to your everyday life.

Before you reflect on the questions that follow, take a moment to review your Possible Self-Image Profile. We suggest that you focus on those personality dimensions for which your Unified and Ideal Self-Images differed most strongly, as well as those in which your Unified and Feared Self-Images do not differ very much. You may also wish to refer to the sections of the interpretation guide that refer specifically to your scores.

1. Consider those dimensions of your personality for which your Unified Self-Image is very different from the Ideal Self-Image to which you aspire. Focus, specifically, on those aspirations that you have personally chosen for yourself. These ideals may include, for example, such concepts as being fun-loving, youthful, self-confident, or versatile. How do you feel about not yet living up to these ideals? Are there some aspirations that you consider more realistic and attainable than others?

2. Think of a specific person who has a clear-cut idea of what *he or she* wants for you, or thinks is best for you in your life. What type of personality would this person like you to develop? How have the

ideals he or she sets for you influenced your own self-image? In what ways are his or her ideals similar to the ideals you set for yourself, and in what ways are they different? Have there been times when these ideals have helped you to achieve more than you previously thought you could?

3. Consider those dimensions of your personality in which your Unified Self-Image is very different from your Feared Self-Image. Is it possible that your deepest fears might be motivating you, in a positive direction, to take all necessary steps to avoid ever allowing them to manifest in your life? How have your fears about the sort of person you could become in a worst-case scenario motivated you to take certain positive steps that have actually improved your life circumstances?

4. Are there other ways in which you may be allowing unrealistic fears about your true capabilities to prevent you from reaching for the brass ring that you feel you deserve and aspire to possess? Have you resisted taking certain calculated risks out of concern that the end result might be the realization of your worst possible fears? Have these fears of experiencing a negative outcome led you to acquiesce—almost by default—to other negative outcomes in your life?

5. Consider those dimensions of your personality in which your Unified Self-Image is not very different from your Feared Self-Image. Does some part of you feel relieved at the thought that you have already hit very close to what is, for you, rock bottom and cannot slip downhill much farther? Is it possible that you are using this negative image of yourself as an excuse not to try to improve your life circumstances and personality?

6. Finally, consider the ways in which your Unified, Ideal, and Feared Self-Images all converge and interact to help make you a unique individual. How might your life change, for better or for worse, if you were simply to envision yourself as a different kind of person, or if you were to strive more actively toward fulfilling your ideals while refusing to allow your fears to hold you back? Are there positive

steps you can take, starting right now, to consciously become less like your Feared Self-Image and more like the Ideal Self-Image that serves as your positive role model?

Notes

1. For a complete treatment of possible selves, see H. Markus and P. Nurius, "Possible Selves," *American Psychologist* 41 (1986): 954–69.

2. For further information about self-actualization, see Abraham Maslow, *Toward a Psychology of Being* (New York: Van Nostrand Reinhold, 1968).

3. For further information on Rogers's views concerning self/ideal discrepancies, see C.R. Rogers and R.F. Dymond, eds., *Psychotherapy and Personality Change* (Chicago: University of Chicago Press, 1954).

4. For more on Higgins's self-discrepancy theory and research, see E.T. Higgins, "Self-Discrepancy: A Theory Relating Self and Affect," *Psychological Review* 94 (1987): 319–40.

Navigating Your Social Roles

In everyday life, all of us play many different social roles. In the course of your own life, for example, you may find yourself playing the role of a student, an athlete, a lover, a manager, an employee, a parent, and a son or daughter. Each of these entails different demands and societal expectations. You may be expected to show restraint and self-control at work yet be expected to be openly, physically aggressive when performing as an athlete. You may be expected to be calm, patient, and virtuous as a parent yet spontaneous and passionate as a lover.

For each significant role that you play in your life, you develop a *role identity*, or image of your personality within that role. Your ongoing life experiences influence the type of role identity you form within each of the roles you play. Each role identity, in turn, influences your behavior and your general perceptions of your personality. If you see yourself as a principled person with clearly defined morals and expectations, for example, this perception may affect the approach you take toward raising your children. The role identity you form as a parent, in turn, may lead you to experience yourself as a strong and supportive person overall.

Some people feel that they adapt their personalities to form customized identities that allow them to meet the specific demands and expectations of particular roles. These *specialized* role identities lead these people to see themselves as having very different personality characteristics in the various roles that they play. Other people feel that they express their personalities in stable and consistent ways, regardless of the roles they are playing. These people have more *uniform* role identities, meaning that they see their personalities as essentially the same in each of their roles. If you have specialized role identities, you may find yourself feeling like a different person on the job than you are at home. If you have uniform role identities, you probably feel that your personality remains very much the same in spite of the shifting demands of particular situations.

To help you explore the way you respond to different circumstances in your own life, the Berkeley Personality Profile now focuses on your specific role identities at work, as a romantic partner, as a friend, and in another social role that you identify as especially meaningful to you. Using the Big Five, you'll compare the Unified Self-Image you developed in chapter 3 with the changes in your self-image within the context of these roles.

Later, you'll be given the option of computing your Total Role Identity Difference Score, which will give you a sense of whether your role identities are basically uniform or very specialized. After completing this section of the Berkeley Personality Profile, you'll have a chance to examine the implications of your scores in light of recent research findings concerning the consequences of adopting uniform or specialized role identities. The Points for Reflection at the end of this chapter will then help you explore how your individual role identities, and the uniformity or specialization among them, may be influencing your interpersonal relationships, your major decisions and lifestyle choices, and your emotional experiences.

How to Take and Score the Test

Once again, turn to the pullout test materials. Cut out the vertical, multicolored scorecards numbered 6 through 9 to rate, one at a time, your Work Role Identity (Scorecard 6), your Romantic Partner Role Identity (Scorecard 7), your Friend Role Identity (Scorecard 8), and an "Other" Role Identity of your own choosing (Scorecard 9).

Begin rating each role identity by stopping for a few moments to think about precisely how you see yourself in the specific role named on the scorecard. Next, place the scorecard alongside the thirty-five statements and rate, as honestly as possible, the extent to which you agree or disagree that the statement is true of you in that role. Then take a five- or ten-minute break before moving on to your next role identity rating. For the most accurate assessment of your personality, do not change any of your responses once you have completed each scorecard. *Do not* look back to the previous scorecards while you are describing the way you see yourself within each of your social roles.

Of course, the roles named on the scorecards will have different meanings for different people. If you are not currently employed, for example, use the Work Role Identity scorecard to describe your personality in a previous job, in the work you do at home, or in volunteer activities. If you are not currently involved in a romantic relationship, use the Romantic Partner Role Identity scorecard to describe yourself in a previous romance, or in another especially intimate relationship. For the "Other" Role Identity, you may describe yourself in any other role that is currently important in your life, such as your role as a parent, sibling, son or daughter, student, athlete, religious or community leader, and so forth. If more than one of these additional roles is important to you, such as your role as a parent *and* a son or daughter, you may use the extra scorecards we've provided to score yourself for each of these other roles.

After you have completed Scorecards 6 through 9, turn to the Role Identity Profile in the perforated section and follow the instructions to compute and graph your scores. Your Role Identity Profile shows all your role identity scores together in one convenient, color-coded chart. It allows you to see at a glance where your various role identities differ dramatically and where they are quite similar.

Role Identity Interpretation Guide

To learn more about your scores, begin by looking up, on the pages that follow, your Role Identity Difference Score for each color-coded dimension, found on the Role Identity Profile you just completed. Once again, you may wish to circle the portion of the interpretation guide that corresponds to your score in each section so that it will be easy to review your test results at a glance later on.

We also remind you that the interpretations provided are based on the way you described yourself in the Unified Self-Image and Role Identity portions of the Berkeley Personality Profile. If you feel that any of the interpretations do not suit you at all, check for possible mistakes in marking your responses or computing your scores. Also check to be certain that you are looking up the scores in the correct portion of the interpretation guide.[1]

Role Identity Difference Scores—Expressive Style (Orange)

- *If your score falls between 0 and 3:* You see yourself as very consistent in your Expressive Style across your roles. You do not feel, for example, that one role requires you to be more outgoing or enthusiastic than you would otherwise be, nor do you find any role unduly restricting your expression of opinions and ideas. All four of your Expressive Style Role Identity scores are probably quite close to your Unified Self-Image Score for Expressive Style, indicating that you find it easy to be yourself in all of your roles, at least with regard to sociability and expressiveness.

- *If your score falls between 4 and 13:* You feel that at least one of your roles demands or encourages a different level of frankness, enthusiasm, dominance, or social interaction than your other roles. In one of your roles, for example, you may be offered more of a chance to be active, adventurous, and outgoing, while another role that is more stable and predictable may bring out the quieter and more reserved side of your nature.

- *If your score is 14 or greater:* You see dramatic differences in the level of energy, assertiveness, or sociability you are permitted to show in one role as opposed to the others. You may find, for example, that you are encouraged to take charge and be a leader in one of your roles, while another role requires you to follow the directions of other people—either preventing you from expressing your ideas and opinions or simply making it futile for you to do so. Alternatively, you may enjoy the stimulation of interacting with a wide variety of people from different backgrounds in one role environment, while also enjoying the solitude afforded to you within another of your roles.

Role Identity Difference Scores—Interpersonal Style (Green)

- *If your score falls between 0 and 3:* You feel that you are quite consistent in the way that you prioritize your own needs relative to those of other people across your various roles. You do not feel, for example, that one role requires you to "shut off" your natural tendency to take a personal interest in others. Nor do you feel that one role so emotionally drains you of patience and compassion that you find yourself running short on these reserves in another area of your life. All four of your Role Identity Interpersonal Style scores are probably very close to your Unified Self-Image Score for Interpersonal Style, so you most likely feel comfortable with this aspect of your personality in all your roles.

- *If your score falls between 4 and 13:* You feel that at least one of your roles requires you to be either somewhat more helpful and cooperative or somewhat more self-protective than you usually feel comfortable being. Although these differences are not dramatic, you probably feel more satisfied in some roles than in others because they make it easier for you to "be yourself" in the way that you balance your needs with those of other people.

- *If your score is 14 or greater:* You see dramatic differences in the level of sympathy and compassion you show for the needs of others in one role as opposed to another. One role, for example, might require you to show a good deal of patience for others in need, while another role calls for you to be substantially more self-centered, aggressive, or argumentative. These differences in the demands, or opportunities, you associate with one role as opposed to another are so strong that you actually have come to see yourself as virtually a different person in each situation.

Role Identity Difference Scores—Work Style (Yellow)

- ***If your score falls between 0 and 3:*** You feel that your commitment to responsibilities and the level of efficiency and effectiveness you display is quite consistent across all your roles. You do not feel that any single role is so demanding of your time and resources that you must sacrifice your ability to perform in one role in order to meet the demands of another. All four of your Role Identity scores for Work Style are probably very close to your Unified Self-Image Score for Work Style. You may or may not be satisfied with your progress in your various roles, but you probably feel that you are at least being yourself with respect to your Work Style in every situation.

- ***If your score falls between 4 and 13:*** You feel somewhat more capable, efficient, or organized in some roles than in others. This may be because you feel that your skills are better suited to the demands and challenges of one role as opposed to another. In short, you may feel that you simply are not cut out for a particular role. You are likely to feel somewhat more motivated in the roles in which you have experienced success, compared to those in which you have repeatedly suffered failure or achieved only mediocre results.

- ***If your score is 14 or greater:*** You see dramatic differences in the way that you accept and respond to schedules, plans, and responsibilities in your various social roles. You may, for example, find the work more enjoyable and the rewards more satisfying when you successfully meet the demands of one role as opposed to another. You may, therefore, be considerably more motivated to apply yourself and be productive in one area of your life than in another. Or you may recently have experienced a failure or a crushing blow—such as the loss of a job or the loss of a loved one—that has temporarily squashed your drive to meet the challenges confronting you in a particular role.

Role Identity Difference Scores—Emotional Style (Red)

- *If your score falls between 0 and 3:* You feel that you experience and express difficult emotions such as frustration, anxiety, and self-doubt to about the same degree in all of your roles. If you are someone who often feels nervous or upset, you find that all of your roles are equally difficult for you in this respect. Conversely, if you tend to keep a cool head and typically feel relaxed and self-assured, you find that all of your roles are equally easy for you in this regard. All four of your Emotional Style Role Identity scores are most likely very close to your Unified Self-Image Score for this dimension.

- *If your score falls between 4 and 13:* You see some modest differences in the type or level of negative emotions you experience and express in one role as opposed to another. You may, for example, feel calm, cool, and collected most of the time but find that you have a tendency to become anxious, upset, or unsure of yourself in one particular role. Or you may find yourself riding an emotional roller coaster most of the time, except when you are engaged in a specific role that makes you feel more comfortable, stable, relaxed, or self-assured than you generally feel in your other roles.

- *If your score is 14 or greater:* You feel that your level of emotionality is closely linked to events in your environment and differs dramatically depending on the role you are playing at any given time. You may, for example, feel that someone with whom you must deal in a particular role has an uncanny ability to provoke you or get under your skin. Or you may feel that the level of stress is so acute in one of your role environments—because of the noise level, task demands, interpersonal rivalries, or other factors—that you constantly feel on edge and may even sometimes wonder whether you can continue to cope in that particular environment for very much longer. Your score suggests, in fact, that you may wish to consider whether you can redefine your more troublesome role(s) in a way that puts you back in control of your emotional responses.

Role Identity Difference Scores—Intellectual Style (Blue)

- *If your score falls between 0 and 3:* You feel quite consistent in your approach toward new ideas and experiences across your various roles. You do not feel, for example, that your artistic, imaginative, or analytic skills are more appreciated by those with whom you interact in one role as opposed to another. Nor do you feel that one role unduly restricts your opportunities to explore new ways of doing things as compared to your other roles. You probably rated all four of your Role Identities as very similar to your Unified Self with respect to Intellectual Style. You probably also feel free to "be yourself" when it comes to the level of conventionality or progressiveness you prefer in all of your roles.

- *If your score falls between 4 and 13:* You feel that, in some of your roles, you act more in accordance with your artistic, intellectual, or philosophical preferences than in others. You may, for example, be a little bored with the activities and personal relationships you associate with one or two of your roles. Roles such as these may simply not offer you enough opportunities to use your more abstract creative and intellectual abilities. On the other hand, you may feel that certain of your roles push you toward changing tried-and-true traditional ways before you feel comfortable that alternative approaches constitute an improvement over old ways of doing things.

- *If your score is 14 or greater:* You see a dramatic difference in the extent to which you exercise your creative, analytic, artistic, and intellectual abilities in some roles as opposed to others. Your profile probably shows a marked schism between the roles in which you consistently deal with change or creative and intellectual challenges, as opposed to those in which you are tied in some way to tradition or your usual routine. If you feel more at ease in more routine role situations, you may wish to consider whether the less predictable situations are expanding your horizons in some important way. If you feel more at ease in unpredictable role environments, you may wish to consider whether the time you spend in routine situations somehow makes your imagination more fertile.

Optional Scoring:
Your Total Role Identity Difference Score

If you completed the Optional Scoring section of the Role Identity Profile, you are probably wondering what your Total Role Identity Difference Score indicates about your personality. Historically, theorists have disagreed about the psychological consequences of having specialized role identities (which emphasize the differences in your personality across roles), as opposed to uniform role identities (which are essentially the same across your various roles). Some, including Carl Rogers, assert that having a "core" sense of self that you carry with you from role to role is an essential component of mental health. Others, such as Kenneth Gergen, have argued exactly the reverse: that differentiating your role identities, so that each suits the specialized actions you must carry out in one particular role, is a sign of exceptionally good adjustment.[2]

Despite the disagreements among theorists, research findings in this area are becoming quite clear. A series of recent studies conducted by Eileen Donahue Robinson, Richard Robins, Brent Roberts, and Oliver P. John at the University of California at Berkeley demonstrates that individuals with very specialized role identities (corresponding to Total Role Identity Difference Scores of about 40 or greater) can suffer a wide variety of personal and interpersonal difficulties.[3]

Robinson and her colleagues found that compared to individuals whose role identities were very uniform across roles, those with highly specialized role identities were more likely to be anxious, depressed, neurotic, and low in self-esteem. They also tended to be less socialized, lower in self-control, and more resistant to accepting society's norms and standards for behavior. Such people also tended to report that they had unusual difficulties with their parents while growing up and that their current relationships were likewise unsatisfying or problematic. Not only were they less content with their current social roles and relationships (for example, their jobs, their family lives, and their friendships), but they also were more likely to have changed jobs and to have divorced and remarried more frequently than those whose role identities were more uniform across their social roles.

It is important to emphasize, however, that having a high Total Role Identity Difference score on the Berkeley Personality Profile is not *always* a sign of personal or interpersonal difficulty. *What is most important is that you feel comfortable with your particular style of negotiating your own self-image within your various social roles.*

Subsequent research by Brent Roberts and Eileen Donahue Robinson has shown that people feel most satisfied in roles in which they feel they are being themselves—that is, in those roles for which their role identity is closest to their Unified Self-Image. If your Total Role Identity Difference score is moderate (between 25 and 39) to high (40 or greater), you may find it useful to compare your Big Five scores for each role identity you graphed on your Role Identity Profile, with your scores on the Unified Self-Image Profile you completed in chapter 3. If the scores you gave yourself for a single role differ widely from your Unified Self-Image Scores in several of the Big Five domains, while your other role identities resemble your Unified Self-Image more closely, this could be a sign that you are simply unsatisfied with that particular role. You may feel somewhat awkward, uncomfortable, or pressured in that role but still feel generally satisfied with other areas of your life. For example, consider a person who projects a dynamic work identity that is much more assertive, demanding, and disciplined than the personality she projects in other roles. This difference would be reflected in Work Role Identity Scores that are markedly higher in Expressive Style and Work Style, and lower in Interpersonal Style, as compared to her Unified Self-Image Scores, and as compared to her Friend and Romantic Partner Role Identity Scores. Although she finds her career stimulating and rewarding, she may nevertheless find it difficult to be "on" all the time at work, and may also feel uncomfortable or ill at ease in her work environment. In her more insecure moments, she may even feel like she is "faking" this dynamic work identity and exist in daily fear of being "found out." However, if she feels happy, comfortable, and at ease in her friend and romantic partner roles, her overall sense of life satisfaction may be quite high.

These recent research findings clearly support the position that a core, integrated self-concept is essential to mental health. But how can we resolve these findings with the claim that specializing your role identities can help you cope more flexibly with the changing demands placed upon you in various social roles? One possible explanation is that the secret to adaptive self-differentiation may lie in the eye of the beholder. While it is important to be able to change your *behavior* in response to the varying demands placed upon you in different social roles, you need not necessarily change your *self-image* to fit each role. The key to maintaining a healthy self-image may be to approach each role by trying to figure out, "How can I do what is expected of me in this role and yet still be *myself*?"

Another possible link between role identities and adjustment revolves around the capacity we all have to *choose* the roles in which we participate. From this perspective, psychologically healthy people would be expected to seek out roles and relationships in which they can be themselves and thrive, and to forsake those roles and relationships in which they are unhappy and feel that their personal evolution is being held back. By contrast, those who are less well adjusted may feel trapped in social roles in which they are miserable and feel they can never be themselves, compounding the personal and interpersonal problems they are already experiencing. Because they feel their behavior is dictated by the demands of each role that they play, they develop very different pictures of themselves—very different role identities—in different situations.

Points for Reflection

After completing this section of the Berkeley Personality Profile, you may find yourself contemplating the ways in which the demands of particular roles influence your personality and behavior, and whether you always feel that you are being yourself in every situation. The Points for Reflection that follow are designed to help you explore these questions as you apply your latest results to your everyday life.

1. Take a moment to review your Role Identity Profile, stopping to consider each of the color-coded Big Five personality dimensions

separately. Take special note of any personality dimension(s) for which your Role Identity Difference Score is 7 or higher. For any such dimension(s), consider the underlying *motivations* that might be leading you to express that particular aspect of your personality differently in various situations. Is this an aspect of your personality about which you feel at all insecure? If so, why? Would you like to become more bold in expressing this side of your personality uniformly across all of your social roles?

2. Now look back, once again, at your Role Identity Profile, this time focusing on your four Role Identities (Work, Romantic Partner, Friend, and Other) one at a time. Compare your overall profile for each Role Identity with the Unified Self-Image Profile you completed in chapter 3. The role identities in which your scores differ most from your Unified Self-Image Scores represent those roles in which you feel that you are not entirely being yourself for some reason.

If you feel that you are not being yourself in a particular role, we suggest that you stop and consider why you feel this way. Does anything about the demands of this role prevent you from expressing some aspects of your personality or lead you to exaggerate other aspects? Do you feel that this situation is healthy for you? Would you like to take steps to be more open about your personality in the circumstances in question, or do you like things the way they are? Or, do you feel that you must accept this situation whether you like it or not?

3. Take a moment to review the Ideal/Feared Self-Image Profile you completed in chapter 4. Compare your Ideal Self-Image Scores (shown in the second row of boxes) for the five personality dimensions with your Role Identity scores shown in the first four rows of boxes on the Role Identity Profile you just completed. In which role is your Role Identity score closest to your Ideal Self-Image for each personality dimension? In which role are your Role Identity scores closest to your Ideal Self-Image overall? What is it about playing this particular role that makes you feel most like your Ideal Self-Image? Are there changes you can make in other aspects of your life that might make you feel equally satisfied with your other role identities?

4. Once again, review the Ideal/Feared Self-Image Profile you completed in chapter 4. This time, compare your Feared Self-Image Scores (shown in the third row of boxes) for the five personality dimensions with your Role Identity scores, shown in the first four rows of boxes on the Role Identity Profile you just completed. In which role is your Role Identity score closest to your Feared Self-Image Score for each personality dimension? In which role are your Role Identity scores closest to your Feared Self-Image overall? What is it about playing this particular role that makes you feel most like your Feared Self-Image? If you are not satisfied with the way that you feel about yourself in this particular role, consider your alternatives. Would you be better off leaving this situation, or trying to change it, or simply letting things be for now?

5. An old adage holds that friends should never do business together, and that coworkers should never have a casual romantic affair. If your personality comes across quite differently in particular roles, you may be able to understand the basis for this recommendation. If you are an especially hard-edged or competitive businessperson, for example, these personality characteristics could adversely affect your relationship with a friend who has never experienced this side of your nature. Or if you have always felt that you could depend on your parents for advice, support, or financial assistance, you may find the role reversal very difficult should your parents suddenly become dependent on you due to a serious illness or other crisis.

If you have ever experienced such difficulties as a result of blurring the distinctions between your various role identities, consider the effects that you and others have experienced when you suddenly find yourselves exposed to aspects of one another's personality that are not usually revealed in the roles you typically share.

6. It is widely believed that your personality can be radically altered by a crisis situation. According to physician Elisabeth Kübler-Ross, for example, *all* terminally ill patients manifest the identical series of responses in learning to cope with their conditions—gradually progressing from "denial" to "acceptance."

Researchers and practicing clinicians have found, however, that crisis situations rarely produce dramatic changes in personality style. In counseling terminally ill patients in a major medical center, for example, Keith Harary found that their responses to their conditions were largely determined by the ways they had learned to cope with other crisis situations throughout the course of their entire lives. Recent personality research likewise has found that unusually stressful circumstances most often affect us by *magnifying* certain patterns already present in our personalities rather than by imposing radically unfamiliar behavior upon us.[4]

Have you ever experienced a crisis situation in which the role you were compelled to play led you to exaggerate certain aspects of your personality? How has your response in such situations been influenced by other experiences you have had in the past and the specific coping skills you have developed throughout the course of your life?

7. Sometimes an unfamiliar role can cause a dramatic short-term change in your personality. This is especially likely when strict role requirements are actively imposed upon you. In a classic study, for example, psychologist Philip Zimbardo found that his students radically altered their behavior when randomly assigned to the role of "prisoner" or "guard" in a mock jail. The experiment had to be called to a halt, in fact, because the "guards" began abusing the "prisoners" under their charge.

In a similar example, while directing a counseling program for the survivors of the notorious Peoples Temple cult following the Jonestown holocaust, Keith Harary studied the role taken by its leader, the Reverend Jim Jones. In an effort to manipulate and gain power over them, Jones assumed the guise of "heavenly father" and encouraged his followers to take on the role of his "children." The technique, which is common among cult leaders, is surprisingly effective—and dangerous—perhaps because some part of many of us enjoys the notion of being relieved of all responsibilities by a "benevolent" parent figure, and also associates being "children" with being relatively submissive in our relationships with other people.[5]

If you have ever experienced powerful changes in your personality style associated with taking on a particular role, consider what this situation tells you about your own human strengths and weaknesses and the ways in which you might benefit from this knowledge and experience. If you have not experienced such a situation, this does not mean that you are immune to it. Consider the ways in which your human vulnerabilities could conceivably leave you open to such an experience in the future.

By mentally preparing yourself for such an eventuality, you may be able to take some helpful steps to prepare yourself—emotionally and otherwise—to deal with it effectively. If you feel comfortable doing so, therefore, we suggest that you take some time to imagine yourself being thrust into a completely alien role and trying to cope effectively with any challenges you may confront. As you do so, you may also wish to consider any underlying personal weaknesses and strengths that this particular exercise in fantasy may reveal to you.

Notes

1. For those who have a professional interest in the design of the Berkeley Personality Profile, the scoring categories in this portion of the test are based on conceptually derived cutoff scores. Role identities that differ by an average of less than ½ point per test question for a particular personality style (that is, a total 0 to 3 points across seven test questions) are considered approximately the same with regard to that personality style. Role identities that differ by an average of ½ to 2 points per test question are considered to be somewhat different, while role identities that differ by an average of 2 points or more per test question are considered to be very different on the personality style in question.

2. For details, see C.R. Rogers, "A Theory of Therapy, Personality, and Interpersonal Relationships as Developed in the Client-Centered Framework," in S. Koch, ed., *Psychology: A Study of a Science*, vol. 3 (New York: McGraw-Hill, 1959), 184–256; and K.G. Gergen, *The Concept of Self* (New York: Holt, 1971).

3. For details, and a review of previous work in this area, see E.M. Donahue, R.W. Robins, B.W. Roberts, and O.P. John, "The Divided Self: Concurrent and Longitudinal Effects of Psychological Adjustment and Social Roles on Self-Concept Differentiation," *Journal of Personality and Social Psychology* 64 (1993): 834–46; and B.W. Roberts and E.M. Donahue, "One Personality, Multiple Selves: Integrating Personality and Social Roles," *Journal of Personality* 62.2 (1994): 199–218.

4. For further information, see E. Kübler-Ross, *On Death and Dying* (New York: Collier, 1969); A. Caspi and T. E. Moffitt, "Individual Differences Are Accentuated During Periods of Social Change: The Sample Case of Girls at Puberty," *Journal of Personality and Social Psychology* 61 (1991): 157–68; and K. Harary, Thanatology Internship Final Report: "A Critical Analysis of the Clinical Theories of Kübler-Ross" (Durham, NC: Duke University School of Nursing, 1974).

5. For further information, see C. Haney and P. G. Zimbardo, "The Socialization into Criminality: On Becoming a Prisoner and a Guard," in J. L. Tapp and F. L. Levine, eds., *Law, Justice, and the Individual in Society: Psychological and Legal Issues* (New York: Holt, Rinehart & Wilson, 1977), 198–223; and K. Harary, "The Truth About Jonestown: Fourteen Years Later. Why We Should Still Be Afraid," *Psychology Today* (March/April 1992): 63–67, 72, 88.

Personality Dynamics and Intimate Relationships

In every personal relationship, your feelings about another person are strongly influenced by the way your interaction makes you feel about yourself. In the healthiest relationships, you gravitate toward those who bring out the best in you rather than those who encourage you to fall into destructive patterns of behavior or otherwise prevent you from achieving your full potential.

In intimate relationships, the partners reinforce and challenge one another's perceptions on an ongoing basis. In the process, they create a shared reality that affects the image they have of themselves and each other, as well as their views of people and events in the world around them. In strong relationships, the partners do not always agree on every issue but are able to communicate openly and with mutual respect about areas of disagreement. Their disagreements may even concern their perceptions of one another.

Your partner may perceive certain qualities in you that you do not recognize in yourself. He or she may also overlook some important aspects of your personality, perhaps because you rarely express them within this specific relationship. Your partner may also have a more intimate knowledge than others have of certain aspects of your character. But you may also reveal some facets of your personality to others that you do not expose to your partner.

In addition, both you and your partner are likely to interpret various aspects of your own and one another's personality within the context of your personal biases and self-perceptions. If you see yourself as shy, for example, you may view your partner as an especially outgoing person by comparison. If you see yourself as flexible, you may consider your partner to be a relatively stubborn person—at least in comparison to you.

The closest relationships often develop a nearly transpersonal quality, in which the partners move beyond their isolated senses of self and experience themselves as part of an integrated whole. They may even feel that the relationship is an essential part of their personal identities. In healthy relationships, the partners are able to experience this feeling of connectedness without sacrificing their individuality. Yet they are powerfully affected in countless ways by this pivotal relationship.

To help you better understand the way your personality influences—and is influenced by—your intimate connection with a special person, this section of the Berkeley Personality Profile provides an opportunity for you to explore the perceptions that you and a selected partner have of one another. This partner may be someone with whom you are romantically involved or the person you consider to be your closest personal friend.

By taking part in this exercise together, each of you will have an opportunity to compare the way you see yourself with how the other sees you. The common ground you find will confirm your areas of agreement, while any differences you discover should be treated as topics for further discussion and exploration of your feelings and perceptions. Keep in mind that such differences do not necessarily represent a failing on your own or your partner's part, or any underlying weakness in your relationship. Instead, these differences may reveal normal variations in style and the individual standards of comparison that both you and your partner bring to your relationship.

How to Take and Score the Test

You will be using the scorecard marked Partner B: Partner Image (Scorecard 12). Your romantic partner, or the best friend you have chosen for this section of the Berkeley Personality Profile, will be using the two scorecards marked Partner B: Unified Self-Image (Scorecard 11), and Partner A: Partner Image (Scorecard 10). You will find these three score-cards on the flip side of Scorecards 7, 8, and 9, which you cut out for the previous chapter. *Please note: If your partner is also completing the entire Berkeley Personality Profile, he or she may use the Unified Self-Image Scores already calculated in chapter 3 instead of using Scorecard 11 in this section of the test.*

Begin by placing Scorecard 12 alongside the thirty-five statements in the Berkeley Personality Profile, making certain the colored rows on the test questions match up with the colored rows on the scorecard. Then stop and consider your view of your *partner's* overall personality. Answer as honestly as possible the extent to which you agree or disagree with each statement as a description of your partner.

Then give Scorecards 10 and 11 to the partner with whom you have chosen to share this section of the Berkeley Personality Profile. Ask your partner to use Scorecard 11 to describe honestly his or her Unified Self-Image, using the instructions provided in chapter 3. *(It would be best if your partner first completed the exercise provided in chapter 2 as well, in order to perform this assessment with the same background you had when you computed your own Unified Self-Image.)* Then ask your partner to take at least a five- to ten-minute break. After the break, have your partner use Scorecard 10 to describe, as honestly as possible, your overall personality as he or she experiences it.

For the most accurate assessment, remind your partner not to go back and change any responses once a scorecard has been completed, and not to refer to Scorecard 11 while filling out Scorecard 10. In addition, you and your partner should not compare your responses until after you both have completed your scorecards for this section.

After you and your partner have completed your respective score-cards for this section, turn to the Self/Partner Image Profile in the perfo-rated section and follow the instructions to compute your scores and graph your profiles. Your Self/Partner Image Profile allows you both to see at a glance where your respective views of yourself and one another differ dramatically and where they are quite similar. It also allows you to compare the relationship between the views you have of each other and the Unified Self-Image that each of you has provided of yourself.

Self/Partner Image Interpretation Guide

To learn more about your scores, look up your five color-coded Self/Partner Difference Scores, from the *third* row on your profile for Partner A or the *sixth* row for Partner B, in the appropriate section below. If you wish to circle the sections of the interpretation guide that refer specifically to your scores, we suggest that you each mark the sections with your own initials or circle the sections that correspond to Partner A's scores in a different color ink than the sections that correspond to Partner B's scores.[1]

Self/Partner Difference Scores—Expressive Style (Orange)

- *If your score falls between 0 and 2:* Your partner sees you in very much the same way as you see yourself with respect to your Expressive Style. That is, the two of you agree about your characteristic level of energy and enthusiasm, the extent to which you speak your opinions frankly or keep them to yourself, and the extent to which you prefer small, quiet gatherings or group activities and large parties.

- *If your score is 3 or greater and you marked a star next to your Unified Self-Image Score:* Your partner sees you as more shy, quiet, reserved, or inwardly focused than you see yourself. Scores between 3 and 10 signify a modest difference, and scores greater than 10 signify a substantial difference in your perspectives. Most likely, you and your partner had different aspects of your attitudes and behavior in mind when answering the orange test questions. Your partner, for example, may have been thinking primarily of the side of your personality that you show in private moments when the two of you are alone together.

- *If your score is 3 or greater and you marked a star next to your Partner Image Score:* Your partner sees you as more active, outgoing, assertive, or fun-loving than you see yourself. Scores between 3 and 10 signify a modest difference, and scores greater than 10 signify a substantial difference in your perspectives. It may be, for example, that you see yourself as somewhat shy overall but that your partner was thinking of the way you express yourself in family gatherings or other situations in which you shine. A partner who is especially outgoing and extraverted is likely to draw out your own more extraverted side as well.

Self/Partner Difference Scores—Interpersonal Style (Green)

- *If your score falls between 0 and 2:* You and your partner see eye to eye when it comes to your Interpersonal Style. Whether you see yourself as exceptionally giving and cooperative or somewhat more stubborn and self-centered, your partner agrees with your self-assessment on this dimension. Although this is an area in which it is sometimes easier to idealize one another than to be completely honest, your level of agreement with your partner suggests you both were candid and evenhanded in describing your Interpersonal Style.

- *If your score is 3 or greater and you marked a star next to your Unified Self-Image Score:* Your partner described you as somewhat less thoughtful or cooperative than you described yourself. One likely reason is that it is easy, from time to time, in intimate relationships to inadvertently hurt or inconvenience those you care about and scarcely realize it. If your partner doesn't find it necessary to remind you of your minor transgressions, you will probably forget about them sooner than your partner.

- *If your score is 3 or greater and you marked a star next to your Partner Image Score:* Your partner described you as more helpful, good-natured, and considerate than you described yourself. If the difference between your self-image and your partner image is small (10 points or less), your partner may simply bring out the warmest, most sympathetic side of your nature. If the difference is large, you and your partner may wish to discuss the particular attitudes or aspects of your behavior that each of you was considering in answering the green test questions. It may be that your partner sees a level of warmth and compassion in your behavior toward others that you tend to downplay yourself. Or it may be that you recognize certain faults in yourself, perhaps stubbornness or self-interest, that your partner has not noticed or prefers to overlook.

Self/Partner Difference Scores—Work Style (Yellow)

- *If your score falls between 0 and 2:* Your partner described your Work Style in much the same way that you described yourself on this dimension. You and your partner agree, for example, about your orientation toward plans, schedules, responsibilities, and hard work. Confirmation from your partner that your perspective on your Work Style is evenhanded and accurate can be especially gratifying if your Unified Self-Image Score is high (around 28 or greater), because it indicates that those who depend on you recognize the time and effort you devote to your commitments.

- *If your score is 3 or greater and you marked a star next to your Unified Self-Image Score:* Your partner sees you as somewhat more forgetful, disorganized, or carefree than you see yourself. If the difference between your respective assessments is small (10 points or less), it may be that your partner had in mind a more haphazard side of your personality that you show when you are frazzled and overcommitted. If the difference is large (greater than 10 points), you and your partner may wish to discuss the way you prioritize various tasks. You may find, for example, that one or two responsibilities that you have given low priority are more important to your partner than you previously realized.

- *If your score is 3 or greater and you marked a star next to your Partner Image Score:* Your partner sees you as more effective, efficient, or serious about work and responsibilities than you consider yourself to be. If you are a high achiever who measures your performance against extraordinary personal standards, you may be underestimating your level of productivity and accomplishment while your partner sees you in a more natural light. Or, if you are juggling a wide variety of commitments and responsibilities and often feel frazzled or as though you are always one step behind, your partner may be trying to tell you that your efforts are more successful than you realize.

Self/Partner Difference Scores—Emotional Style (Red)

- *If your score falls between 0 and 2:* Your partner has confirmed the view of your Emotional Style that you portrayed in your Unified Self-Image Profile in chapter 3. The similarity between your opinion and your partner's suggests, first, that your self-image represents an honest and accurate appraisal of your tendency to experience negative emotions such as frustration, anxiety, and self-doubt, on one hand, or, on the other hand, to remain calm and self-confident even in the face of stress. Your Self/Partner similarity also indicates that your partner has a good understanding of your emotions and recognizes when you are trying to cope with and work through feelings that may be difficult for you to handle.

- *If your score is 3 or greater and you marked a star next to your Unified Self-Image Score:* Your partner sees you as more calm, cool, and collected than you see yourself, or perhaps less prone to anxiety or frustration than you believe yourself to be. If you discuss this difference with your partner, you may find that you have underestimated your own ability to cope with stress. If you make a concerted effort to hide your emotions so as not to trouble your partner, however, you might actually be distancing yourself and depriving your partner of the opportunity to offer emotional support when you need it most.

- *If your score is 3 or greater and you marked a star next to your Partner Image Score:* Compared to your own self-image, your partner sees you as somewhat more moody or susceptible to fear, frustration, and self-doubt than you believe yourself to be. If your Self/Partner Difference Score for this dimension is large (greater than

10), you may wish to discuss this situation with your partner in an effort to illuminate the source of your disagreement. You may find, for example, that you express negative emotions more forcefully in the presence of your partner than you realize. Alternatively, your partner may be able to sense that you are grappling with emotional conflicts even when you try to repress those feelings.

Self/Partner Difference Scores—Intellectual Style (Blue)

- **If your score falls between 0 and 2:** You and your partner share very similar views of your Intellectual Style. Whether you see yourself as a person who prefers the comforts of simplicity and convenience, as someone who enjoys experimenting with new ways of doing things, or as someone who welcomes change in some moderate degree, your partner has confirmed this image of your personality.

- **If your score is 3 or greater and you marked a star next to your Unified Self-Image Score:** Your partner sees you as somewhat less interested in philosophy, the arts, and technology, or a little more tied to tradition and routine, than you see yourself as being. One reason for this pattern may be that partners often share a large part of their daily routine and household chores. Because of the predictability that common ground necessarily ensures, partners may come to see one another as creatures of habit. Your partner, however, may be unaware of the more fanciful thoughts that occupy your imagination while you trudge through the daily grind.

- **If your score is 3 or greater and you marked a star next to your Partner Image Score:** Compared to your own self-image, your partner sees you as somewhat more open to abstract ideas and new approaches to solving old problems. You may wish to discuss this difference with your partner—particularly if your difference score is large (10 or greater). You may feel artistically or intellectually deprived at the moment, perhaps because you see yourself as having fewer opportunities to explore new ideas and experiences than you did at some other point in your life. Your partner may nevertheless have noticed that you apply your creative and analytical skills to everyday situations more often than you realize.

Common Ground and Self-Disclosure

What factor most influences the extent to which your partner understands your personality? If you consider this question, you might speculate that couples with similar educational and occupational backgrounds, or those who are very close in age, might find it easier to understand one another and would therefore know their partners especially well. Or you might suspect that couples who have known one another for a long time, or are married or living together, or have raised children together, might know each other better than couples who have shared fewer life experiences. At least these are some of the factors that *we* thought might have an important bearing on how well partners knew one another when we began studying the responses of more than two hundred people who responded to our couples survey in *Psychology Today*.

We discovered instead that several other, more critical factors influenced how well our respondents' partners actually understood them. First, we found that people with certain personality characteristics appeared to be easier for their partners to get to know. Specifically, those who scored themselves high on Expressive Style, Work Style, Emotional Style, or Intellectual Style tended to have partners who agreed about these particular aspects of their personalities. It may be that the characteristic behavior of those who score high on these dimensions is highly noticeable and provides particularly informative clues about their personalities. Second, we found that your partner's personality is likely to influence how much he or she agrees with your assessment of your own personality. If your partner is especially high in Interpersonal Style or Work Style, he or she is somewhat *less* likely to share your view of your own personality—but will tend to err in a positive direction. This may be because those who score high on these dimensions make an extra effort to sustain positive relationships with their partners.

By far, the most important factor affecting how closely a person's self-image will match his or her partner's image, however, appears to be the quality of the *communication process* they share. This process turns out to be quite unrelated to the other facts and figures of a relationship, such as whether the partners come from similar backgrounds and have known one another for a long time, or even the personality styles of the people involved. According to our findings, the strongest predictor of how well your partner will understand you is *how well you, in turn, understand your partner*. If your description of your partner's personality closely matches his or her own self-description, then your partner's description of *your* personality is more likely to closely match the way you describe yourself.

If it isn't essential to be married, to spend many years together, or to have a personality that is especially well suited to developing empathy and understanding in order to create a common ground of mutual understanding in a relationship, then just how do some couples get to know one another so well? Based on our own findings and those of other researchers, we believe the most likely explanation is mutual self-disclosure. Communicating well with your partner, however, requires more than merely talking about yourself a lot and listening to your partner in return.

In order for your partner to really get to know you, you have to be willing to make yourself vulnerable by sharing your innermost feelings—even when it isn't easy for you to find the words to explain these sentiments and their origins to your partner. This is the only way your partner can come to understand *why* you think, act, and feel the way you do. You may even find that this process helps you learn more about yourself as well.

Researchers call this process of sharing intimate, private information about yourself with another person *self-disclosure*. They have found that opening up and sharing some private detail about yourself usually leads your partner to open up and reveal some private information in return.[2] This piggyback process, called *mutual self-disclosure*, has been shown to play a critical, constructive role in forming and nourishing close relationships, and to be positively related to marriage satisfaction.[3]

As you and your partner continue your own voyage of mutual discovery, we encourage you both to keep in mind that learning about each other may be difficult at times but is well worth the effort and commitment required. Developing a stable and satisfying relationship does not require some mysterious, innate talent that is bestowed upon only certain kinds of people. It depends on a deliberate process of mutual self-disclosure and careful, attentive listening. It's not *who you are* but *what you do* that strengthens your relationship.

Scenes from a Marriage

In the process of illuminating the inner workings of an intimate relationship, we need not only to examine the extent to which each partner shares a common view of the other's personality but also to pinpoint any areas of disagreement. By doing so, we may uncover patterns that suggest systematic biases in the way each partner views the other. Commonly, even in the healthiest relationships, partners have different views of one another with respect to *particular* personality dimensions, such as those you explored in the interpretation guide above. A systematic bias occurs, however, when partners consistently disagree, and always err in the same direction on all or most of the five personality dimensions. Let's take a look at three couples who responded to our survey to explore these principles in action. (We have changed their names to protect their privacy.)

Through Rose-Colored Glasses: Ben and Judy

A common bias couples hold is the tendency for the partners to see one another through rose-colored glasses. Judy and Ben were in their early forties at the time of our survey. They had been married for twenty-two years and had two sons, ages eighteen and twenty-one. Neither had attended college, but they had worked together to build a small family business. In the area of Interpersonal Style, each partner's Unified Self-Image Score was within a few points of the score their partner gave them on that dimension. As we can see on their Self/Partner Image Profile, however, on every *other* dimension Ben described Judy much more positively than Judy saw herself (by 5 to 12 points per dimension), while Judy described Ben much more positively (by 6 to 10 points) than Ben

Judy and Ben
Self/Partner Image Profile

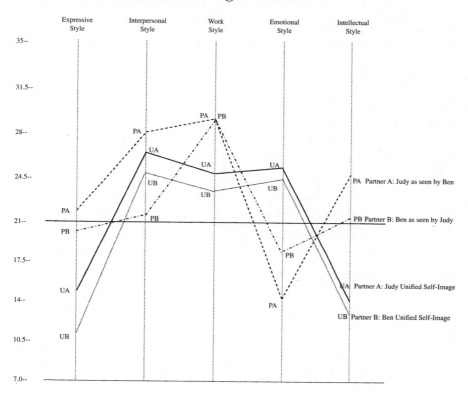

saw himself. (Within the scoring system of the Berkeley Personality Profile, higher scores on Expressive Style, Interpersonal Style, Work Style, and Intellectual Style, and lower scores on Emotional Style, are considered more positive or favorable because they represent the way the majority of people say they would ideally like to be.)

What does this suggest about their relationship? Evidently, either Judy systematically undervalues her own personality strengths or Ben systematically overestimates his wife's positive qualities, or both. Likewise, Ben either undervalued his own, more positive side or Judy is overly positive about him, or both. This apparent tendency toward modesty on the part of both partners, coupled with the positive bias each appears to show in describing the other's personality, might help to create the subtle ambiance of a "mutual admiration society" within the marriage itself. This may indicate that, even after decades together, Ben and Judy still view one another through the idealistic eyes of young lovers. It may also indicate, however, that Judy and Ben have an implicit reluctance to be completely honest with one another, or simply have a tacit agreement to be overtly complimentary when describing each other. This situation may help things to run smoothly in their relationship, but it may also prevent them from clearly perceiving certain aspects of one another's personality. It could also inhibit their ability to communicate on certain levels.

The risk in this relationship is that one partner may, at some point, fail to live up to the other's high expectations. If this should occur, and the other partner should have the poor judgment to be less than sympathetic, then both partners may end up disappointed in one another—thereby potentially throwing the entire relationship into question. Since both Ben and Judy seem to be modest people, however, they might each find it easy to admit being wrong, thereby opening the door for further growth in their relationship and a continuing commitment based upon the idealistic love they appear to feel for one another. The encouraging news in their relationship, of course, is that many couples have far more serious problems to worry about than a tendency to see one another in an overly positive light after twenty-two years of marriage.

Whom Do We Believe? Barbara and Dwight

A bias in the opposite direction might cause a great deal of friction in a relationship. Consider the case of Barbara and Dwight. They were in their mid-fifties at the time of our survey, had been married for twenty-six years, and had two grown children. Barbara had a bachelor's degree in history and was working part time in an administrative position. Dwight was a corporate attorney. They each saw themselves in a decidedly more positive light than they were seen by the other—by as many as 11 points on several dimensions, as shown in their Self/Partner Image

Barbara and Dwight
Self/Partner Image Profile

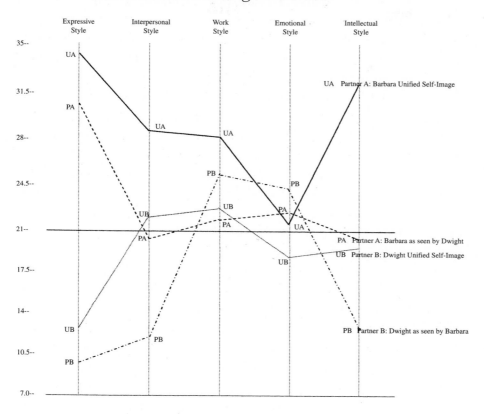

Profile. Is there any way to know whether Dwight and Barbara's self-appraisals are unrealistically positive and their partner appraisals more honest? Or conversely, are their self-appraisals accurate but their partner appraisals unrealistically negative?

All of Barbara's Unified Self-Image Scores, with the exception of Emotional Style, are extremely high. She indicates that she is remarkably sociable and enthusiastic, exceptionally kind and giving, unusually dedicated and responsible, and extremely open-minded and creative. Dwight agrees that she is remarkably sociable but sees her as only moderately kind, responsible, and open-minded. Although Dwight also sees himself in a more positive light than Barbara sees him, his Unified Self-Image

Scores are very different. He mentions a few particular strengths he sees in his character, such as being reasonably cooperative, hardworking, and emotionally stable, but also emphasizes particular areas of weakness, including shyness and a certain ambivalence in his approach to new ideas and experiences. Barbara agrees that Dwight is, indeed, hardworking and responsible. She describes his Interpersonal Style, however, as cold and inconsiderate, his Emotional Style as nervous and ill-tempered, and his Intellectual Style as being quite disinterested in the arts and other imaginative pursuits. It is also worth noting that while he describes Barbara in a less positive light than she describes herself, Dwight nevertheless describes Barbara more favorably than he describes himself on every dimension but two. Although Barbara may feel that Dwight is being somewhat unforgiving when describing her personality, therefore, he apparently is making an effort to be even more brutally honest about his own personality.

Whom do we believe?

Barbara's self-descriptions were almost universally positive, while her descriptions of Dwight were almost universally negative. Dwight, on the other hand, had both positive and negative things to say about them both. This suggests that Dwight may have been making an effort to be more objective because his responses appear to be specific to the questions themselves. He was also, evidently, not trying to make himself look like a saint. Barbara, however, simply appeared to be using the test questions as an opportunity to say positive things about herself and negative things about Dwight, although she did pause to give him credit for working hard.

How should we interpret the totality of Dwight's and Barbara's responses? It appears to us that Barbara may have been using the Berkeley Personality Profile to communicate her extreme dissatisfaction with the present state of affairs in her marriage. Perhaps she feels less than appreciated by Dwight and is saying, in effect, "Look how wonderful I am, and all the things I put up with from you." Dwight, meanwhile, appears to be willing to admit his own weaknesses, but also seems to be trying to honestly remind Barbara that she isn't perfect either. It is possible that both Dwight and Barbara were just having a bad day when they filled out their Berkeley Personality Profile scorecards, but we believe that more serious problems may be brewing in the undercurrents of their marriage.

A Shared Perspective: Marlene and Steve

You may be wondering what a relationship looks like when the partners enjoy a shared view of each other's personality. Consider the case of Marlene and Steve. They were in their late forties, and each had been previously divorced, when they responded to our survey. At the time, they had known one another for only a year and a half, and had been married for less than a month. Marlene had a high school education, worked as an office manager, and had two children from a previous marriage. Steve had attended college and was working in middle management, supervising a team of air traffic controllers. From their history alone, you might conclude that Steve and Marlene, as newlyweds, could hardly know one another as well as our other two couples, who had been married for more than twenty years. But you'd be wrong.

As we can see on their Self/Partner Image Profile, on four of the Big Five dimensions, Steve's descriptions of Marlene were within 3 points of her self-description; the only disagreement was that Steve described Marlene as somewhat less open to new experiences than she saw herself. Similarly, Marlene's descriptions of Steve were within 4 points of his own self-descriptions on every dimension, with the exception that she saw him as slightly more emotional than he saw himself. This is exactly the kind of scoring pattern that we would expect from partners who communicate well and engage in mutual self-disclosure. In the brief time they have been together, Steve and Marlene apparently have developed an admirable level of trust and acceptance in their marriage, thereby setting the tone for continued open communication in the years to come. They each appear to feel comfortable honestly expressing their areas of disagreement, and self-confident and clearheaded enough not to feel the need to exaggerate their partner's positive qualities.

Marlene and Steve
Self/Partner Image Profile

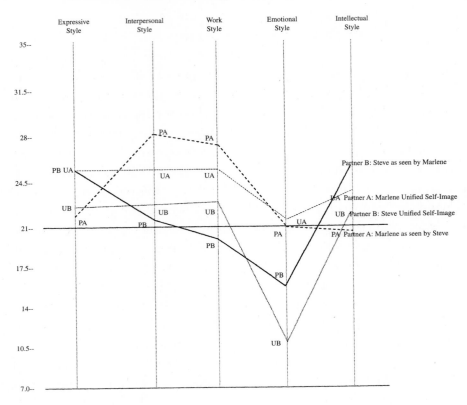

Points for Reflection

After completing this section of the Berkeley Personality Profile, you may find yourself considering the way your relationship with a special person makes you feel about yourself. You may also find yourself contemplating the differences in the way that you and your partner perceive each other's personality, and the possible impact these differences may be having on your relationship. The Points for Reflection that follow are designed to help you explore these questions as you continue to apply your findings to your everyday life. We recommend that you and your partner individually consider the questions that follow, and then get together to discuss them.

1. Consider the way you felt about yourself just before you met your partner. How did these feelings change when the two of you first got together? How have they changed over the course of your relationship? Which of these changes are attributable to outside factors, such as ongoing events in your career or other aspects of your life not directly connected with your partner, and which do you associate with this specific relationship?

2. Do you ever feel as though you are somehow a different person when you are alone with your partner than when you are around other people, or that your partner is somehow different with you? If so, consider the particular qualities that your relationship seems to bring out in each of you. What is it about your relationship that seems to lead one or both of you to magnify certain traits in your personality while downplaying others? Are you entirely comfortable with these changes, or would you like to modify them in some fashion?

3. Consider the aspects of your partner's personality that first led you to find him or her attractive—either as a romantic partner or best friend—and the sides of your nature that led you to feel drawn to these characteristics. Were you looking for someone who would embody the personality characteristics you believed you were lacking in yourself? Or were you looking for a kindred spirit—one whose personality was so similar to yours that you would have no difficulty understanding one another's idiosyncrasies? For what may turn out to be some especially provocative insights, you may also wish to compare the way you described your partner with your Ideal and Feared Self-Image as described on your Possible Self-Image Profile.

4. Are there some aspects of your own and your partner's personality that seem consistently to lead to difficulties between you, such as a tendency for one or both of you to become agitated too easily, or to

become too caught up in the pressures of work to devote the time that is needed to nurture your relationship? Is there something about the way you both react to this situation that leads to additional problems and that somehow sets up a destructive pattern in your relationship? In what ways do the personality traits of each of you help to set you both up for this pattern? What steps might you both be able to take to deliberately break this pattern in the future?

5. Do you ever feel as though your partner is being insensitive to your needs and feelings? Do you find yourself maintaining a secret list of petty resentments instead of bringing them up with your partner? Counselors refer to this practice as "gunnysacking," because those who engage in it tend to carry their resentments around, and store them all up, only to dump the entire bag of complaints on an unsuspecting partner all at once—typically in the midst of an argument. A more reasonable, more positive, and more effective approach would be to bring any hurt feelings or complaints to your partner's attention as they arise. Doing so requires a skillful process of self-disclosure that is directly focused on your partner's specific actions and the feelings they invoke within you.

It is more useful to say something like "It hurts my feelings when you make fun of my big feet" than it is to say something like "At least I'm not a lousy lover like you." The former statement gives your partner an opening to respond to your hurt feelings by apologizing and modifying a specific action, while the second statement is likely to invoke a hostile and defensive response that escalates into a heated argument.

Consider some past situations in which an argument with your partner was precipitated by a failure on the part of one or both of you to communicate effectively about your feelings. Are there steps you can take to be more immediately communicative with your partner about any problem areas rather than allowing your concerns to build into full-scale resentments? Are there ways in which you can facilitate a positive process of mutual self-disclosure with your partner rather than setting off a destructive pattern of defensiveness and accusations? Are there aspects of your own personality, or your partner's, that are likely to make this self-disclosure process easier or more difficult for both of you?

6. Have you ever found yourself feeling as though your partner simply doesn't understand you and wondered how he or she could be so oblivious? Consider the possibility that you may be partly responsible for this situation, since you cannot expect your partner to be a mind reader. Are there ways in which you can help your partner to understand you better, perhaps by making an effort to be more open about certain of your thoughts and feelings? Are there aspects of your partner's personality that you also do not really understand yourself, about which you might be able to get your partner to be more open?

Notes

1. For those who have a professional interest in the structure of the Berkeley Personality Profile, the scoring categories in this section of the test were designed to highlight fairly subtle but common differences between the way people saw themselves and the way they were seen by their partners. The specific cutoff scores chosen were based on our research on couples who responded to our third survey in *Psychology Today*. For each of the five personality styles, approximately 35 to 45 percent of the respondents had Self/Partner Difference Scores between 0 and 2, suggesting that their partners basically agreed with their own self-images. Likewise, for each personality style, approximately 25 to 35 percent scored their Unified Self-Image 3 or more points *higher*, and approximately 25 to 35 percent scored themselves 3 or more points *lower*, than their partners scored them.

2. For further information, see J. H. Berg and V. J. Derlega, *Self-Disclosure: Theory, Research, and Therapy* (New York: Plenum, 1987); A. L. Chaikin and V. J. Derlega, *Self-Disclosure* (Morristown, NJ: General Learning, 1974); P. C. Cozby, "Self-Disclosure: A Literature Review," *Psychological Bulletin* 79 (1973): 73–91; and S. M. Jourard and P. Lasakow, "The Effect of High-Revealing Subjects on the Self-Disclosure of Low-Revealing Subjects," *Journal of Humanistic Psychology* 10 (1970): 84–89.

3. For further information, see G. Levinger and D. J. Senn, "Disclosure of Feelings in Marriage," *Merrill-Palmer Quarterly of Behavior and Development* 13 (1967): 237–49; and L. A. Peplau and D. Perlman, "Blueprint for a Social Psychological Theory of Loneliness" (paper presented at the Swansea Conference on Interpersonal Attraction and Love, Swansea, Wales, September 1977).

Reflections of the Self

If you ever have looked at yourself in a roomful of fun-house mirrors, you know that each reflected image exaggerates certain aspects of your physical appearance while minimizing others. Every time you interact with another person, a similar process occurs. The other person responds to you in a way that suits his or her *image* of you, thereby shaping the interchange the two of you will have and influencing your behavior. Over time, the reflected images that you decipher from the way others approach and respond to you can influence your own self-image as well.

We have already discussed some of the ways in which others form impressions of you. People who know you well, such as your romantic partner or best friend, base their impressions on their past experiences with you, including how you behave while you are around them and what you reveal to them about your innermost feelings, your childhood experiences, and other intimate details of your life. People who know you only in a particular setting or social role, such as at work, form impressions of you based on your behavior in that setting, which may be defined in part by what others expect of you. Finally, people who meet you for the first time form impressions of you based upon your behavior at that particular moment, as well as on stereotypes drawn from their experiences with others whose physical appearance, posture, clothing, speech, mannerisms, and so forth are similar to yours. Regardless of the source of these impressions, their power to shape your behavior and life experiences can be dramatic.

How do your family's, friends', and coworkers' perceptions of you differ from one another? How do their images of you differ from your own self-image? When combined with the perceptions that your best friend or romantic partner has of you, what does the overall pattern reveal about your personality?

This section of the Berkeley Personality Profile offers you an opportunity to answer these questions by working directly with your other friends, coworkers, and family members. All of these individuals probably know you fairly well, and together they have witnessed the way you act in a wide variety of life settings—such as working with clients, appeasing your boss, disciplining your children, relaxing on a camping trip, and driving in traffic. They have a lot of information about you and may even have noticed certain things about your behavior that you tend to overlook yourself or take for granted.

The Reflected Self

The perceptions that others develop of you are based, in part, on the differing aspects of your personality that you reveal in various situations. They are also based on the subjective values and relative standards of comparison that other people bring to your relationships. You may, for example, be greatly admired by a child who views your spontaneity and indifferent attitude toward work as signifying an enviable quality of independence. These same qualities, however, may lead your spouse and coworkers to regard you as immature and irresponsible. Your drinking buddies, on the other hand, may consider you an exceptionally reliable person because they can always count on you to show up at the local tavern at the same time every night.

Just as your own view of yourself is affected by the role you are playing at any given time, the way that others respond to you in each situation also influences your overall self-image and future behavior. If you see yourself as an effective and supportive manager who has won the respect and affection of those working under you, for example, this Work Self-Image might inspire you to be lenient when employees come to you with personal problems. This self-image might be shattered, however, if your employees begin taking advantage of you, start slacking off, and fail to take your reprimands seriously. In addition to changing your Work Self-Image, you would probably alter your managerial tactics as well.

We have found in our research that people display many basic personality traits in the same way across a wide variety of roles and situations. We have learned, however, that people also sometimes exhibit certain very specific differences depending on the circumstances they are in. If you reveal distinctive sides of your nature in different situations, it is not surprising that those in diverse settings will often develop dissimilar views of your personality. This is precisely why we developed the reflective approach that we use in the Berkeley Personality Profile.

A typical personality test is administered in only one life situation, such as while you are applying for a job. It may provide an accurate assessment of those personality characteristics that you display in a consistent way. But it will not provide a complete picture of the aspects of your personality that are more variable and that are perceived differently by others in diverse situations. No single measure can provide the kind of multifaceted information that is essential to describe the complex changes in personality that occur across situations.

One way to find out which of your personality characteristics are most stable across a variety of roles is to use the identical set of questions to describe the way you see yourself in each individual role, as you did in chapter 5. This tells us whether you *experience yourself* as the same person in each of these social situations, but your own self-ratings could potentially be distorted by your personal biases. Another way to examine the consistency of your behavior is to ask a "panel of independent judges," comprised of individuals who interact with you in a variety of settings, to describe the way they view your personality. To the extent that all of their answers are consistent, you display similar personality traits in a wide variety of settings.

Of course, just as your own perceptions might be colored by your innermost values and biases, the impressions that others form of you are likely to be influenced by their personal values and biases as well. Personality researchers have found, however, that the reported perceptions of a large number of individuals who each have slightly different prejudices usually balance each other out. The *consensual* or average image of your personality as seen through the eyes of *many* people who know you, therefore, tends to be relatively free of bias—and represents a relatively objective view of how you come across to other people.

We refer to the consensual picture that others develop of your personality in all of the social roles you play in your life as your Reflected Image Average Score for each personality dimension. In our ongoing research concerning the reflective approach to personality assessment, we have found that people's Reflected Image Average Scores and Unified Self-Image Scores are often closely related. Those with whom you interact in specific social settings may not individually perceive a complete picture of your personality. Their combined perceptions may, however, add up to an overall view that is closely related to the way you see yourself.

Once you have gathered this information, you may also compare the descriptions you obtained from those who know you in a particular setting with the way you envision yourself in each situation. In so doing, you may discover that you generally see yourself as others see you, or you may find that there are certain dimensions of your personality on which you see yourself quite differently—either overall or in specific situations. This process is the focus of the reflective approach you'll be taking in this section of the Berkeley Personality Profile.

How to Take and Score the Test

Turn to the pullout test materials provided in the perforated section of this book. Locate Scorecards 13 and 14 on the flip side of Scorecards 5 and 6, and cut out Scorecards 15 through 18 as well. Now give the two Scorecards marked Coworker 1 and Coworker 2 to two professional associates whom you feel know you well. Ask these colleagues to use these scorecards to respond independently to the thirty-five statements in the Berkeley Personality Profile, rating as honestly as possible the extent to which they believe each statement does or does not apply to your personality. Then give the scorecards marked Friend 1 and Friend 2 to two personal friends, and ask them also to respond to the thirty-five statements. If you did not already include your best friend's responses in the scores you collected previously from your Partner/Best Friend, now would be the proper time to solicit these responses for Friend 1. Finally, give the two scorecards marked Family Member 1 and Family Member 2 to two family members, and solicit their responses to the thirty-five questions as well. (If you do not have two family members available, you may give these two scorecards to additional friends. Note your relationships with the individuals who complete Scorecards 17 and 18 in the blanks provided at the top of the cards.)

Ask each of the individuals you select to fill out the scorecards without consulting anyone else, honestly rating your personality as they each experience you. Ask them to keep in mind that there are no right or wrong answers. *We recommend that you do not tell any of your respondents the identity of the other people who will be filling out your Reflected Image scorecards. You should also be sure to request that they not discuss their responses with anyone else.* We also recommend that you keep all of the responses confidential, although this is ultimately a matter of personal discretion. You may wish to remind your respondents that you intend this to be a learning experience and that they can help you in this effort by being completely honest. Once you receive the completed scorecards from your respondents, you should not be critical of the information they have provided. After all, you solicited their honest opinions—and do want to know what they really think. One of the strengths of the reflective approach is its ability to help you explore the divergent images that other people may have of you, particularly when these do not completely mesh with your own view of yourself, or with the image you have attempted to present to others in any given area of your life.

When you have collected all of your completed scorecards, you will be ready to analyze the results. Turn to Reflected Image Profile 1 and Reflected Image Profile 2 in the perforated section and follow the instructions to compute and graph your scores. *(Please keep in mind, in computing your scores, that your results will be more reliable if you collect all of the requested scorecards from your respondents. If you have collected fewer scorecards, you should divide the total of these scores in each dimension by the number of respondents whose scores you have actually entered in computing your Reflected Image Average scores on Reflected Image Profile 2.)* For example, if you collected scores from seven people, add together the Expressive Style scores from all seven people, and then divide by seven to obtain your Reflected Image Average Score for Expressive Style. Do the same to compute your Reflected Image Average Scores for each of the other personality styles. However, if you collected scores from only four people, you would divide the total of their Expressive Style scores by four when computing your Reflected Image Average Score for Expressive Style, and then do the same for the other personality styles.

Reflected Image Interpretation Guide

Your *Reflected Image Difference Score* on each of the Big Five personality dimensions reflects the extent to which the people in different areas of your life *agree* or *disagree* about your personality with respect to that dimension. Your *Unified/Reflected Difference Score*, meanwhile, reflects the extent to which your own self-image accurately represents the way others see you.

It is crucial to examine these two pieces of information as a unit because the implications of your Unified/Reflected Difference Score depend upon the size of your Reflected Image Difference Score. The pattern of the scores really counts.

To learn more about the significance of your own scores, look up your Expressive Style Reflected Image Difference Score from the eighth row of boxes on your Reflected Image Profile 1, and your Expressive Style Unified/Reflected Difference Score from the tenth row of boxes on your Reflected Image Profile 2. First, find the paragraph below that corresponds to your Reflected Image Difference Score. Second, find the subparagraph beneath it that corresponds to your

Unified/Reflected Difference Score. Do the same with your scores for the remaining Big Five personality dimensions.[1]

Reflected Image Scores—Expressive Style (Orange)

- ***If your Reflected Image Difference Score falls between 0 and 6:*** Your friends, family members, and coworkers all agree about the level of energy and expressiveness—or the level of privacy and reserve—that you show in your dealings with them. This indicates that the Expressive Style you display is quite consistent across a variety of interpersonal situations. *In addition:*

  If your Unified/Reflected Difference Score falls between 0 and 2: Your self-image on the Expressive Style dimension accurately portrays the way you are perceived by others in a variety of different settings, at least with regard to the way you focus your attention toward private, internal matters or toward group activities and interpersonal experiences.

  If your Unified/Reflected Difference Score is 3 or greater and you starred your Unified Self-Image Score: According to the observations of others, you consistently behave in a way that is somewhat more low-key, soft-spoken, or perhaps passive than is indicated by your self-image. You may, for example, feel more confident, cheerful, and engaged than your behavior suggests. Or you may feel that you lead others silently by example, and therefore see yourself as asserting more authority than they may ever know.

  If your Unified/Reflected Difference Score is 3 or greater and you starred your Reflected Image Average Score: Your behavior strikes others as consistently more upbeat, outgoing, or spontaneous than you realize. This pattern is common among those who feel acutely aware of their own social anxieties but successfully camouflage these feelings in their dealings with others.

- ***If your Reflected Image Difference Score is 7 or greater:*** Your friends, family members, and coworkers described you very differently with respect to your Expressive Style. This indicates that you are more lively and animated in some situations than in others. It is likely that the people whom *you* find most stimulating, and who therefore draw out your more spirited side, are those who rated your Expressive Style the highest. Conversely, your lowest scores on Expressive Style probably came from people whom you find *either* boring or intimidating. *In addition:*

If your Unified/Reflected Difference Score falls between 0 and 2: Although your Expressive Style varies across situations, your own self-image accurately portrays your *average* level of energy, assertiveness, and involvement in social activities.

If your Unified/Reflected Difference Score is 3 or greater and you starred your Unified Self-Image Score: According to the observations of your friends, family members, and coworkers, your average tendency to hesitate or hold back in social situations is somewhat greater than you may realize. It is likely that your expressive behavior fails to communicate to others how you really think and feel in some situations.

If your Unified/Reflected Difference Score is 3 or greater and you starred your Reflected Image Average Score: Although your Expressive Style varies across situations, the average impression you create for others is more upbeat or dynamic than you may realize. You may, for example, experience a certain degree of shyness or social anxiety, but your outwardly focused behavior indicates that you successfully overcome these feelings in at least some situations.

Reflected Image Scores—Interpersonal Style (Green)

- *If your Reflected Image Difference Score falls between 0 and 6:* Others who know you all presented a similar view of your Interpersonal Style. That is, they all agreed about the extent to which they find you especially easy or especially difficult to get along with. *In addition:*

If your Unified/Reflected Difference Score falls between 0 and 2: Your own self-image as either a thoughtful and agreeable person or as someone who is rather impatient or inconsiderate accurately portrays the impression that you consistently make on other people.

If your Unified/Reflected Difference Score is 3 or greater and you starred your Unified Self-Image Score: Others consistently interpret your behavior as somewhat more aggressive, impersonal, or impatient than you intend. You may be unaware of something in your manner or tone of voice that strikes others as harsh, competitive, or abrupt. Alternatively, it may be that you feel much more sympathy and compassion for others than you reveal in your outward behavior.

If your Unified/Reflected Difference Score is 3 or greater and you starred your Reflected Image Average Score: Others see you as consistently more kindhearted, cooperative, or understanding than you give yourself credit for being. You may show a certain warmth or sympathy in your smile that strikes others more strongly than you know. Or perhaps the modesty revealed in your Unified Self-Image is the very quality that makes others trust you implicitly.

- *If your Reflected Image Difference Score is 7 or greater:* The people you surveyed presented rather different perspectives on your Interpersonal Style. Some people described you as more thoughtful, agreeable, or cooperative, while others portrayed you as a little more stubborn or difficult. *In addition:*

If your Unified/Reflected Difference Score falls between 0 and 2: Although those who know you indicated that you are more good-natured and warmhearted in some settings than in others, your own self-image accurately portrays the average stance you take in your relationships with other people.

If your Unified/Reflected Difference Score is 3 or greater and you starred your Unified Self-Image Score: The discrepant views of your Interpersonal Style reported by those who know you indicate that you are warmer and more thoughtful in some settings than in others. On the average, however, others see you as running somewhat shorter on sympathy or patience than you realize. This might occur if you focused only on your comfortable and rewarding personal relationships when rating your own Interpersonal Style, while overlooking those relationships that need a little work.

If your Unified/Reflected Difference Score is 3 or greater and you starred your Reflected Image Average Score: Although the differing perspectives of those who know you indicate that you are more self-focused or protective in some of your relationships than in others, on average you come across more favorably than you realize. Some people score in this way because one difficult relationship has led them to be overly self-critical concerning their ability to get along with others. Others score in this way because they are so accustomed to being focused on *other* people that they fail to recognize the essential component their own personality plays in determining the quality of their relationships.

Reflected Image Scores—Work Style (Yellow)

- *If your Reflected Image Difference Score falls between 0 and 6:* For better or worse, everybody you asked offered a similar opinion of your Work Style. In short, those who have observed you working toward a wide variety of family, social, and career goals all roughly agreed about the level of effort, persistence, and direction you show. *In addition:*

If your Unified/Reflected Difference Score falls between 0 and 2: The impressions of your friends, family, and coworkers confirm that you take a very honest and accurate view of the way you respond to plans and schedules, and the extent to which you apply your personal resources toward achieving your goals.

If your Unified/Reflected Difference Score is 3 or greater and you starred your Unified Self-Image Score: The other people in your life consistently described you as more easily distracted, disorganized, or ineffective than you see yourself as being. Sometimes this pattern of scores signals a classic "underachiever," who sets low goals and subjectively feels successful in meeting them, but who others believe has the potential to achieve far more.

If your Unified/Reflected Difference Score is 3 or greater and you starred your Reflected Image Average Score: People in various areas of your life consistently described you as more hardworking, effective, and productive than you see yourself as being. Most likely, this is because you judge your own performance and effectiveness by standards that are far higher than those to which others hold you.

- **If your Reflected Image Difference Score is 7 or greater:** People who have observed your behavior in different settings, in the course of family events, leisure activities, and occupational pursuits, offered very different opinions of your Work Style. Those in some settings saw you as more dedicated and responsible, while those in other settings saw you as somewhat more informal, carefree, or unconstrained. *In addition:*

If your Unified/Reflected Difference Score falls between 0 and 2: Although, according to the observations of others, you are more serious about commitments in some areas of your life than in others, your own self-image accurately portrays your average level of diligence, discipline, and efficiency in all these aspects of your life combined.

If your Unified/Reflected Difference Score is 3 or greater and you starred your Unified Self-Image Score: It appears that you evaluate your own Work Style on the basis of only certain areas of your life, most notably those in which you feel you are most organized, effective, and achievement oriented. However, based on the opinions and observations of those who deal with you in a variety of life settings—and who on *average* see you as somewhat more forgetful, disorganized, or undependable than you see yourself—you may want to reevaluate the priorities you assign to responsibilities in certain areas of your life.

If your Unified/Reflected Difference Score is 3 or greater and you starred your Reflected Image Average Score: Although the effort you apply toward your goals is somewhat variable, the average view of your Work Style based on the reports of those in several areas of your life suggests that you may be underestimating your overall effectiveness. It is possible that you are being too hard on yourself, perhaps because in one area of your life you have had difficulty mustering up the motivation to achieve, or perhaps because your continued efforts have recently met with little success.

Reflected Image Scores—Emotional Style (Red)

- **If your Reflected Image Difference Score falls between 0 and 6:** Others who know you provided a very consistent picture of your Emotional Style in the various domains of your life. It therefore appears that you show the same even temperament and self-assurance—or the same amount of tension or frustration—in each of these social settings. *In addition:*

  If your Unified/Reflected Difference Score falls between 0 and 2: Your friends, family members, and coworkers would all concur that your self-image is accurate with respect to the level and type of negative emotion that you experience and express in your dealings with others.

  If your Unified/Reflected Difference Score is 3 or greater and you starred your Unified Self-Image Score: Others consistently interpret your behavior as evidence of greater confidence and stability than you feel you possess. It may be, for example, that you subjectively experience more anxiety, frustration, or self-doubt than you openly display in the presence of others.

  If your Unified/Reflected Difference Score is 3 or greater and you starred your Reflected Image Average Score: Regardless of the setting you are in at any given time, your expressions of emotion are interpreted by others as more negative, intense, or severe than you realize or intend them to be. Some people score in this range because they are prone to short-lived outbursts that they themselves quickly forget but which nevertheless form a lasting impression on others. Others score in this range because something in their behavior or demeanor is interpreted by others as a sign of nervousness or insecurity, although none is consciously present.

- *If your Reflected Image Difference Score is 7 or greater:* Your experience and expression of negative emotions apparently differ depending on the context in which you find yourself and the people with whom you are interacting, as evidenced by the conflicting views of your family, friends, and coworkers. There may be something in the social climate, such as political issues, extreme competitiveness, and distrust at your place of work, or sensitive and complicated family issues, that leads you to experience greater stress, discomfort, insecurity, or frustration in certain life settings than in others. Alternatively, one particular individual who is overly sensitive about your comments and suggestions, and who therefore sees you as a much more volatile person than you actually are, may have rated you differently than everyone else whom you surveyed for this test. *In addition:*

If your Unified/Reflected Difference Score falls between 0 and 2: Although your self-certainty and composure, as contrasted with expressions of anxiety, frustration, and self-doubt, are somewhat variable, others have confirmed that your self-image accurately portrays the average level of emotionality that you display in various life settings.

If your Unified/Reflected Difference Score is 3 or greater and you starred your Unified Self-Image Score: According to the observations of others, the emotionality that you display in the presence of your friends, family members, and coworkers is, on average, less intense than might be expected on the basis of your own self-image. It may be that in evaluating your own emotional style, you focused on the particular settings and situations that make you feel less in control of your emotions than you ordinarily are.

If your Unified/Reflected Difference Score is 3 or greater and you starred your Reflected Image Average Score: According to the observations of others, you often underestimate the average level of intensity that you show in your interactions with family, friends, and coworkers. It may be that others take your expressions of uncertainty or discontent more seriously than you take them yourself. It may also be that, in evaluating your Emotional Style, you focused on particular situations that make you feel at ease. This may especially be the case if you feel that your emotional responses in other, more difficult situations are justified by frustrating circumstances and therefore indicate little about your personality.

Reflected Image Scores—Intellectual Style (Blue)

- **If your Reflected Image Difference Score falls between 0 and 6:** Your family members, friends, and coworkers all noticed the same fondness for tradition and simplicity, or the same level of interest in science, philosophy, and the arts, expressed in your behavior. *In addition:*

  If your Unified/Reflected Difference Score falls between 0 and 2: The people whom you surveyed evidently know this aspect of your personality very well, in that their perspectives toward your Intellectual Style are uniformly consonant with your own. Most likely, you openly express your feelings about the complications that modern advances in society can sometimes introduce, as well as your appreciation of music, art, and literature.

  If your Unified/Reflected Difference Score is 3 or greater and you starred your Unified Self-Image Score: Others consistently interpret your behavior as indicating that you have a greater level of attachment to traditional ways of life or to comfortable daily routines than you believe yourself to have. At the same time, the others whom you surveyed underestimated your interest in artistic and imaginative pursuits. It may be that others feel that you pay only lip service to progressive ideas and fail to follow up with action. Alternatively, it may be that your interest in technology, creativity, or the arts is something that you pursue primarily in private, and therefore represents a side of you that others rarely see.

If your Unified/Reflected Difference Score is 3 or greater and you starred your Reflected Image Average Score: Others consistently see you as more interested in abstract ideas, technological change, or artistic pursuits than you described yourself as being. You may, for example, appear to others to be perfectly adapted to your complicated life, or very devoted to science and technology, while at the same time you privately yearn to live in a simpler time or place.

- *If your Reflected Image Difference Score is 7 or greater:* Your friends, family members, and coworkers have very different impressions of your Intellectual Style. Some see you as wedded more to tradition and simplicity, while others see you as complex, contemplative, or cultured. It is likely that you display your interests in such pursuits differently depending on the role you are playing or the people with whom you are interacting at any given time.

If your Unified/Reflected Difference Score falls between 0 and 2: Your own self-image pays homage to your attachment to the simpler things in life, as well as to your interest in innovation, progress, and sophistication. Moreover, your Unified Self-Image on this dimension accurately portrays the average level of interest in progressive and innovative thinking that you display in the presence of others.

If your Unified/Reflected Difference Score is 3 or greater and you starred your Unified Self-Image Score: While others disagree about your Intellectual Style, the average portrait of your personality gleaned from the responses of those you surveyed indicates that, on average, your behavior displays less affection for the innovative and analytic pursuits than you personally espouse. It is likely that you reserve the intellectual or creative side of your personality for those who share your interests and appreciate your ideas.

If your Unified/Reflected Difference Score is 3 or greater and you starred your Reflected Image Average Score: Although others disagree about your Intellectual Style, they nevertheless describe you, on average, as more analytic, original, or philosophical than you described yourself. It may be that you are currently feeling discouraged about your Intellectual Style because you feel the people or activities in one area of your life are failing to provide sufficient intellectual stimulation.

Through the Looking Glass

Reviewing your individual pattern of Reflected Image Difference Scores and Unified/Reflected Difference Scores can lead you toward important insights about the way you come across in your everyday life. You may also gain further insights by comparing your results with those of our research participants. What lies beyond the looking-glass view of your reflected image as described by those who know you?

In addition to their completed self-image scorecards, over 1,000 of our 1,300 *Omni* survey respondents included Reflected Image scorecards completed by four or five people who knew them well in different areas of their lives, such as coworkers, friends, parents, children, and romantic partners. When we compared the Reflected Image scorecards describing each individual, we found that people's scores tended to be more consistent for some personality dimensions than others.

If you found that those who know you disagreed more about your Emotional Style than any other area of your personality, you are in the good company of many of our *Omni* respondents. Emotional Style was the dimension that was disagreed upon by friends, family members, and coworkers more often than any other in our survey. In fact, 84 percent of our respondents had Reflected Image Difference Scores of 7 or greater for Emotional Style. The most likely explanation for this situation is that people express their emotions differently depending upon the social context—in part because different things lead them to feel frightened, upset, or insecure in each situation, and in part because unwritten rules exist for how emotions should be displayed in particular circumstances. On average, however, our respondents' Unified/Reflected Difference Scores were not any higher for Emotional Style than for any of the other personality dimensions, suggesting that in spite of their emotional variability across situations, most people have a reasonably accurate idea of the *average* level of emotionality they display. Intellectual

Style, by contrast, tended to be the easiest dimension for observers from different areas of people's lives to agree upon. Specifically, we found that for 41 percent of our respondents, all of the observers agreed about their Intellectual Style to within 6 points. This suggests that people display a relatively even level of interest in intellectual and artistic pursuits in a wide variety of social situations.

Relationship Strategies and Personality

When is your conduct likely to be varied, or tailored to meet the demands of particular relationships—thereby leading those who know you in disparate settings to see you quite differently? Under what conditions does your personality "take over" and lead you to engage in similar actions, regardless of the setting or situation? Researchers have found that the strategies you employ to develop and maintain your relationships, and even the strategies you use to influence others to do what you want, are closely linked both to your personality and to the nature of your relationships with specific individuals.

In a study focusing on the specific kinds of tactics people use to encourage, influence, and manipulate others to do what they want in relationships, psychologist David Buss of the University of Michigan found several interesting patterns.[2] First, he found that different tactics tended to be used in different types of relationships. The tactics that the participants in his study used more frequently with their spouses than with their friends or parents included *coercion* (criticizing, making demands, and yelling), *responsibility invocation* (setting a deadline and getting a commitment), *charm* (flattering and sweet-talking), and *regression* (pouting, sulking, and whining). Tactics used more frequently with friends than with parents and spouses included *reciprocity reward* (giving up something else or doing favors in return) and *social comparison* (pointing out that other people would do what you want). With parents, Buss found that *reason* (pointing out the benefits of doing what you want) was used more often than it was with friends or spouses. Finally, he found that two more troublesome strategies, *hardball* (withholding money and using physical violence, threats, lies, deception, and degradation) and *debasement* (lowering oneself in various ways—including by feigning sickness) tended to be used more often with friends and parents than with spouses.

Second, Buss found that—regardless of the relationship—those who scored high or low on each of the Big Five personality dimensions tended to prefer particular tactics. The personality test scores Buss used in his research corresponded roughly to the Unified Self-Image and Reflected Image Average Scores you computed for yourself in the Berkeley Personality Profile. Buss found that, when attempting to influence or manipulate other people, those scoring high on Expressive Style tended to use the tactics of responsibility invocation and coercion, while those scoring low on this dimension tended to use debasement. Individuals scoring high on Interpersonal Style tended to use reason, while those scoring low on this dimension tended to use coercion, along with another tactic commonly known as the *silent treatment* (failing to respond verbally and otherwise ignoring a person). Those scoring low on Emotional Style tended to use regression; and those scoring high on Intellectual Style tended to use reason, while those scoring low on this dimension tended to use social comparison.

Please keep in mind that, while these findings highlight interesting patterns that are common among *many* people in certain types of situations, and *many* individuals with particular personality characteristics, these patterns are by no means universal. You may find it interesting to consider the situations and relationships in which you tend to rely on certain tactics yourself. You may also find it worthwhile to consider whether these approaches are, for you, somehow encouraged within the context of particular relationships or if they are somehow rooted in your own personality. We also encourage you to bear in mind that these patterns may apply differently to you than they did to those who took part in Buss's research.

Points for Reflection

After completing this section of the Berkeley Personality Profile, you may find yourself contemplating the differences and similarities in the ways that those from different aspects of your life perceive you. You may also find yourself considering the impact that these perceptions have on your relationships with people in particular social settings. The Points for Reflection that follow are designed to help you explore these questions and make the most of your exploration of your Reflected Images.

1. If your overall description of your personality is similar to the way others describe you in a wide variety of situations, you probably have a realistic sense of the way you generally come across. There may, however, be underlying aspects of your personality—for example, characteristics that might come to the surface in a crisis situation—that you have not yet fully explored or revealed to other people.

   If you found most people concurring in their overall descriptions of your personality, and their views closely matching your own perspective, consider those sides of your nature that might nevertheless surprise other people. What special circumstances do you believe would be required to bring these sides of your personality to the surface?

2. Information about your personality that comes up in several people's descriptions is likely to represent accurately the way you come across. The greater the number of people who describe you in a particular way, the more likely it is that their perceptions represent something true about your personality, rather than the biased perceptions of certain individuals. If you disagree with their perceptions, you may be overlooking an important component of your personality or taking it for granted.

   If many other people have described an aspect of your personality that does not correspond with your own self-perceptions, consider the possible source of this disagreement. Is there something about your outward behavior that misleads people about your underlying feelings and motivations? Is your own self-description overly flattering, or overly modest—at least with regard to specific personality dimensions?

3. Take special note of any striking differences in the way various people described you. Sometimes a number of people from a single social setting may describe your personality in a similar fashion, even though this description is at odds with your self-image and the descriptions people in other areas of your life provided. Such differences may indicate a tendency to express one side of your personality to a greater degree in a particular social setting while downplaying this aspect of your nature in other situations.

If you have found a striking difference in the way people drawn from a particular part of your life describe your personality, consider what this tells you about your behavior in this particular setting. Do you feel that you are more "yourself" when in this setting, or do you feel that you are not yourself at all in this situation? What does the way that others drawn from this setting describe your personality tell you about the nature of your personal relationships in this situation?

4. The Big Five personality styles for which your Reflected Image Difference Scores (from your Reflected Image Profile 1) were *the highest* indicate the particular dimensions of your personality that are seen by other people as *varying the most* across the important social contexts of your life. Did you see yourself as most variable on the *same* personality dimensions—that is, were your Role Identity Difference Scores (from the Role Identity Profile you completed for chapter 5) also the highest for these same personality styles? If so, you are probably skilled at both adapting your personality style to meet the demands of a variety of social contexts and at managing the impressions other people form of you in those situations.

5. Take a few minutes to compare your Ideal Self-Image and Feared Self-Image, as described in chapter 4, to the way others have described you within each role. Do others tend to perceive you as being more like your Ideal or Feared Self-Image? Which individuals described your personality as closer to your Ideal Self-Image? Which individuals described you as closer to your Feared Self-Image? What do these patterns tell you about the dynamics of your relationships with these individuals?

6. Is there some aspect of your personality that seems especially well suited to a particular social setting, so that everyone who interacts with you within this setting seems to have a positive impression of your personality? Is there something about being in this type of social climate that seems to bring out the best in you? What steps might you be able to take to use this setting as a model of how you should select other social environments in the future, or restructure existing situations so that they will more readily permit you to flourish?

Notes

1. For those who have a professional interest in the design of the Berkeley Personality Profile, the scoring categories for the Reflected Image Difference Scores were constructed so that, for each dimension, a person's reflected images were considered to be approximately the same if the ratings made by others differed by *less* than 1 point per item, on average, across the seven items. For each of the five personality styles, we found that 16 to 41 percent of our respondents had Reflected Image Difference Scores of 6 or less.

   The scoring categories for the Unified/Reflected Difference Scores are more stringent because we found that most people in our survey had Unified Self-Image Scores that were quite close to the way that others, on average, viewed them. Specifically, for each of the five personality styles, we found that 45 to 59 percent of our respondents had Unified/Reflected Difference Scores of 2 or less.

2. For further information on tactics used in relationships, see D. Buss, "Manipulation in Close Relationships: Five Personality Factors in Interactional Context," *Journal of Personality* 60 (1992): 477–99.

Chapter 8

Personality Progression Through Time

Although well known for his studies of personality traits, influential psychologist Gordon W. Allport (1897–1967) believed that personality itself is best understood not as a fixed collection of traits but rather as a lifelong *process*, in which an individual's uniqueness grows and develops over time. He called this the process of "becoming."[1] Few would question the idea that your current personality is shaped by experiences in your past, including important events and relationships from each stage of your past, as well as the self-images you actually had of yourself at significant points in your past, and your current, retrospective account of the person you believe yourself to have been in *hindsight*. However, not everyone recognizes the ways in which your current personality development is also affected by *foresight*, or your forecast of the person you realistically expect to become at significant points in your future. Your Past and Future Self-Images provide points of reference that help you determine what is appropriate for you at this particular point in your life and help you to evaluate the progress you have made to date in your process of personal "becoming."

Because your personal experiences unfold in a wide variety of contexts that shift over time, you have probably developed a complex array of Temporal Self-Images that form the timeline of your life. Your Past Self-Images begin with your earliest memories and continue through your childhood, adolescence, early adulthood, and every intervening era up to and including the most recent months. Your Unified Self-Image represents your overall view of yourself at your present stage of life, while your Future Self-Images represent the person you believe will emerge as you face each of the many important time periods to come.

Temporal Self-Images change over time in two important ways. Most people feel their personalities have developed and changed over the years, so that the images they have of their childhood personalities differ somewhat from the images they have of themselves when they finished school, met their first lovers, and progressed through various jobs and living situations. Your images of yourself in the future likewise differ depending on which period of your life you are considering, be it five, ten, or thirty years from now. A second, more subtle process causes your Temporal Self-Images to change over time. As your present self matures and experiences more of life, this process affects the context or perspective from which you view each period of your life. For example, when you were a teenager, you had a particular, retrospective view of yourself as a child. Moving out of your parents' house and beginning your life as an independent adult, however, probably led you to modify your view of your childhood in important ways. Having children of your own can also cause dramatic changes in the way you view yourself as a child. Similarly, your view of yourself at any given point in your future, such as after you retire from work, changes as you gradually come closer to that eventuality.

In the two-part exercise that follows, we provide you the opportunity to first explore and learn from an image you have of yourself at some earlier point in your life and later to explore the personality you might develop at some point in your future. The hindsight you gain from first exploring your Past Self and its relation to your Unified Self might strongly affect or inform the way you project your personality into the future. Therefore, we recommend that you complete the Past Self-Image scorecards, profile, and interpretation guide before moving on to your Future Self-Image.

Part I: A Snapshot of Your Past

Select a period from your past that you feel influenced your personality development and is of special interest to you. Some people choose a broad period of several years during which their personalities were stable, such as the period of their early childhood, high school, or college years, or the span of their twenties, thirties, or forties. Other people choose narrower, more specific points in their pasts that were a time of personal and interpersonal change, such as the time of starting their first jobs, or when they first married, first became a parent, or first retired. Still others like to choose a time during which they were at distinct high or low points in their lives.

Once you choose a time in your life on which to focus, you can use several techniques to refresh your memories of the time. One way is to review artifacts from that period—look at old photos or newspaper clippings, rummage through the attic, handle old toys or clothes that you saved, listen to the music of that era, or watch a movie that reminds you of those days. Another is to visit places or engage in activities that defined that time of your life—go to a ball game, take a long drive, eat your favorite foods, call up an old friend to reminisce. People who have vivid sensory memories sometimes find that thinking about the sensory experiences of a particular point in time can trigger a whole host of other memories that virtually transport them to the past. To try it, just close your eyes and remember the smell of your first puppy, the force of the wind as you raced your bike down the biggest hill in town, the pinch of the fabulous shoes you wore to your junior prom, or the distinctive flavor of the gyros at your favorite varsity hangout. Perhaps you can recall the hunger you endured to fit into the wedding dress that was a size too small, the cry of a new baby, the laughter of neighborhood children, or the heat of the sun on your family vacation.

The questions in the space below are designed to help you identify and describe the particular Past Self-Image that you would like to focus on in this section of the Berkeley Personality Profile. Select a brief label or name to describe that particular Past Self (for your convenience in labeling your scorecards and profile), and write down your approximate age (or range of ages) at that time of your life. Next, think about the reasons you chose this Past Self as one you would like to focus on, and describe the elements of your living situation that made this time important (e.g., I was on my own for the first time; I was struggling financially; I had just moved to a new city; my children had just moved out of the house). Finally, try to reflect on how you felt about yourself during that period and how you would have characterized yourself. For example, were you generally confident and happy, or did you feel lost, lonely, and completely miserable? Would you have characterized yourself as a young go-getter with a bright future, a hapless person stuck in a rut, a successful professional who was unlucky in love, or a rebel with (or without) a cause?

Be sure to jot down your answers regarding your Past Self in the space provided *before* you complete the Past Self-Image scorecard. Doing so will help refresh your memory of your life at the time and help get your mind "into" reliving the role. If you would like to explore several periods in the development of your personality, simply use another piece of paper to label and describe the following questions for each additional Past Self-Image:

Characterize Your Past Self-Image

Past Self-Image label: _____

Your age at this time in your past: _____

Distinctive elements of your life situation at this time: _____

_____

Your general feelings about yourself at this time: _____

_____

_____

_____

How to Take and Score the Past Self-Image Test

Turn to the test materials at the back of the book. Cut out the vertical, multicolored Scorecard 19, and write the label you have assigned to your Past Self-Image on the top of the card. Place this scorecard alongside the thirty-five statements in the Berkeley Personality Profile, making certain the colored rows on the test questions match up with the colored rows on the scorecard. Use the scorecard to respond to the thirty-five statements, rating as honestly as possible the extent to which you believe each statement did or did not apply to you at this particular time in your past. If you used the questions above to characterize any additional Past Self-Images, cut out some of the extra scorecards (22 to 24) provided in the back of the book, label them accordingly, and use the scorecards to respond to the thirty-five questions for each additional Past Self-Image.

After you have completed your scorecard(s), turn to the Temporal Self-Image Profile in the back of the book and follow the instructions to compute and graph your scores. This profile shows your Past Self-Image Scores, together with your Unified Self-Image Scores from chapter 3, in one convenient, color-coded chart. (You will be adding your Future Self-Image Scores to this profile in Part II of this chapter.) Inspect the graph to form a visual impression of the differences and similarities between your Past and Unified Self-Images, then look up the meaning of your Past-Unified Difference Scores in the Temporal Self-Image Interpretation Guide that follows on page 162 of this chapter. (This interpretation guide is designed so that you may look up the meaning of your Past-Unified Difference Scores in the same chart that you will later use to look up your Future-Unified Difference Scores.)

Part II: A Glimpse into Your Future

Select an important period in your anticipated future that is of special interest to you. As you did in the case of your Past Self-Image, you may define your Future Self-Image as a given decade during which you expect your personality to be stable, such as your forties, sixties, or eighties, or you may choose a narrower, more specific time that represents a point of important personal or interpersonal change, such as the time when you expect to embark upon a new career or new relationship, or when you expect to complete a significant project or other endeavor.

Your Future Self-Image Profile and results will be more meaningful to the extent that you select a time that represents a *foreseeable* future—that is, a future life course that is realistically possible for you to experience and that you can imagine in detail. Many people find it easier to form a clear image of their Future Self-Image if they select a future period that is not too far distant from the present. Begin by thinking about the specific ways in which you expect your life to change in the upcoming years, as well as the significant factors that you expect to remain stable. Do you expect to receive a promotion, change jobs, or retire soon? Do you expect to undergo significant changes in your financial status or living situation? In what ways do you anticipate your personal, professional, and family relationships will change or remain the same?

Next, consider your emotional responses to the events in your predicted future. Major life transitions are often accompanied by strong emotional responses, which can affect, in turn, the way you express your personality. How do you feel today, as you anticipate these events—hopeful, excited, fearful, ambivalent? And how do you expect you will feel in the future, when you believe these events will come to pass? Most of us have had the experience of looking forward to a life change, such as growing up and becoming independent from our parents, only to find that the fantasy is in some ways better than the reality. Similarly, sometimes we worry for months or even years in anticipation of difficult life changes, such as sending our children off to college, only to find that as we mature and become ready for it, the adjustment is not as bad as we once feared.

If you find it difficult to predict how your expected life changes will affect your internal feelings and external behavior, try thinking about other people you know who have already encountered this situation, such as your parents, siblings, or friends of the family. These people can serve as either positive or negative role models to help you determine how you should (or should not) respond to your own future life changes.

The questions in the space below are designed to help you identify and describe the particular Future Self-Image that you would like to focus on in this section of the Berkeley Personality Profile. Select a brief label or name to describe this particular Future Self (for your convenience in labeling your scorecards and profile), and write down the approximate age you expect to be when this projected Future Self-Image will apply. Next, think about the reasons you chose this particular point in your future, and describe the defining elements of your life situation as you expect it to be (e.g., reaching the pinnacle of your career, upsizing or downsizing your family home, or having to care for your aging parents). Finally, try to reflect on how you expect to feel about yourself when this future situation comes to pass, and how you would characterize your projected self at that time. For example, do you see your Future Self as anxious or confident about your abilities, satisfied or disappointed with your relationships, enjoying good health or coping with an illness? If you would like to explore several periods in the future development of your personality, simply use another piece of paper to label and describe the following questions for each additional Future Self-Image.

Characterize Your Future Self-Image

Future Self-Image label: _____

Your estimated age at this time in your future: _____

Distinctive elements of your life situation as you project them to be at this time: _____

_____

General feelings you expect to have about yourself at this time: ___

_____

_____

_____

How to Take and Score the Future Self-Image Test

Find the vertical, multicolored Scorecard 20 (on the reverse side of the Past Self-Image Scorecard 19 that you cut out previously), and write the name you have assigned to your Future Self-Image on the top of the card. Place this scorecard alongside the thirty-five statements in the Berkeley Personality Profile, making certain the colored rows on the test questions match up with the colored rows on the scorecard. Use the scorecard to respond to the thirty-five statements, rating as honestly as possible the extent to which you believe each statement will or will not apply to you at this particular point in your future. If you used the questions above to characterize any additional Future Self-Images, cut out some of the extra scorecards (22 to 24) provided in the back of the book, label them accordingly, and use the scorecards to respond to the thirty-five questions for each additional Future Self-Image.

After you have completed your scorecard(s), turn to the Temporal Self-Image Profile in the back of the book, and follow the instructions to compute and graph your scores. This profile will now show your Past, Unified, and Future Self-Image Scores together in one convenient, color-coded chart. Inspect the graph to form a visual impression of the differences and similarities between your Past, Unified, and Future Self-Images, then look up the meaning of your Future-Unified Difference Scores in the Temporal Self-Image Interpretation Guide that follows.

Temporal Self-Image Interpretation Guide

We designed this interpretation guide so that you may use the same chart to look up the Past-Unified Difference Score you completed in Part I of this chapter and the Future-Unified Difference Scores in Part II. The term "Temporal Self-Image" refers to both your Past Self-Image and your Future Self-Image, because these are simply two different types of Temporal Self-Images. Remember, we recommend that you complete the Past Self-Image exercise and look up the meaning of all five of your Past-Unified Difference Scores before you begin the Future Self-Image exercise. Because you are already more than familiar with the Big Five, we spend less time *describing* the meaning of your scores and more time explaining the possible reasons why your self-images may have changed or remained stable on each dimension.

To compare your Past and Unified Self-Images, look up your five color-coded Past/Unified Difference Scores, from the fourth row of your Temporal Self-Image Profile, in the appropriate section below. Small scores (between 0 and 2) indicate stability over time for a particular personality dimension; simply look up your score and the interpretation will provide some possible reasons why you have remained stable over time in this respect. For larger scores, the interpretation first explains the meaning of each score and then provides a general explanation of the possible reasons for your changing over time.

After you have finished with your interpretations of your Past/Unified Difference Scores, begin the Future Self-Image exercise. Then use your scorecard and profile to guide you through the interpretation in the same way as you did for your Past/Unified Difference Scores.

Temporal Difference Scores—Expressive Style (Orange)

- *Difference Score between 0 and 2:* You see your Unified Self's current level of activity, sociability, and positive affect as very similar to your Temporal Self-Image Expressive Style. Temporal stability in Expressive Style can be related to preserving over time your priorities for balancing your private and social life. Stability in your fitness, health status, and energy level, as well as your inborn, genetic predisposition toward sociability, activity level, and positive emotion, also tends to maintain Expressive Style, across years, decades, or even an entire life span.

- *Difference Score 3 or greater:* You see moderate (*scores 3 to 6*) or large (*scores 7 and above*) differences in your Temporal Self-Image as compared to your present Unified Self-Image with regard to your Expressive Style. For your *Unified/Past Difference Score*, a star next to your Past Self-Image indicates that you feel you were more upbeat, sociable, or assertive in the past than you are today; a star next to your Unified Self-Image indicates that you feel you were somewhat more quiet or self-restrained in the past. For *Your Unified/ Future Difference Score*, a circle next to your Future Self-Image indicates that you expect to be more sociable and energetic in the future than you are at present; a circle next to your Unified Self-Image indicates that you expect to be relatively more muted or restrained in your Expressive Style in the future.

Reasons for the Change: Changes in Expressive Style can be related to changes in health, fitness, or lifestyle that affect the energy and enthusiasm with which you face the daily tasks and special challenges of your life. Changes in Expressive Style can also result from dramatic differences in the number and nature of your interpersonal relationships. The loss of an intimate friendship might make you feel less fulfilled in your social relationships more broadly. An upward change in status, such as a job promotion, might make you feel more confident and self-assertive, but also more distant from your former peers. Moving to a place where people still smile at strangers on the street may make you feel more sociable yourself.

Temporal Difference Scores—Interpersonal Style (Green)

- ***Difference Score between 0 and 2:*** Your Temporal Self's level of warmth and cooperativeness differs little, if at all, from that of your Unified Self. Deep-rooted values and morals, especially those that emphasize caring for others' needs before one's own, can help you maintain a steadfast commitment to compassion and an unwavering generosity of spirit, even over an entire life span, as reflected by high scores in Interpersonal Style that last over a long period of time. Conversely, early-learned lessons regarding the dog-eat-dog world and the need to watch your own back can lead you to maintain a cold, hesitant, or suspicious stance in your dealings with others, leading to low scores on Interpersonal Style that remain stable over time. Genetic predispositions and evolutionary pressures may also contribute to stability over time in Interpersonal Style. Theorists in the field of evolutionary psychology have argued that millions of years of living in social groups has created in all persons innate tendencies that lead to cooperation and altruism under certain living conditions, as well as innate tendencies that lead to selfishness and even violence under other living conditions.[2]

- *Difference Score 3 or greater:* You see moderate (*scores 3 to 6*) or large (*scores 7 and above*) differences in the Interpersonal Style of your Temporal Self as compared to your present Unified Self. For your *Unified/Past Difference Score*, a star next to your Past Self-Image indicates that you feel you were more trusting, caring, or cooperative in the past than you are today; a star next to your Unified Self-Image indicates that you see yourself as more helpful or compassionate today than in the past. For *Your Unified/Future Difference Score*, a circle next to your Future Self-Image indicates that you expect to be more committed to the needs and concerns of others in the future than you are at present; a circle next to your Unified Self-Image indicates that you expect some change in your life to require you to become somewhat more careful about protecting your own interests in the future.

Reasons for the Change: Changes over time in Interpersonal Style can be related to changes in the lessons you learn from your interpersonal relationships. For example, if your childhood relationships were cold and distant but you are lucky enough to find friends and partners in adulthood who offer you consistent, unconditional acceptance and support, you may eventually learn to return it. If your early relationships led you to trust and accept others quite easily but in your later relationships your trust is repeatedly betrayed, you will gradually find it harder and harder to approach others with charity and compassion. Developments in your life events that improve your empathy for others, such as having children or facing a difficult illness, can also improve your level of sympathy and compassion. On the other hand, during periods of your life when your ability to cope is tested to its limits, you may feel restricted in the patience and help you are able to offer to other people.

Temporal Difference Scores—Work Style (Yellow)

- **Difference Score between 0 and 2:** You see your Unified Self's current level of responsibility, efficiency, and productivity as very similar to that of your Temporal Self-Image. Children who are raised with a strong work ethic, especially one in which a person's value to the community is closely tied to his or her being hardworking and dependable, often preserve those priorities over long periods of time. On the other hand, children and adolescents who see that the hard work of parents and other role models often goes unrewarded, or often occurs at too high a price (e.g., poor health, no time left to enjoy family and other simple pleasures of life), may spend their adult lives making a conscious attempt to work only as hard as necessary in order to avoid becoming workaholics. Temporal stability in achievement motivation can also be related to aspects of a person's temperament that are present at birth, even though observable, behavioral signs of a high or low Work Style may not be evidenced until several years later.

- **Difference Score 3 or greater:** You see moderate (*scores 3 to 6*) or large (*scores 7 and above*) differences in your Temporal Self-Image as compared to your present Unified Self-Image with regard to your Work Style. For your *Unified/Past Difference Score*, a star next to your Past Self-Image indicates that you felt more disciplined, responsible, or effective in the past than you do today; a star next to your Unified Self-Image indicates that you feel you were relatively more aimless, distractible, or perhaps disorganized in the past as compared to today. For *Your Unified/Future Difference Score*, a circle next to your Future Self-Image indicates that you expect to be more organized, conscientious, or hardworking in the future than you are at present; a circle next to your Unified Self-Image indicates that you expect your Future Self to be rather more laid-back and less detail-oriented than your present Unified Self.

Reasons for the Change: You may score higher in Work Style at a time in your life when hard work is encouraged and appreciated by others.

Conversely, at a time when your efforts at work, at home, or elsewhere are underappreciated, you may be less motivated to apply yourself and consequently feel less focused and effective. Similarly, you may score yourself as highest in Work Style at a time when you have just enough duties and responsibilities to keep you busy. Being overcommitted can leave you feeling overwhelmed and ineffective; being undercommitted might leave you feeling aimless and undirected.

Temporal Difference Scores—Emotional Style (Red)

- **Difference Score between 0 and 2:** You see your current level of emotional adjustment as very similar to your Temporal Self-Image Emotional Style. Temporal stability in Emotional Style can be related in part to inborn temperament; that is, some of us are born with a biological makeup that leaves us more (or less) susceptible to anxiety, overreaction, and self-doubt. At the same time, periods of extreme stress may make even the healthiest among us feel more irritable, vulnerable, or uptight than we normally feel, at least until we learn to cope with the new challenges thrown our way. Hence, if your level of Emotional Style is similar across two periods in your life, you have probably chosen two times in your life for which the ratio between your stress level and your ability to cope was approximately equal, two time periods in which you felt equally capable (or incapable) of handling your daily dose of stress.

- **Difference Score 3 or greater:** You see moderate (*scores 3 to 6*) or large (*scores 7 and above*) differences between your Temporal and Unified Self-Image with regard to your level of anxiety or tension. For your *Past/Unified Difference Score*, a star next to your Past Self-Image indicates that you felt more uptight or insecure in the past than you do today; a star next to your Unified Self-Image indicates that you saw yourself as somewhat more calm, cool, and collected in the past than you see yourself today. For *Your Unified/Future Difference Score*, a circle next to your Future Self-Image indicates that you expect to be more irritable, anxious, or troubled in the future than you are at present; a circle next to your Unified Self-Image indicates that you expect to be more comfortable and even-tempered in the future than you are at present.

Reasons for the Change: Changes in Emotional Style can be related to changes in the overall stress level you feel in your life. Major transitions, even those that you feel good about, such as beginning a new career, getting married, having children, or retiring from work, redefine your place in the social world in subtle but important ways. During these transitions, when you are learning new skills and meeting the new expectations that others have for you, you may find it somewhat more difficult than usual to rein in your negative emotions. Conversely, you may find it easiest to keep your emotionality in check during periods when your life is relatively predictable.

Temporal Difference Scores—Intellectual Style (Blue)

- ***Difference Score between 0 and 2:*** You see your current level of intellectual and creative activity as very similar to your Temporal Self-Image Intellectual Style. Temporal stability in Intellectual Style can be related to preserving over time your priorities for keeping your mind stimulated with new experiences and new ideas. If your Intellectual Style is consistently high, you probably take steps to be sure you are always stimulated by at least one thing in your life, be it your career, your interest in the arts, a love for books, or surrounding yourself with provocative people. If you saw your Intellectual Style as tending toward the simple or unpretentious end of the spectrum both for your Unified and Temporal Self-Images, you may feel sufficiently occupied by the details of your everyday situation that you prefer not to complicate matters unnecessarily.

- ***Difference Score 3 or greater:*** You see moderate (***scores 3 to 6***) or large (***scores 7 and above***) differences in your Temporal Self-Image as compared to your present Unified Self-Image with regard to your Intellectual Style. For your *Past/Unified Difference Score*, a star next to your Past Self-Image indicates that you felt more creative, cultured, or intellectual in the past than you do today; a star next to your Unified Self-Image indicates that in the past you saw yourself as more narrow, conventional, or naive. For *Your Unified/Future Difference Score*, a circle next to your Future Self-Image indicates that you expect to be more cultured, articulate, or analytic in the future than you are at present; a circle next to your Unified Self-Image indicates that you expect your future self to be somewhat more traditional or uncomplicated than you see yourself at present.

Reasons for the Change: People usually describe themselves as highest in Intellectual Style during periods of their lives in which they feel they are actively exercising their minds on a daily basis. Having challenging problems to solve at work, pursuing an interest in literature or the arts, or surrounding yourself with fascinating people can contribute to feeling intellectually stimulated. Conversely, feeling that your life at a particular point in time is dominated by the boring details of an unchanging routine might lead you to score yourself somewhat lower in Intellectual Style.

Personality Change in the Context of Your Life

A reminder: We recommend that you complete your Temporal Self-Image Profile and look up the meaning of your scores in the interpretation guide, above, before reading on.

Personality traits are tied very closely to genetic inheritance and, secondarily, to early experience. Thus, it is not surprising that most people experience a good deal of stability in their personalities over time. Although the circumstances of your life have changed dramatically from your earliest childhood memories through your adolescence and each successive decade of your adult life, you probably feel like you're still pretty much the same person in most of the ways that matter. If you were the most even-tempered teenager you knew, you are probably still more calm and emotionally stable than most of your adult friends. If you were irritable and impatient as a child, you're probably no Dalai Lama today, even if you *have* mellowed a bit with age. If you were a slacker in college, you're probably still more laid-back than most of your peers at work, even if adulthood has forced you to step up the pace a bit since college.

Personality does change in important ways throughout the entire life span, but for most people the change is neither random nor dramatic. Personality change occurs in systematic ways, and as a matter of degree. Put simply, your personality matures in ways that help you deal with the major events and changes in your life.

Recently, a convergence of research on personality change across the life span has helped us to understand how personality development occurs in response to the normative, or typical, life changes a majority of people experience. For example, most people experience a moderate increase in Work Style in early adulthood, as society expects them to become more and more productive and responsible. Similarly, the majority of people experience mild to moderate increases in Interpersonal Style throughout middle adulthood, while they are focused on so-called generative concerns such as raising children and/or finding other ways to give something back to society. In Intellectual Style, most people seem to become a little more creative and open-minded during the course of their twenties but gradually become more conventional again through the course of their thirties, forties, and fifties.

Changes over time in Emotional Style and Expressive Style differ somewhat for women as compared to men. On average, teenage girls tend to have more difficulty with anxiety and low self-esteem than do teenage boys; however, as they grow and mature over time, women learn to deal with those negative emotions much better, so that the Emotional Styles of men and women become increasingly similar as they mature. Young women also tend to score higher in Expressive Style than men, but over the life span women tend to become a bit less gregarious than in their youth, so that by the age of sixty their Expressive Styles become closer to that of men.

These research results for the five personality styles come from a study of over 100,000 people of different ages who took a slightly longer version of the Big Five Inventory, the same test on which the

Berkeley Personality Profile is based.[3] Your results in the Temporal Self-Image Profile may show some patterns of personality development that are similar to the temporal differences observed among this large group of people, particularly if your life has followed a fairly typical course, and if the Past and Future Self-Images you chose to explore reflect the same stages of life. Of course, your personality is unique, so your Temporal Self-Image results will be unique in many important ways as well. As you think about the Points for Reflection that follow, keep in mind that your personality matures in ways that help you to adapt to the events and transitions in your own life, especially those that are of the greatest significance in your own mind.

Points for Reflection

Your memory of the kind of person you were in the past—your Past Self-Image—can have a profound impact on your present sense of self and overall approach toward life. In a similar way, your image of the person you expect to become in the future—your Future Self-Image—can also have a powerful influence on the way that you see yourself now. The Points for Reflection that follow are intended to help you explore the way that these two opposite perspectives may be influencing your current view of yourself and the sorts of possibilities that you believe are available at this point in your life.

Before you reflect on these questions, take a moment to review your Temporal Self-Image Profile. We suggest that you first focus on those personality dimensions for which your Unified and Temporal Self-Images differ most strongly, followed by those in which these scores do not differ very much. You may also wish to review the sections of the interpretation guide that refer specifically to your scores.

1. How does the way that you currently see yourself differ from the kind of person you remember being at significant points in your past? Do you feel that you have "grown beyond" some of your previous perceptions, or do you still sometimes feel that you are too caught up in times gone by? How have your most important memories influenced

your personal development? If you remember yourself as someone who was brutalized as a child, for example, you may be predisposed toward seeing yourself as a victim and being defensive toward others. Alternatively, you may think of yourself as a survivor who has overcome adversity and may therefore approach new challenges with a powerful sense of possibility. Do you tend to think about your own disappointing past experiences with feelings of sadness or bitterness, or do you consider them more as valuable lessons learned that will help guide you in the future?

2. Are there elusive qualities of your Past Self-Image with which you have somehow lost touch but that you would like to recapture? If one or more of your past selves, such as your childhood self, could communicate directly with you now, what insights would you want to be reminded about that you may have lost touch with over time? Conversely, if you could go back and communicate with one of your previous selves, drawing on the insights you have gained from your subsequent life experiences, what would you want to say to yourself as a child, or at other significant periods in your life? How would that conversation influence your view of yourself now?

3. Has anyone special influenced your Past Self-Image, for better or for worse? What effect did that person have on the overall course of your life? The individual in question may be a parent, for example, or a teacher, friend, or former spouse. Did you incorporate this person's feelings and messages about you into your own self-image at that time? Looking back, do you believe this person's ideas about you were accurate? How have those messages helped you in your life since then, and how have they held you back? How have they influenced your relationships with other people? Since that time, have you questioned or rejected any of those notions, or replaced them with different concepts and values that were more of your own choosing? If you could go back to the past and respond to the messages your significant person gave you about yourself, what would you want to tell them about the person you have become and the way your life has turned out?

4. Focus on those dimensions of your personality for which your Unified Self-Image is very different from the way you see yourself at a significant point in your future. Your Future Self may be the person you will become following retirement, for example, or in an important new relationship, different job, or following another equally significant life transition—such as getting out of prison, sending your children off to college, or entering the military. Do you eventually expect to "grow beyond" some of the ways in which you currently experience yourself? Are you concerned about potentially losing touch with any valuable aspects of your personality that seem to be deeply intertwined with your present situation? Do you believe your future expectations are realistic?

5. If you could create a mental "time capsule" to remind your Future Self of the most important lessons you have learned up to the present point in your life, what kinds of reminders would you want to include in the package? Are there certain mistakes you have made in the past that you would like to remind your Future Self not to repeat? Are there other, more positive things that you would like to keep in mind as a model for the future?

6. Consider those dimensions of your personality for which your Unified Self-Image is not very different from either your Past or Future Self-Image. Do the most consistent aspects of your personality represent immutable qualities that you believe comprise the fundamental core of who you really are? Or do they also represent some ways in which you may have become fixated on unhealthy patterns that are keeping you from finding true fulfillment? Considering the most constant aspects of your nature, which ones have proven most beneficial over time, and which do you believe have held you back? For example, if you have always been adventurous, perhaps you feel this has helped you take the necessary risks that have gotten you ahead. On the other hand, if you have always had a hard time controlling your temper, perhaps this has gotten you into trouble more than once. Are there ways in which you can build more effectively on the positive while better managing the downside of your nature in the future?

7. Is your Past Self-Image basically consistent, or have you been rewriting your memories over time? Do ongoing changes in your Unified Self-Image influence the way you look back on the person you were before? For example, has your view of yourself in adolescence been fixed since your early twenties, or has it evolved as you have continued to gain perspective? Has the way you look back on the person you were in a previous relationship been influenced by the quality of your subsequent relationships?

8. Consider the ways in which your Unified, Past, and Future Self-Images all converge and interact to help make you a unique individual. How does this complex array of self-images across interconnected points in time influence your relationships with other people and the way you choose to live your life? Are these images primarily realistic and helpful, or can you correct and enhance your self-images in a way that may enrich your life in the process?

Notes

1. For further information, see G. W. Allport, *Becoming* (New Haven, CT: Yale University Press, 1955).

2. For more information, see M. E. Price, L. Cosmides, and J. Toobu, "Punitive Sentiment as an Anti-free-rider Psychological Device," *Evolution and Human Behavior* 23 (2002): 203–31. See also J. Duntley and D. M. Buss, "The Evolution of Evil," in Arthur Miller, ed., *The Social Psychology of Good and Evil* (New York: Guilford Press, 2004), 102–23.

3. For more information, see S. Srivastava, O. P. John, S. D. Gosling, and J. Potter, "Development of Personality in Early and Middle Adulthood: Set Like Plaster or Persistent Change?" *Journal of Personality and Social Psychology* 84 (2003): 1041–53.

The Road Not Taken: Exploring Your Alter Ego

One of the principal ways in which personality influences your life course is by influencing your decision-making process. Some of the decisions you make feel monumental, like the choice of a particular college, career path, or life partner. Other decisions may seem small at the time you make them, such as choosing how much warmth, vulnerability, or leadership you display in different social roles and settings. Keep in mind that major decisions and subtle choices can have important consequences that accumulate as your life progresses over time.

We hope that your experiences with the Berkeley Personality Profile so far have helped you understand how the decisions you have made in your life were influenced by internal factors, such as your personality and priorities at the time, combined with external considerations and constraints—such as the jobs you were offered or the amount of money you had available. You have also likely realized that the choices you have made in the past have affected, in turn, your personality development and the course of your life that followed. But, have you ever wondered whether the opportunities that you passed by—the roads *not* taken—have also had an important and lasting effect on the person you are today?

Every time you have made an important life decision, you have always necessarily embraced certain sides of your nature while placing less emphasis on others. If you had taken an alternate path at some significant point in your development, perhaps by choosing a different career or spouse, by adopting a different culture, or by committing yourself to different priorities, you might have turned out to be a "different person," not literally, of course, but in the ways that those experiences influenced your personality and individual evolution. Every time you stop to think about the way things might have been, this very exercise affects the way you think and feel about the person you have become, and the person you might still become in the future. Each image of the person you believe you could have become given any pivotal life change represents an alter ego, or alternative aspect of your personality.

Many psychologists emphasize the benefits of getting more in touch with your alter ego. Jung believed the suppressed elements of our personalities converge to form a secondary constellation of traits and feelings that he called the "shadow self."[1] Jung saw the shadow self as having its own complex character and value system, which, although normally suppressed, remains accessible or "on call" to the conscious side of our nature. The shadow self allows us to call upon the lesser utilized aspects of our personality when we are forced to confront an unusual situation. A normally meek and unassertive person may draw upon an aggressive alter ego when her sense of propriety is threatened. The alter ego, however, does not necessarily involve the dark side of the soul. You may also have enlightened dimensions of your personality hidden within that do not ordinarily emerge in your everyday life. A hard-as-nails military drill instructor might uncover the patience and sensitivity of a saint when tragedy strikes his family.

Alter egos are perennial topics of fascination in literature, fairy tales, and pop culture. Robert Louis Stevenson encourages us to explore the darker, repressed sides of our own identities by engaging us in the story of the kindly, refined, and materially successful Dr. Jekyll, who struggles for control when he unleashes his terrifying, animalistic alter ego in the form of Mr. Hyde. Cinderella's fairy godmother intervenes to free her from the control of her cruel stepmother so that Cinderella may explore her alter ego as a gracious princess, reminding us that we need not remain the victim of unfortunate conditions. Even the all-powerful

Superman learns that his mild-mannered and socially awkward alter ego, Clark Kent, has certain advantages; Clark is able to form rewarding, reciprocal personal friendships, whereas Superman is isolated by his invulnerability.

Alter egos can be multifaceted and exceedingly complex. Just as your conscious, working self-images are specialized to represent a variety of perspectives, such as your Inner and Outer Self-Images, your Role Identities, and so forth, your suppressed alter ego may also be viewed from a variety of perspectives. Your alter ego is not a single image but rather a subsystem of the self that shifts somewhat as you view it from different vantage points. For example, you may have one alter ego that represents the side of yourself you suppressed when you decided not to go to college, and another that represents the hidden feelings of hostility that you keep under wraps at work. Each alter ego represents *the person you have not become* as seen from a particular perspective.

This section of the Berkeley Personality Profile invites you to think about some of the ways in which your life might have turned out differently. It helps you "look down" one of the paths not taken to discover the alter ego aspects of your personality that may have emerged if your life had taken this alternate course. This exercise stresses the realistic elements of your alter ego, the person you actually *could* have become if your life were somehow different. Because the Berkeley Personality Profile is designed to assess personality characteristics within the normal, so-called healthy range of the Big Five personality dimensions, it is well suited to exploring your "realistic" alter egos.

By providing a reasonable standard against which to compare the progress of your personality development to date, and to advise your future choices, realistic alter egos can serve an important function in your everyday life. But you can also learn different lessons by exploring the more unlikely elements of your alter ego, the shocking extremes hidden deep within your personality that might come to light under truly remarkable circumstances, leading you to act in ways that challenge the bounds of your normal, everyday behavior. "Exceptional Alter Egos" is a special bonus section at the end of this chapter that provides a series of compelling thought experiments designed to help you explore the more fantastic sides of your alter ego using unstructured techniques.

We recommend that you first complete the Alter Ego scorecard, profile, and interpretations for a realistic perspective. The basic insights gained from your realistic alter ego will help prepare you for the unstructured techniques of the fantasy exercise that follows.

How to Take and Score the Test

To gain the most from the experience, the Alter Ego you choose to explore in this section of the Berkeley Personality Profile should be realistic, specific, and of special importance to you. This Alter Ego should reflect your *clearest possible portrayal* of the person you might actually have become as a consequence of some *specific,* alternate course of events in your life. This alternate life course may revolve around:

1. an influential decision that you might have made differently;

2. a change in your goals or priorities that might have led you to do many things differently, causing your everyday behavior and awareness to be dominated by a different side of your personality; or

3. a specific change in the events, circumstances, or persons in your life that would have made things either easier or more challenging for you in particular ways.

If you are curious about how your decisions have affected your life, you may wish to explore the Alter Ego, or alternate personality, that would have developed if you had made different choices—if you had married your first love, gone to a different school, or taken a different job. If you learned difficult lessons from a decision that you now regret, such as becoming involved with alcohol, drugs, or crime, you might like to explore the Alter Ego that would have come to light if your life had not been overshadowed by this pivotal mistake. If you are interested in the way that your values influence your behavior, you may wish to explore an Alter Ego that would have emerged if you had pursued different goals or adopted different priorities. Would your whole life have changed if you had been more ambitious about your career goals, more dedicated to a social or political cause, more family oriented, or more willing to break away from what others expected of you? If you feel you have led an easy life, you may wish to explore an Alter Ego that would have developed if you had been born to poverty, lost a parent at an early age, or suffered a difficult disease or disability. If you feel life has thrown too many challenges your way, you may wish to explore an Alter Ego that would have developed if your life had been less taxing—for example, if you had the benefit of good health and good fortune, if you had been raised in a less complicated family, or if you had the support of a strong network of friends.

You may choose an Alter Ego for an alternate life course that has been in the back of your mind for a long time, or for an alternate life course that you have never before stopped to ponder. Begin by choosing just one Alter Ego associated with one alternate life course. If you enjoy the exercise, you may use some of the extra scorecards in the back of the book to explore other Alter Egos later on.

Once you have identified an alternate life course of special interest to you, take a few moments to form a clear image in your mind of how this change in circumstances might have realistically affected the way you experience and express yourself as a person. Use the space provided below to jot down a brief name or label for this particular Alter Ego, and a description of the alternate life course or circumstances that would have been involved.

Choose a label to describe this Alter Ego: _____

Describe the choices, events, or circumstances that might have given rise to this alternate expression of your personality: _____

_____

_____

_____

Turn to the test materials at the back of the book. Cut out the vertical, multicolored Scorecard 21 and write the label you have assigned to this Alter Ego on the top of the scorecard. Place this scorecard alongside the thirty-five statements in the Berkeley Personality Profile, making certain the colored rows on the test questions match up with the colored rows on the scorecard. Use the scorecard to respond to the thirty-five statements, rating as honestly as possible the extent to which you believe each statement would or would not apply to this Alter Ego expression of your personality.

After you have completed the scorecard, turn to the Alter Ego Profile in the back of the book and follow the instructions to compute and graph your scores. Your Alter Ego Profile shows your Alter Ego Scores, together with your Unified Self-Image Scores from chapter 3, in one convenient, color-coded chart.

Alter Ego Interpretation Guide

Locate your Unified/Alter Ego Difference Scores in the third row of your Alter Ego Profile. Be sure that you marked a *star* on the profile next to either your Unified Self-Image Score or your Alter Ego Score, whichever was larger, in each color-coded column. Look up your color-coded Unified/Alter Ego Difference Scores—orange for Expressive Style, green for Interpersonal Style, and so forth—in the corresponding sections below. The interpretations for each of the five personality styles are designed to help you learn more about how one particular change in the course of your life might have led you to express an Alter Ego side of your personality that is in some ways similar to, and in other ways different from, your current Unified Self-Image.

Unified/Alter Ego Difference Scores—
Expressive Style (Orange)

- *If your score falls between 0 and 2:* You see your Alter Ego as very similar to your Unified Self with respect to your typical level of energy, enthusiasm, and sociability. In other words, you feel your Expressive Style would have been essentially untouched by the change in events that would have led to the emergence of this Alter Ego.

- *If your score is 3 or greater:* You see moderate (*scores between 3 and 6*) to large (*scores 7 or greater*) differences between your Alter Ego and your Unified Self with respect to Expressive Style. *More specifically:*

If you marked a star next to your Alter Ego, you feel you would have been more active, adventurous, or outgoing if this Alter Ego had been permitted to emerge. You may believe that the alternate life course you are exploring would somehow lift the physical limitations or social inhibitions that are currently keeping your positive emotions in check. Perhaps you would have more energy available to do things that you are currently too exhausted even to consider. Perhaps you would be more confident and less concerned about what other people might think of you. You may have found yourself becoming more of a leader, and less of a follower, under this alternative scenario.

If you marked a star next to your Unified Self, you feel your Alter Ego would have been more shy, retiring, or inhibited than you currently experience your Unified Self as being. Perhaps the life course you are exploring would have led you into a more isolated lifestyle. You may have found yourself restricted, by your health or your responsibilities, in a way that made it more difficult for you to be spontaneous, have fun, or pursue adventures. Perhaps this alternate scenario would have led you to protect your privacy more carefully, or to be less likely to meet new people, initiate conversations, or take on the responsibilities of leadership.

Unified/Alter Ego Difference Scores— Interpersonal Style (Green)

- *If your score falls between 0 and 2:* You see your Alter Ego as very similar to your Unified Self with respect to your tendency to be kind, helpful, and supportive of others. This suggests that you felt it would not have been necessary to adapt your current Interpersonal Style in response to the change in events you imagined would have led to the emergence of this Alter Ego.

- *If your score is 3 or greater:* You see moderate (*scores between 3 and 6*) to large (*scores 7 or greater*) differences between your Alter

Ego and your Unified Self with respect to Interpersonal Style. *More specifically:*

If you marked a star next to your Alter Ego, you saw your Alter Ego as significantly more caring, cooperative, or agreeable than your Unified Self. Perhaps the change in events or circumstances associated with this Alter Ego would have afforded you more time and patience to give to the other people in your life. Being in a situation in which your own material, emotional, and spiritual needs have already been met might also have helped you open up to others more easily, showing them more empathy, compassion, and generosity.

If you marked a star next to your Unified Self, you saw your Alter Ego as somewhat less thoughtful, generous, or cooperative than your Unified Self. Perhaps this Alter Ego would have emerged from a circumstance in which you had to struggle to get your own material, emotional, or spiritual needs met, leaving you less time and energy to worry about the needs of others. Fear of getting hurt or becoming vulnerable might also have led your Alter Ego to become cold, distant, or antagonistic toward others. Or, this Alter Ego might have become particularly ambitious and preoccupied with getting ahead, even at the cost of hurting, undermining, or manipulating others.

Unified/Alter Ego Difference Scores—Work Style (Yellow)

- *If your score falls between 0 and 2:* You see your Alter Ego as very similar to your Unified Self with respect to your approach toward work and responsibility. This suggests that the alternate scenario you imagined would not have affected your ability to get things done.

- *If your score is 3 or greater:* You see moderate (*scores between 3 and 6*) to large (*scores 7 or greater*) differences between your Alter Ego and your Unified Self with respect to Work Style. *More specifically:*

If you marked a star next to your Alter Ego, you see your Alter Ego as more capable, effective, or goal oriented than your current Unified Self. The scenario you imagined might have led to your feeling more challenged and motivated than you currently feel. Your motivation might have been improved by work that is more stimulating, by a social setting in which your efforts are better recognized and appreciated, or simply by virtue of a higher salary. Being more self-confident or less troubled by distractions might also have improved your Alter Ego's ability to concentrate, and therefore your ability to get things done in a productive and efficient manner.

If you marked a star next to your Unified Self, you see your Alter Ego as somewhat less motivated, effective, or hardworking than your current Unified Self. This Alter Ego might have emerged from a situation in which you felt overwhelmed and pulled in all directions by more demands and responsibilities than you could have reasonably met. Or, your Alter Ego may have made a conscious decision to be less preoccupied with material concerns and more willing to take time out to relax and enjoy life once in a while. If your Unified/Alter Ego Difference Score for Work Style was extremely high (10 or greater), your Alter Ego may have manifested in a situation that caused you to feel aimless, inept, or discouraged, making it almost impossible to accomplish even the simplest tasks.

Unified/Alter Ego Difference Scores— Emotional Style (Red)

- *If your score falls between 0 and 2:* You see your Alter Ego as very similar to your Unified Self with respect to your overall level of emotional adjustment. In other words, you feel that the change in circumstances that might have given rise to this Alter Ego would not have affected the way you dealt with negative emotions such as anxiety, disappointment, and self-doubt.

- *If your score is 3 or greater:* You see moderate (*scores between 3 and 6*) to large (*scores 7 or greater*) differences between your Alter Ego and your Unified Self with respect to Emotional Style. *More specifically:*

If you marked a star next to your Alter Ego, you see your Alter Ego as somewhat more troubled by anxiety, disappointment, or self-doubt than your current Unified Self. Your Alter Ego may be associated with a situation in which you would have lost one of the major sources of love and support that presently helps your Unified Self to remain calm and well balanced. Or, your Alter Ego might have emerged from a situation that was significantly more stressful, traumatic, or threatening than the life you currently enjoy. If your Unified/Alter Ego Difference Score for Emotional Style is extremely high (14 or greater), you may see your Alter Ego as poised at the precipice of sanity, afraid of losing all emotional control, and barely holding it together.

If you marked a star next to your Unified Self, you see your Alter Ego as somewhat more calm, confident, and relaxed than your current Unified Self. Your Alter Ego might have been enjoying a situation that would be less stressful or traumatic than your current life situation. Your Alter Ego may have been less threatened by the loss of a job or an important relationship, less afraid of alienating others, or just less pessimistic about human nature in general. Alternatively, your Alter Ego might have experienced the same sources of stress you currently confront on a daily basis, but might have somehow managed to show more grace under pressure, perhaps feeling more confident and having better coping strategies available to handle pressure and uncertainty.

Unified/Alter Ego Difference Scores—Intellectual Style (Blue)

- *If your score falls between 0 and 2:* You see your Alter Ego as very similar to your Unified Self with respect to your approach toward intellectual and creative pursuits and your tendency to seek out, or shy away from, new experiences. You feel your Intellectual Style would have remained more or less intact if this Alter Ego had been permitted to emerge.

- *If your score is 3 or greater:* You see moderate (*scores between 3 and 6*) to large (*scores 7 or greater*) differences between your Alter

Ego and your Unified Self with respect to Intellectual Style. *More specifically:*

If you marked a star next to your Alter Ego, you see your Alter Ego as more creative, imaginative, or open-minded than your current Unified Self. You may envision this Alter Ego as having benefited from a more worldly or well-rounded education than you actually experienced, or as having been blessed with more raw talent for artistic and intellectual pursuits. Perhaps you imagined that this Alter Ego had more time to devote to creative endeavors, being less preoccupied by the mundane concerns of family and finances. This Alter Ego may simply have been less afraid to break out of the mold and try new things. It may also have been supported by others who were more willing to listen to your insights and ideas than those who currently surround you.

If you marked a star next to your Unified Self, you see your Alter Ego as having less time or interest to devote to intellectual matters, perhaps feeling reluctant to express unconventional ideas or afraid to explore new places and experiences. This Alter Ego might have emerged from a home or work environment in which curiosity was not encouraged, in which intellectual and artistic pursuits were considered frivolous, or in which you felt bored by a daily routine of passive activities that failed to challenge your intellect.

More Than Child's Play

Alter egos fascinate children. It's a delight to watch a young child climb a tree and belt out a Tarzan yell, fly to another star in a cardboard box, or swim like a mermaid in the bathtub. Some like to role-play favorite characters; others like to daydream about what they want to be when they grow up, or plan how things would be different if they were bigger and stronger than the neighborhood bully. Some children create invisible playmates that represent some suppressed aspect of their own developing identities.

In addition to being good, wholesome fun, alter egos can serve important functions in a child's cognitive, social, and personality development. We know a delightful five-year-old who has dozens of outfits that each represent a different identity, ranging from Batman and Superman to Underdog and Jiminy Cricket. He has such fun with his identities that he has rarely appeared as "Andrew" since before his third birthday. In addition to exercising his imagination, the identities he plays help him explore the notion of reality and the difference between fantasies that can come true and those that cannot. Perhaps most importantly, he has used his identities to compensate for a motor delay that makes his speech somewhat difficult to understand; becoming a character creates a specific context that facilitates communication and gives him the confidence to draw friends, family, and even total strangers into his game. Recently, when disembarking from a long flight, he spotted the airline captain in uniform and said boldly, "Excuse me, I'm Inspector Gadget. Who are you being?" Smiling warmly, the man replied, "Oh, today I'm only the pilot."

Although the alter egos we work with as adults may not be as exciting as our childhood heroes, they continue to serve important psychological functions. By helping us to gaze down the roads not taken, and illuminating the consequences of our choices, alter egos create a context that can help us to define, evaluate, and take responsibility for our own personality development. By reminding us what we could have been, alter egos provide a valuable store of potential behavior that we can call upon at a moment's notice, whenever an unusual situation might demand an unusual response. By helping us to imagine what we might become if put in someone else's shoes, alter egos can help us to empathize and identify with people whose personalities and priorities might otherwise frighten, confuse, or offend us. And finally, by highlighting the multiplicity of our options, alter egos can help us imagine a wider variety of possible futures for our own lives and the lives of the people we love.

Special Section: Exceptional Alter Egos

Now that you have completed the Alter Ego exercise by focusing on a critical point in your past, you may also wish to consider the ways in which some specific and dramatic event might conceivably impact your personality at some point in the future. In our own firsthand clinical experience, we have found that even under extraordinary circumstances most people do not dramatically change their personalities. For example, as we discussed in chapter 5, in counseling the terminally ill, we have found that individuals do not suddenly shift into the popular myth of a standardized pattern of grieving that gradually evolves into acceptance.[2] Instead, they tend to handle the crisis using the skills and emotional strategies they have developed over a lifetime, often cycling back and forth between disjointed and contradictory emotions.[3]

Nevertheless, under exceptional circumstances ordinary people really do sometimes find themselves reacting in extraordinary—even unprecedented—ways for them. Sometimes we can find heroes in unexpected places—in the manager of a fast-food restaurant, for example, who instinctively sacrificed his life to save one of his workers by throwing himself in front of a knife-wielding killer, and in the members of a traveling entertainment troupe who stayed behind to rescue the passengers aboard a sinking liner after the captain and crew abandoned ship—proving that cowards are also sometimes found where they are least expected. The real-life phenomenon takes a dramatic fictional turn in the classic film *Straw Dogs*, in which Dustin Hoffman's mild and retiring leading character aggressively emerges as his violent shadow self when his peaceful home is threatened, then returns to his usual polite and accommodating personality once he's handled the threat. Even science fiction and horror movies such as *The Wolfman* and *The Hulk* explore the concept of an ordinary person forced to cope with an extraordinary alter ego—the shadow self in full regalia spontaneously dominating the personalities, and even the physical forms, of the title characters.

If you sometimes wonder how you might react if you were thrown into the midst of a remarkable (or even frightening) scenario, now is your chance to let your imagination go as far as you dare. What if you were to find yourself being kidnapped by terrorists, or discovered that the planet Earth was under attack by hostile aliens? What if you won the lottery, lost everything you owned to a nuclear accident, or found yourself—as in the shocking case of the Hutus and the Tutsis in Rwanda's notorious ethnic conflict—suddenly cast into the role of a potential mass murderer or victim in a genocidal call to arms that pitted neighbor against neighbor? Many of us cannot help but consider such thoughts whenever we hear about some incredible event that has occurred in a faraway land. As you allow yourself to think about all the possible implications of encountering the most unusual dimensions of your alter ego, however, we invite you to carry the following exercise through to its most personal conclusion.

Begin by choosing an imaginary scenario that you believe would push your personality to such an exceptional extreme that some unprecedented dimension of your alter ego would spontaneously rise to the surface. What if you were suddenly to lose your job, or leave your mate, or if circumstances left you no choice in the matter and you found yourself destitute and entirely alone in a country where you didn't speak the language? What if you found yourself accused of a crime that you didn't commit, or if you really did commit an unexpected crime of passion? What if the stock market crashed, or you found that you were being held for ransom, or you were suddenly forced to fight in a war for your country's or the world's survival? What would it take to call upon some underlying, hidden aspect of your personality—your shadow self or more enlightened nature—that currently resides within your deepest alter ego?

Take a deep breath, close your eyes, and imagine that you really are immersed within that situation. Allow yourself to imagine that you hear the sounds, can smell the atmosphere, and feel the physical sensations that are associated with the situation you have chosen. Who are you now? How does it feel to experience the world through the extreme reactions and emotional perceptions of your exceptional alter ego? Is there a part of you that you still recognize, and another part of you that seems completely unfamiliar? While such an exercise can only go so far without your actually finding yourself in the midst of an extraordinary situation, are there any aspects of your own imaginary responses that really do surprise you? Perhaps it is your own most exceptional alter ego, calling to you from an unexplored and still mysterious perspective on your personality.

Points for Reflection

In completing this section of the Berkeley Personality Profile, you have had an opportunity to explore an unusual dimension of your personality that most of us rarely consider: the person you could have become had the circumstances of your life been very different. The Points for Reflection that follow are designed to help you integrate this information into your overall sense of self-awareness. They will also help you carry this particular exercise to a deeper level as you consider the alternatives still open to you in the future.

1. How do you feel about the Alter Ego you described? In answering this question, you may find it especially useful to compare your Alter Ego with the Ideal vs. Feared Self-Image you described in chapter 4. Do you want to become more, or less, like your Alter Ego, either in general (Unified Self) or in some particular area of your life (Role Identities)? Look at the particular Big Five dimensions that would need to be changed, and consider the specific changes in your behavior, interpersonal style, or life circumstances that might help you to accomplish this objective.

2. Which Self-Images that you rated in previous chapters seem most closely aligned with your Alter Ego? Does this particular area of your life serve a special purpose—perhaps providing an escape from your usual routine and even allowing you to become something of a different person in the process? Do you feel that this area of your life represents a healthy or an unhealthy influence, or perhaps a little of both?

3. Are you satisfied with the choices you have made and how they have influenced your personal development? If your Alter Ego is based on a different path you might have taken that involved your career, visually

compare your Work Role Identity to your Alter Ego by transferring and plotting Work Role Identity scores from your Role Identity Profile onto your Alter Ego Profile. If it is based on an alternate choice for your life partner, plot and compare your Romantic Partner Role Identity to your Alter Ego. If it is based on the image you would like to project to others, plot and compare your Outer Self-Image Scores or your Reflected Image Scores. Do the differences you see appear significant?

4. If you are considering an Alter Ego based upon a different path you could have taken in the past, plot the Past Self-Image you described in chapter 8 on your Alter Ego Profile and visually compare these two perspectives. Notice the similarities and differences between your Past Self-Image and your Alter Ego. Is your Alter Ego only a voice from your past or does it represent an entirely separate formulation of your present personality?

5. If you are considering an Alter Ego based upon a dramatic change you could still make in your life at some point in the future, plot the Future Self-Image you described in chapter 8 on your Alter Ego Profile and visually compare these two perspectives. Notice the similarities and differences between your Future Self-Image and your Alter Ego. Do you believe that a dramatic change in your individual circumstances could potentially trigger an equally dramatic change in your personality, perhaps bringing your suppressed Alter Ego to the surface? Do you believe that such a change would be positive or negative, or both? Do you believe your expectations are entirely realistic?

Notes

1. For details, see Carl Jung, *The Archetypes and the Collective Unconscious* (Princeton: Princeton University Press, 2nd ed., 1981).

2. For further information, see E. Kübler-Ross, *On Death and Dying* (New York: Collier, 1969).

3. For further information, see K. Harary, Thanatology Internship Final Report: "A Critical Analysis of the Clinical Theories of Kübler-Ross" (Durham, NC: Duke University School of Nursing, 1974).

Chapter 10

More Than the Sum of Your Parts

As you enter the final phase of the Berkeley Personality Profile, you may be wondering how you can possibly consolidate the complex array of information you have gathered by examining your character from so many different perspectives. In the first four sections of the test, you explored what psychologists call your *multifaceted self-concept*, or your myriad self-images, each of which serves a particular function in helping you to motivate, plan, and evaluate various aspects of your behavior. You then expanded the focus to incorporate the perceptions of others—first those of an intimate partner who knows you well and with whom you feel relatively safe and comfortable, and then those of friends, family members, and coworkers whose perspectives on your personality may be further removed from your own. You also explored the similarities and differences between the images you hold of yourself at some significant point in the past, the way you perceive yourself at this particular moment, and how you envision yourself turning out at some significant point in the future. Finally, you entered the fascinating realm of your alter ego—your image of the sort of person you could potentially have become if the circumstances of your life were somehow different. Even if you have never taken the time to think about it before, images drawn from these self-perspectives and other people's viewpoints have been influencing your actions, your experiences, your relationships, and your sense of self-esteem since childhood.

But which point of view is correct?

Since you are the only one with direct access to your own hopes, fears, goals, attitudes, obsessions, emotions, and innermost perceptions, you might reasonably conclude that you alone possess an accurate and comprehensive view of your personality. Your romantic partner or best friend, however, combines an intimate knowledge of your inner experiences gained through self-disclosure, with an external perspective on your actions and expressions as they come across to other people. So he or she might actually be in the best position to know your personality, but at the same time might be influenced by his or her own biases toward you. But if it is your public actions, rather than your private intentions, that ultimately determine who you are, perhaps only a panel of independent observers from different areas of your life can offer a completely impartial view of your personality.

How can you reconcile the inconsistencies that emerge when your personality is viewed from several different perspectives? Is your personality ultimately defined by who *you* think you are or by what *others* think about you? When you stop to consider the ways in which your various self-perspectives and the views that others have of you continuously interact to shape the course of your life, it becomes clear that *both* must be integral components of your personality.

Your personality consists of all the coherent patterns in the way that you act, think, feel, and impress others that make you a unique person. Even when your self-perspectives and the impressions you create in the minds of other people stand sharply in contrast, both convey crucial information about your character. If you feel, for example, that you are naturally shy and introverted, yet others see you as a fun-loving extravert, then that exactly describes your Expressive Style: an individual who feels shy but is perceived and treated as an extravert by others. It is up to you to determine whether this delicate balance is helpful or harmful to you.

Who Are You?

By now, you may be considering the unsettling possibility that if you strip away all the subjective perceptions, perhaps nothing at all remains of your "true nature"—that your so-called personality may be nothing more than a complex web of partially shared illusions. Is there a single, consistent self that transcends all situations and perceptions, the existence of which remains continuous throughout all your life's adventures? Are you essentially the same individual at this point in your life that you were in your early childhood, and that you will be for many years to come? These fundamental questions about the nature of human personality must be resolved partly in the realm of science and partly in the realm of philosophy.[1]

The evidence we presented in the opening chapter regarding the validity of the Big Five dimensions certainly demonstrates that human beings do, in fact, possess "real" personalities. How else could your individual personality attributes be partially inherited, observable from birth, and capable of exerting such powerful influences on your behavior, lifestyle, relationships, and major life experiences? Yet, as highlighted by the exploration of Past and Future Self-Images, powerful life experiences—such as falling in love, joining a powerful social movement, or suffering a debilitating illness—can sometimes have a major impact on your behavior, your view of yourself, and the way others view you. Even ordinary life experiences, such as the process of growing older, can affect your personality in ways that are no less dramatic. Does this mean that your personality actually changes, or that you merely experience different aspects of the same personality you have had all along? Although this question has preoccupied philosophers for centuries, researchers are only beginning to understand the complex psychological processes involved.[2]

We would not presume to offer a universal answer to these fundamental questions, but we do have a suggestion for how you might use the Berkeley Personality Profile to begin exploring it for yourself. Many philosophical and religious systems have emphasized the significance of letting go of the individual "ego" or "self" as a primary tenet of achieving a higher level of personal fulfillment. Viewed from a psychological perspective, this might imply that learning to overcome a limited, self-centered view of your own existence is a crucial element in personal growth. One way to accomplish this objective is by learning to see yourself from many different perspectives, so that you may incorporate this more expansive view into your evolving self-image. In so doing, you may develop a greater sense of kinship and connectedness with those around you, as well as a greater degree of insight into the nature of your own existence. Whether your personality is singular and immutable, or whether it continues to re-create itself in its own expanded image throughout your lifetime, the end result of such an exploration will inevitably be a greater degree of personal knowledge, which will inform and empower you in the years to come.[3]

The Integrator Matrices

The Self-Image Integrator Matrix and the Reflected Image Integrator Matrix are designed to work together as a guide or map of your overall personality structure. The two matrices use a single, common format to describe your personality according to the Big Five personality styles, each viewed from a wide variety of perspectives. The two matrices compile data from nineteen distinctive scorecards and nine comparative profiles in order to illuminate trends and patterns in the way you view yourself and the way others view you. Your Self-Image Integrator Matrix draws together all the information you provided regarding the way you see your own personality from different perspectives, while your Reflected Image Integrator Matrix draws together all the information you obtained from other people regarding their impressions of your personality. Everything you need to complete both integrator matrices can be found in the color-coded, perforated section of the book.

Begin your Self-Image Integrator Matrix by looking up your Inner/Outer Difference Scores for the five personality dimensions, which appear in the last row of boxes on the Inner/Outer Self-Image Profile you completed for chapter 2. For any Inner/Outer Difference Score that is 3 or greater, place a check mark in the corresponding color-coded box on your Self-Image Integrator Matrix. Then, for each of the five color-coded dimensions, circle "Inner" if your Inner Self-Image Score on the dimension was larger, or "Outer" if your Outer Self-Image Score was larger. (In each case, circle the larger score, whether or not you checked the box. If there is no difference, circle neither score.) Follow the same general procedure for all the other scores called for as you move down the left-hand column of the matrix. *Please note that the size of the difference scores that should be marked with checks differs as you move from one row in the matrix to the next.* For each row, simply look up your difference scores from the appropriate profile, check the boxes that exceed the score listed on the matrix, and circle the larger scores. (The Unified/Feared row differs slightly; in this case, check the boxes for your Unified/Feared Difference Scores that are 3 or *less*.) If your larger score is tied among 2 or more scores, circle all the top scores for that box. To complete the last row of the matrix, copy your scores from the Unified Self-Image Profile you completed for chapter 3 into the corresponding color-coded boxes.

Continue with your Reflected Image Integrator Matrix using the same general method. Look up your Partner Difference Scores from your Self/Partner Image Profile. (If you participated in that exercise as Partner A, you will find your scores in the third row of boxes at the bottom of the profile; if you were Partner B, your scores will be in the sixth row.) For any of your Partner Difference Scores that were 3 or greater, place a check mark in the corresponding color-coded box in the first row of your Reflected Image Integrator Matrix. Then, for each of the five color-coded dimensions, circle "Unified" if your Unified Self-Image Score on the dimension was larger, or "Partner" if your Partner Image Score was larger. (In each case, circle the larger score, whether or not you checked the box. If there is no difference, circle neither score.) Follow the same general procedure for the second and third rows of the matrix, keeping in mind that the size of the difference scores that should be marked with a check differs as you move down the matrix. The Reflected Image Difference Scores needed for the second row of the matrix can be found in the last row of boxes on your Reflected Image Profile 1. The Unified/Reflected Difference Scores needed for the third row of the matrix can be found in the last row of boxes on your Reflected Image

Profile 2. The last row of your Reflected Image Integrator Matrix is different; in this row, simply copy your five Reflected Image Average Scores, which can be found in the eighth row of boxes near the bottom of your Reflected Image Profile 2.

Personality Styles in Your Integrator Matrices

Each of the Big Five personality styles—Expressive Style, Interpersonal Style, Work Style, Emotional Style, and Intellectual Style—is represented by a particular color-coded column that runs lengthwise down your Self-Image Integrator Matrix, and similarly down your Reflected Image Integrator Matrix. To interpret your results for the personality styles, begin by placing the two matrices side by side. Check marks indicate areas of complexity or differentiation in your personality structure, typically arising from behavior patterns that you have adapted to meet the changing demands of particular social contexts, or by implicit comparison to imagined changes in behavior. Hence, personality styles for which your behavior is relatively stable, and for which ratings from different perspectives tend to converge, will receive relatively few check marks. Personality styles for which your behavior is viewed differently depending on the situation or the perceiver will receive relatively more check marks. For example, having a large number of check marks in the orange column of one or both matrices indicates that Expressive Style is a dimension of particular complexity in your overall personality. A preponderance of check marks in the blue columns would draw attention to the complexities of your Intellectual Style. Please note that there is no set number of check marks that is considered high or low for everyone. Rather, what matters is the relative number of check marks that you have placed in the colored columns of one personality style as compared to those of another.

The personality styles or dimensions for which your self-images and reflected images show the greatest complexity, as indicated by the columns with the greatest number of check marks, also tend to be the dimensions for which you are most "at risk" of experiencing psychological discomfort, disillusionment, or difficulties with other people. Of course, while some people find it uncomfortable to be confronted by discrepancies of any kind in their personality structure, other people enjoy or even cultivate marked eccentricities in their personal style over time or across different social contexts. Hence, variability within your personality structure is only a "problem" to the extent that it either makes you feel bad about yourself or somehow interferes with your interpersonal relationships or with your ability to get things done.

It is worthwhile to take note of personality styles that are potential "risk areas" in your personality, even if the personality dimensions in question are not creating significant problems for you or anyone else at the moment. Simply being aware that others may see your behavior as erratic, unpredictable, or out of character might help you to prevent future conflicts and misunderstandings. For example, if you were more of an outgoing party lover in your youth, it might be wise to warn your spouse of what to expect before you bring her to your high school reunion. Many people use "compartmentalization" to keep personality differences in order; they may, for example, leave their worries about work behind at the office in the evening, and forget about that argument over the breakfast dishes as soon as they leave home the next morning. When a strategy such as compartmentalization helps you to cope effectively with variability in your personality style, it is generally advisable to continue using it.

Contextual Perspectives in Your Integrator Matrices

While the columns of your integrator matrices represent the Big Five personality styles, the horizontal rows each correspond to a specific context or perspective from which your personality was viewed in the Berkeley Personality Profile. Although your underlying personality structure tends to create a broad sense of coherence in your behavior, each distinct personal and interpersonal context has the potential to influence the way you experience and express your personality in subtle but important ways. Rows with the most check marks indicate contexts that had the greatest impact on the way your personality was perceived.

Rows with the fewest check marks indicate contexts that exerted relatively little influence on the way your personality was perceived.

In general, people tend to feel uncomfortable in demanding situations that cause them to diverge from their usual personality styles and familiar ways of behaving. For this reason, you may experience relatively more discomfort or distress in the contexts associated with those rows in your integrator matrices in which your check marks are most heavily concentrated.

The rows of your Self-Image Integrator Matrix represent some of the most salient or influential perspectives from which you view your own past, current, and potential personality characteristics. Your basic thoughts, feelings, hopes, dreams, and memories about yourself come together to form your *core sense of self*. A strong, stable core sense of self provides coherence to your self-experience, allowing you to feel very much "like yourself" no matter what situation you are in, even when you change your behavior in dramatic ways to meet the shifting requirements of different social contexts. Maintaining a strong, stable core sense of self helps you in setting your goals, planning your actions, monitoring your progress, and evaluating the extent to which you are satisfied with yourself and your life situation. By contrast, if you feel like your behavior is driven so strongly by external situational factors that you begin to lose touch with your true personality, your core sense of self becomes weakened, and with it your sense of efficacy and control.

If you have placed several check marks in the first row (Inner/Outer Difference Scores) or the fourth row (Role Identity Difference Scores) of your Self-Image Integrator Matrix, this could signify an underlying sense of uncertainty or instability in your core sense of self. You may be experiencing doubts and confusion about the way you should define yourself as an individual. A large number of check marks in the second row (Unified/Ideal Difference Scores) or third row (Unified/Feared Difference Scores) of your Self-Image Integrator Matrix could signal that you are having problems accepting yourself as you are—perhaps because you are not especially pleased with the core sense of self you experience.

A heavy concentration of check marks in the fifth and sixth rows (Unified/Past and Unified/Future Difference Scores) indicates that you have seen, or expect to see, comprehensive changes in your personality over time, a sort of "personality makeover," for better or for worse. The psychological impact of these temporal changes will depend on the nature of the change, the length of the time span involved, and the perceived reasons for the change. When you look back on a Past Self-Image from long ago, you may experience relief, regret, or nostalgia for the sides of your personality that you rarely see today, but these feelings probably affect your current psychological health only to the extent that you dwell on them. Similarly, a large number of check marks in the seventh row, reflecting dramatic differences between your Unified Self and your Alter Ego, may be of greater philosophical than practical significance in your everyday life.

Check marks that recur in row after row of the Self-Image Integrator Matrix may indicate a tendency to dwell heavily on discrepancies across both the realized and unrealized areas of the core self. An individual who checks a large number of boxes in the yellow Work Style column of many rows in the matrix, for example, might be feeling uncertain about what she really wants to achieve in life, wondering whether she has "sold out" the ideals of her youth in favor of material gain or security, wondering whether her work-related behavior is leading her toward or away from what she most values in life, or feeling trapped by a lack of drive or ambition that has resulted from these personal concerns and disillusionment. Because these check marks are concentrated in the Self-Image Integrator Matrix, they indicate that she is feeling uncertain about herself, but this may or may not be affecting her relationships with others.

The rows of the Reflected Image Integrator Matrix refer to various aspects of your relationships with other people. A heavy concentration of check marks in these rows suggests an underlying rift in the interface between your own self-image and the broader social context in which you live. Checks in the Reflected Image Difference row indicate that your behavior, in at least some social settings, may be fundamentally at odds with your core sense of self. Checks in the Partner Difference and Unified/Reflected Difference rows more commonly indicate problems in accurately communicating your thoughts, feelings, intentions, needs, and desires to other people and, in return, failing to gain the unambiguous sense that others understand and appreciate you for who you are.

Without a smooth and relatively seamless interface between your internal vision of yourself and the external images of your personality that are reflected in the way other people approach and respond to you, you may eventually come to feel trapped, alienated, frustrated, or resentful. Furthermore, if others do not accurately perceive your true motivations and intentions, they may fail to open the doors of opportunity that could lead you toward personal, occupational, and intellectual growth and development. Over time, such interpersonal differences in perspective could create internal psychological problems for you as well, leading you to feel unsatisfied with or uncertain about your core sense of self.

As you focus on the rows and columns of your matrices that signal potential problems or challenges for you, the information provided by the perspectives that you circled may prove helpful in outlining the more specific details of these contrasts. In each case, the circled perspectives are those from which you rated yourself (or were rated by others) as highest on the dimension in question. The Unified Self-Image Scores and Reflected Image Average Scores, which appear in the last row of boxes on the Self- and Reflected Image matrices, respectively, also provide a useful frame of reference.

If you have a lot of check marks in the Expressive Style column, for example, you may wish to take special note of the perspectives from which you were rated highest on Expressive Style. If you circled "Ideal" in the Expressive Style (orange) box of row two, then you would ideally like to be more personable or assertive than you currently believe yourself to be. The perspectives that you circled in every other box in the orange column of the matrix are each probably closer to your Ideal Self-Image than any of the other scores to which they had previously been compared because—like your Ideal Self-Image—you rated them the highest. So if you circled "Ideal" in row two and "Partner" in rows four, five, and six, you probably see yourself as closest to your Ideal Self-Image in this particular role identity and are also viewed most favorably by your partner on this dimension.

In another example, if you circled "Feared" in row three of the Emotional Style (red) column, then you fear that you could potentially become more vulnerable, anxious, or irritable than you are at present. In this case, if you circled your Work role in the red box of row four, and were rated highest by your coworkers on Emotional Style, as indicated by circling "Coworker" in row six (Role Identity Difference Scores), then something in your work environment may be leading you to act in a way that is at least superficially similar to your Feared Self. Consequently, you are probably least satisfied with this role identity.

You may wish to incorporate your Unified Self-Image Scores into your integrative picture by examining whether you have more check marks in the color-coded columns of the matrix for which you had the highest and lowest Unified Self-Image Scores. In some cases, scoring yourself extremely high or extremely low on a dimension may increase the chances that this dimension will be a source of disagreement. Consider, for example, a person who scored his Unified Self-Image higher on Interpersonal Style (34) than on any other personality dimension (scores ranging from 12 to 25). If he has many checks in the lower half of the Interpersonal Style (green) column of the Reflected Image matrix, it may be that others agree that he has a warm and sensitive Interpersonal Style but simply found it difficult to agree with the *extremely* high score he gave himself on this dimension.

Or, consider a woman who scored her Unified Self-Image very low (8) on Work Style, and who has a great many check marks up and down the entire Work Style (yellow) column of both matrices. In this case, the disagreement among her own self-perspectives and among the perceptions of her personality by others could have occurred primarily because she rated herself extraordinarily low on Work Style. The others in her life might agree that she has trouble with plans, schedules, and responsibilities but simply see her work-oriented behavior less pessimistically than she sees it herself. At the same time, the difference between her Unified and Ideal Self-Images, as would be indicated by a check mark in the yellow box of row two of her matrix, might be inflated because of her unrealistically low self-image for this personality dimension.

For both the personal and interpersonal domains, we remind you, once again, that check marks do not indicate areas of habitual problems for everyone. As long as you feel in control of the situation, you may be able to make the most of your idiosyncrasies and continue to flourish. You may, however, still find it worthwhile to make a mental note of any highly variable, possibly stressful, or potentially misunderstood aspects of your character that are highlighted in your integrator matrix, for future reference.

Points for Reflection

Now that you have completed your integrator matrices, you may find yourself considering the dimensions of your personality for which you consistently experience psychological challenges concerning your own self-image and your relationships with other people. The Points for Reflection that follow are designed to help you clarify your thoughts and feelings as you apply this final section of the Berkeley Personality Profile to your everyday life.

1. Focus on the color-coded *column* of your integrator matrices in which you have placed the most check marks. This represents a dimension of your personality for which there are inconsistencies in your own self-image or your image as perceived by other people in your life. These inconsistencies may result from fluctuations in the way you actually come across in different situations or from conflicts concerning your personal beliefs about your identity.

   Are you being too hard on yourself on this dimension or do you simply feel that this is an area of your personality that could use some work? Do you agree that other people accurately perceive the fluctuations in the way you act in different situations or do you feel that they are somehow misconstruing this dimension of your personality? Do you feel that your core sense of self is solidly established for this dimension or are you still uncertain about "who you really are" when it comes to this aspect of your personality? Alternatively, is this an area for which you hesitate to commit yourself to a firm, core sense of self, perhaps because you value the flexibility to adapt yourself to the shifting demands of particular roles and settings—or because you fear becoming too set in your ways?

2. Sometimes major life events, such as getting engaged, beginning college, or getting a promotion, can have a powerful impact on your sense of self and the way you are viewed by other people. Have any of the inconsistencies in your self-image, or your image as perceived by others, emerged because you are currently in the process of a major life transition? In responding to this question, focus on the color-coded *column(s)* of both your integrator matrices in which you have placed the most check marks to determine the dimension(s) of your personality that are most affected.

3. Now focus exclusively on your Self-Image Integrator Matrix. If you find that your check marks are concentrated on this particular matrix, the kinds of strains you are most likely to experience concern your own self-image and self-evaluations. You may be having difficulty defining and achieving your goals, perhaps because you are uncertain of your capabilities or perhaps because you fear that your standards and expectations are just too high. You may be suffering from low self-esteem or feel as though you allow other people and external circumstances to have too great an influence over how you feel about yourself. Alternatively, you may just be overly modest in your evaluations of your personality.

If you are experiencing personal problems directly concerning your self-image, stop and consider the possibility that you are being too hard on yourself, or at least underestimating the full extent of your accomplishments and capabilities. The modesty you appear to show in describing your personality suggests that you might have many more positive qualities than you admit. Any fluctuations in your self-image as you move from one setting to the next in your everyday life could indicate a high degree of adaptability rather than a lack of integrity or consistency in your personality.

4. Now focus exclusively on your Reflected Image Integrator Matrix. If your check marks are concentrated in this particular matrix, the kinds of strain you are most likely to experience pertain to the way you are perceived by other people. You may not consider the differences between the way you see yourself and the way others perceive

you to be a problem, however, if you reserve some sides of your personality for certain settings while maintaining a different persona where and when you feel the situation demands it.

Consider the ways in which you frequently find it difficult to clearly communicate your thoughts and feelings to those around you, and the ways in which you feel that you are especially misunderstood. Do other people perceive you as being more like your own Ideal Self-Image or Feared Self-Image? Do their perceptions of you in particular roles agree with your perceptions of yourself in those circumstances? If you are unhappy with the way you are perceived by others, consider the kinds of positive steps you can take to change this situation.

Consider whether you deliberately conceal some aspects of your nature from certain people and whether you feel completely comfortable with this state of affairs. If you feel that particular conditions demand that you remain "undercover" about some aspects of your personality, you may wish to consider whether these situations are healthy for you. Are you comfortable with the circumstances in question? If not, would you like to change them in some way or find a way to move into a more comfortable situation?

5. Now focus on those personality dimensions, or color-coded columns of both integrator matrices, in which you have not placed any check marks. It is very likely that these are dimensions of your personality with which you feel especially comfortable. You may, however, wish to consider whether feeling comfortable about this side of your nature is, for you, a positive or a negative thing. A positive sense of comfort occurs when you have a solid sense of who you are and feel good about yourself and your relationships with other people. A negative sense of comfort occurs when you feel trapped within a certain pattern in the way you think, act, feel, and approach others, and consider yourself incapable of changing for the better; some individuals even find a certain strange comfort in the familiar quality of their unhappiness.

Your own behavior may offer clues about whether the degree of comfort you feel about these aspects of your personality represents a positive or negative state of affairs for you. If you hesitate to take on new challenges or pursue novel experiences that you would otherwise like to explore, your self-certainty may have developed more from habitual patterns than from a conscious decision to foster and maintain this particular aspect of your self-concept.

6. As you review the overall distribution of check marks and circled items in both integrator matrices, consider the source of any recurring patterns in your own perceptions, actions, and experiences, and the source of any recurring opinions that others form about you. Have you adopted either a consistent, or an unusually variable, pattern of behavior in some area of your life because your parents, siblings, or peers encouraged you to adopt this pattern when you were growing up? Do you sometimes find yourself living up (or down) to others' expectations because you find it easier to fit in and be predictable than to try to be yourself?

   Are there any recurrent patterns in your behavior, your self-perceptions, your perceptions of others, or their perceptions of you that may be attributable to broad societal pressures, such as the confusing values promoted by the mass media and advertisers? These values include such contradictory concepts as the notion that a "successful individual" should be ambitious and assertive but never brusque or ruthless, should be a popular member of the crowd while remaining fiercely independent, and should have a healthy appetite and "consume mass quantities" while remaining remarkably fit and thin. If you feel that some of the "risk areas" in your personality may be related to the way you respond to such mixed messages, consider the possibility that you might feel happier if you were more discriminating.

7. What inner strengths and other admirable qualities have you discovered or confirmed about your personality in completing the various sections of the Berkeley Personality Profile? We suggest that you take a few moments to appreciate these positive sides of your personality. Consider the ways in which these qualities have served you well throughout your life. Consider, also, the ways in which you

may consciously nourish these sides of your nature, and use them to continue to flourish and nurture your relationships with other people, now and in the future.

Notes

1. For a more detailed exploration of the issues involved in defining the nature of the self and its perception of reality, see M. Polanyi, *Personal Knowledge: Towards a Post-Critical Philosophy* (Chicago: University of Chicago, 1974); and D. Parfit, *Reasons and Persons* (Oxford: Oxford University Press, 1984).

2. For more on the question of personality change, see T. F. Heatherton and J. L. Weinberger, eds., *Can Personality Change?* (Washington, DC: American Psychological Association, 1994).

3. For more on the philosophical relevance of personal knowledge and related issues, see H. Arendt, *The Human Condition* (Chicago: University of Chicago, 1958); M. Polanyi, *The Study of Man* (Chicago: University of Chicago, 1959); and S. Kierkegaard, *Fear and Trembling and the Sickness unto Death* (Princeton, NJ: Princeton University Press, 1941).

Person to Person

We hope you have enjoyed exploring the many different sides of your nature, using the Berkeley Personality Profile as your guide. By drawing on the insights you have gained from this experience, you may improve your relationships and make the kinds of positive life choices that are most in tune with your personality. We hope you will call upon the inner strengths and resources you have discovered to improve your quality of life.

How can you make the most of what you have learned through the Berkeley Personality Profile? First, know yourself. As you continue to grow and mature during your life's journey, remember your past, which remains a part of you, and be sure to keep your self-image fresh and relevant to who you are today. Keep in mind that certain predispositions within your personality are hardwired and have been with you since birth, for better or for worse. Although these most central aspects of your nature will always influence the way you experience and react to your world, you can learn to make the most of them, to express them in the healthiest way possible.

Your personality has evolved over a lifetime of experiences in a variety of social settings and situations. No doubt, it has become extremely complicated in the course of that adventure. We suggest that you try to accept your dominant tendencies that are stable across perspectives, but that you also allow yourself to adapt to your surroundings as necessary, as desirable, as appropriate, and as possible within the limits of your capabilities. Remember that there may still be surprises hidden deep within your personality. Perhaps other people in your life may recognize something in your character that you never stopped to notice, or perhaps the untapped possibilities that wait within your alter ego will surprise you all.

Through the process of exploring your own personality, we hope that you have also developed a deeper understanding of the significant people in your life. Consider the fact that their personalities are as complex as your own, and try to give them the same latitude you should afford yourself. When possible, try to accept their predominant traits and allow them to be themselves, while also allowing them the freedom to adapt to different circumstances. When trying to interpret their behavior, keep in mind that you are only partially responsible for the way that other people react to you. Sometimes others may treat you unfairly because of some deeply rooted aspect of their own nature, or because of something that happened to them in another relationship. Sometimes another person may idolize you for reasons that likewise have little to do with your own characteristics or the nature of your actual involvement with them. There is an old saying among crisis intervention counselors that "You are only responsible for your part of the interaction," but not for all the life events, individual decisions, and personal predispositions that brought a particular person to a particular point. That is excellent advice to keep in mind in all of your relationships.

You can begin by applying your increased understanding of personality dynamics toward understanding the people closest to you—your immediate family and most intimate friends. The next step is when the real work begins. If you feel the others in your group will be amenable to the process, you can begin to work together to apply your combined insights toward understanding and improving your mutual interactions. Pay attention to the details as you learn to notice the *patterns* in the actions and reactions of each person, including yourself. Which patterns are healthy for the group dynamic, and which patterns put stress on any individuals or the group as a whole? Before sharing your observations with others, you may first want to ask them what patterns they may have observed in the group dynamic and how they feel about those observations. We urge you, however, to be as gentle and subtle as possible as you go about this process. Remember to be sensitive toward others' feelings and to keep an open mind about the ways in which their observations might differ from your own. If there is any possibility of volatile reactions, we suggest that you first consult a clinical professional before opening any individual or group discussion.

The same principles can be applied, with a more modest scope, to understanding the individual characters and group dynamics in other domains of your life. Please keep in mind, however, that in a setting such as your work environment, you are dealing with only a thin slice of each person's daily activities, and with only a thin slice of each individual's personality. It is not always necessary or desirable to learn more about the private lives of your coworkers. Focus on having your work identity get to know their work identity. Then focus on developing effective strategies for getting your work identity to function together in the most pleasant and productive fashion possible with theirs. Attempting to open a psychological dialogue with your coworkers is probably unnecessary and could be disastrous if your relationship is more formal than intimate. However, you may be able to make subtle changes in your own behavior that can improve your relations with coworkers without explicitly drawing their attention to it. In turn, if you can think of some small, specific change a coworker might be able to make to his or her habits that would help the group dynamic, we suggest that you find the correct time and ask nicely if they might consider making that change. Start small in your requests, be sensitive to others' feelings, and always use common sense.

The Berkeley Personality Profile provides a range of tools to aid in your careful analysis of personalities and relationships. But some interpersonal situations require you to "Think fast!" First impressions can have lasting effects, so it is important to present yourself carefully and thoughtfully in a way that makes the right first impression on the other person—that is, an impression that will be healthy for the relationship you wish to have with that individual and an impression that you are able and willing to maintain for the duration of the relationship. The most dominant aspects of your personality—those that you have tended to express in a similar fashion over a long period of time and across a range of social settings—are likely to shine through in your behavior quite naturally in a first-impression situation. The less central aspects of your character, those that you often express differently according to the demands of different situations, are those that you will have the most latitude in managing when creating and maintaining a first impression. The same principle applies when you are forming your first impressions of another person. If you attend carefully to specific cues in that person's verbal and nonverbal behaviors, you will probably form a fairly accurate impression of their most basic traits.

Relationship expert Barbara Rubin, PhD, who cofounded the Women's Center at Jersey City State College, advises that "People will always tell you who they are the first time you meet," if you are listening to them and paying attention to their behavior. We have found this to be true with those who have remarkably advised us, up front, that they cannot remember ever having a healthy relationship with anyone, or that they are generally insensitive and uncaring toward the feelings of others, or that those with whom they become personally involved always end up believing they are crazy. We have likewise found it to be true with those who say they always remain friends with those with whom they have been intimately involved, or that they usually enjoy their professional relationships, or that their interactions with other people include a wide range of individual experiences. Even in the initial days of your interaction, however, and especially in the first blush of a romantic attraction, it is not always easy to see through your own hopes, fears, misconceptions, and overpowering emotions. Some relationship experts believe that it takes at least six months for people to truly let down their guards and begin to recognize each other for who they really are—especially in response to the chemistry of their own personal interactions. Keep in mind that some of the less central features of another person's nature may be expressed differently as your relationship evolves and you come to know them better. We suggest that you take it easy and enjoy the process and, as one wise friend—photographer David Lutz—recently advised, "Allow yourself to discover what the relationship is going to become over time." You can always retouch your first impressions based on later information.

One way to get to know others better is to try to find some common ground in your attitudes, opinions, values, and even those personality predispositions that you might share. Recognizing one of your own central or peripheral traits in another person can help you empathize and understand them better. Observing the way your shared traits are expressed in the other person's behavior might also help you to understand your own tendencies a little better. If you are interested in learning more about your own personality traits by studying the way that similar traits have been played out in other people's lives, look first to the people in your own immediate social world and consider the ways in which their most predominant traits appear to coincide with the Big Five dimensions for which you scored highest and lowest. The closer you are to another person, the more comprehensive your view of their personality and life history. Of course, sometimes it can be fun and exciting, or even inspiring, to compare the role a particular trait has played in your own life with the role the same trait has played in the life experiences of a famous person as portrayed in a biography, autobiography, or historical account. Whether exploring the personality and life experience of someone you know personally, or of a famous person, remember that each perspective from which a person is viewed may differ in subtle but important ways, and that none of these viewpoints represents a source of absolute truth.

We hope the Berkeley Personality Profile has given you some useful insights into the ways that other people—your romantic partner, friends and family, coworkers, and others—each perceive your personality. You should also have come to better recognize the ways in which these perceptions are influenced by the social roles in which you meet, and how you reveal yourself to others in those situations. As you continue to integrate this information into your life and your relationships, you should now have a better sense of the kind of lasting impression you are making on all those around you. You should also, in the process, have gained a heightened awareness of why even strangers tend to respond to you in a particular way. Their first impressions are formed in response to the many clues that you give out about your personality within only moments of meeting you, and the ways in which their perceptions are influenced by their own predispositions. You should also have a better sense of how you form your own instantaneous impressions of other people, and why—as we must all eventually discover—even first impressions can be lasting. At a deeper level, through exploring the nuances and mysteries of your own personality, we hope you have discovered something valuable about the common human ground you share with those around you, and how the patterns of all our individual traits and interactions blend together to help create our individual and collective life experiences.

Your personality is the essence of how your see yourself and how you are perceived by those around you. It is the focal point of your entire life experience, and all your values and perceptions. It is also that essential part of your existence that can never be reduced to simple calculations—that is uniquely and profoundly you. It makes it possible for you to form the irreplaceable connections you have formed with other people. Now that you have completed the Berkeley Personality Profile, we offer our appreciation and congratulations. We hope that you will take the time to celebrate the unexpected things that you have learned about yourself, and to rejoice in your connections with the special people in your life.

About the Authors

Keith Harary, PhD, is a graduate of Duke University and the Union Institute, where he earned his doctoral degree in psychology with emphases in both clinical counseling and experimental research. He is research director of the Institute for Advanced Psychology, a nonprofit consortium of independent scientists. His work has included psychological and physiological studies of altered states of consciousness, laboratory investigations of intuition and perception, field investigations of the psychological methods used in the Peoples Temple and other extremist groups, and the development of the Reflective method of personality assessment in cooperation with colleagues at the Institute of Personality and Social Research at the University of California at Berkeley. His clinical work has included comprehensive training and experience in crisis and suicide intervention and marriage and family counseling. Dr. Harary is the former editor at large of *Omni* magazine and was a key contributor to *Omni*'s award-winning Internet edition. He has published more than one hundred professional journal and popular scientific articles, several other books, and has given dozens of invited lectures, workshops, and presentations sponsored by leading universities and other scientific and cultural organizations. He has also served as an award-winning public relations and marketing consultant and/or media spokesperson for a number of international corporations, ranging from Microsoft to Budget Rent A Car, and as a scientific consultant to various government agencies working on classified projects.

Eileen Donahue Robinson, PhD, earned her doctoral degree in personality psychology at the University of California at Berkeley, where she held a National Science Foundation fellowship. While at Berkeley, she participated in the development of the Big Five Inventory, an original psychological test designed to measure fundamental dimensions of personality. She also worked as personality assessor in intensive longitudinal research programs at the university's Institute of Personality and Social Research, and designed independent personality assessment programs of her own. She later worked as a professor at Wellesley College in Wellesley, Massachusetts, and at Williams College in Williamstown, Massachusetts, where she taught a variety of classes and seminars in personality psychology, as well as courses in general psychology, statistics, and research methods. Her independent research has focused on the Big Five personality dimensions, the multifaceted self-concept, and people's everyday descriptions of self and others. Her empirical work has been published in the *Journal of Personality and Social Psychology, Journal of Personality,* and *Psychological Science.* Dr. Robinson now resides in Hawaii with her husband and three young sons, from whom she draws her greatest inspiration.

Notes

Notes

Notes

Notes

Notes

Notes

Who Do You Think You Are?

Explore Your Many-Sided Self with
THE BERKELEY PERSONALITY PROFILE

*The fascinating new system
that shows you how to see yourself
as you really are with your
partner, family, friends, and coworkers*

KEITH HARARY, PhD, AND
EILEEN DONAHUE ROBINSON, PhD

GENERAL PROFILE INSTRUCTIONS

The Berkeley Personality Profile consists of a series of twenty-one score-cards, nine profile charts, and two integrator matrices. Each of these elements provides a unique perspective on your personality. The materials you need to complete the exercises are located in the color-coded perforated sections of this book.

How It Works

Each of the twenty-one scorecards in the Berkeley Personality Profile represents a unique view of your personality as seen from one particular perspective. Self-Image scorecards reflect the way you view yourself from different perspectives, and Reflected-Image scorecards reflect the way that other people view your personality. Each of the nine profile charts provides a visual comparison showing the results for a small group of thematically related scorecards. To complete each profile, you must first complete the corresponding scorecards for that section of the test.

The color-coded design of the Berkeley Personality Profile greatly simplifies the calculation of your scores. For each section, begin by adding together all the numbers you marked for the orange lines on a particular scorecard. Then enter the total in the corresponding color-coded box provided for that section on the profile itself. Do the same, in turn, for your green, yellow, red, and blue responses on each scorecard, entering the total score for each color in the corresponding color-coded box.

Once you have added up and entered all the color-coded responses for all the scorecards needed for a particular section of the test, follow the additional instructions provided in the section titled "Individual Profile Scoring Instructions" to compare your scores. Look up your scores on the interpretation guides provided for chapters 2 through 9 to learn more about the meaning of your scores for each perspective on your personality.

In each section of the Berkeley Personality Profile, you may visually compare your scores by charting them on the graph provided for that part of the test. To do so, simply mark the initials of the scorecard you are using ("I" for Inner Self-Image, "O" for Outer Self-Image, and so forth) at the level of the number corresponding to your score for a given color-coded personality dimension. Then draw a line to connect all the scores you marked from a particular scorecard, across all five personality dimensions.

A Sample Profile

The sample case we have provided of a completed Inner/Outer Self-Image Profile shows you how easy it is to fill out each profile form. Please note that we have used solid, dashed, and dotted lines to represent the different scores that we've charted for the sample cases we'll be presenting to you in various chapters. You may wish to do the same as you plot your profiles for the various sections of the test, or you may wish to use a different color ink to represent each of the various self-perspectives.

The scores depicted were sent to us by one of our *Psychology Today* survey respondents. First, we added up all the numbers marked from the orange lines on the Inner Self-Image scorecard, writing the result (21) in the first box in the top row, labeled "Inner Self-Image Scores." We followed the same procedure for the green, yellow, red, and blue response on the Inner Self-Image scorecard, again writing the results in the corresponding boxes in the first row. We then followed the identical procedure for the Outer Self-Image scorecard, this time writing the resulting scores in the corresponding boxes for the Outer Self-Image Scores in the second row. We marked these scores at the corresponding level of the graph above each section of boxes, marking an "I" for Inner Self-Image Scores and an "O" for Outer Self-Image Scores, and plotted a line connecting each of these two different sets of scores. We also starred the larger of the two scores shown for each personality dimension, as requested by the Inner/Outer Self-Image Profile instructions, and wrote the difference between these two scores in the

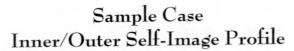

Sample Case
Inner/Outer Self-Image Profile

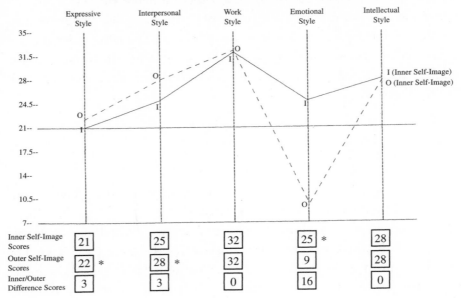

third row of boxes. Using these scores as our guide, we were then able to look up their meaning in the interpretation guide provided for chapter 2.

Individual Profile Scoring Instructions

Instructions for Inner/Outer Self-Image Profile

1. Beginning with the Inner Self-Image scorecard (Scorecard 1), add together all the numbers you marked from the orange-colored lines, then enter the total in the top box of the orange section for Expressive Style. Do the same for the green, yellow, red, and blue responses, entering the scores across the top row of boxes. These are your Inner Self-Image Scores. Next, add together the color-coded numbers you marked on your Outer Self-Image scorecard (Score-

card 2), exactly as you did for the Inner Self-Image Scores, and enter the scores in the second row of boxes. These are your Outer Self-Image Scores.

2. Chart your scores on the Inner/Outer Self-Image Profile. First, write an "I" in the orange portion of the graph at the level of the number that corresponds to your Inner Self-Image Score from the top orange box. For example, if your score is 35, you will mark an "I" at the very top of the orange region. If your score is 7, you will mark an "I" at the very bottom. More moderate scores will be marked somewhere in between these two extremes. Do the same for the rest of your Inner Self-Image Scores, writing an "I" at the correct level of each color-coded region of the graph. Now draw a line that connects all the "I's" that you marked.

   Chart your Outer Self-Image Scores in the same way. This time, write an "O" at the level of each color-coded region of the graph that corresponds to your five Outer Self-Image Scores. Draw a line that connects all the "O's" that you marked.

3. Compare your Expressive Style (orange) scores for your Inner Self-Image and Outer Self-Image. Mark a star next to the larger of these two scores. Then subtract the smaller from the larger score, and write the result in the corresponding (orange) box in the third row. This is your Inner/Outer Difference Score for Expressive Style. (If your Inner Self-Image and Outer Self-Image Expressive Style scores are exactly the same, write a zero in the third box and don't mark a star next to either score.) Follow the same procedure for each color-coded category to compute your Inner/Outer Difference Scores for Interpersonal Style, Work Style, Emotional Style, and Intellectual Style. Record your results in the corresponding boxes in the third row. *(Don't plot your Inner/Outer Difference Scores on the graph. You'll be using these scores later on.)*

   By looking at your Inner/Outer Self-Image Profile, you can see easily where your Inner and Outer Self-Image Scores differ dramatically, and where these scores are very close together. In addition, you can tell at a glance the Big Five personality dimensions on which you scored highest and lowest. The interpretation guide in chapter 2 will help you break down and analyze in detail the meaning behind each important aspect of your profile.

Instructions for Unified Self-Image Profile

1. Add together all the numbers you marked from the orange-colored lines on your Unified Self-Image scorecard (Scorecard 3), then enter the total in the orange box for Expressive Style. Do the same for the green, yellow, red, and blue responses, entering the scores in the corresponding boxes. These are your Unified Self-Image Scores.

2. Chart your scores on the Unified Self-Image Profile. First, write a "U" in the orange portion of the graph at the level of the number that corresponds to your Unified Self-Image Score from the orange box. For example, if your score is 35, you will mark a "U" at the very top of the orange region. If your score is 7, you will mark a "U" at the very bottom. More moderate scores will be marked somewhere in between these two extremes. Do the same for the rest of your Unified Self-Image Scores, writing a "U" at the correct level of each color-coded region of the graph. Now draw a line that connects all the "U's" that you marked.

By looking at your Unified Self-Image Profile, you can tell easily at a glance the Big Five personal dimensions for which you scored highest and lowest. The interpretation guide in chapter 3 will help you to break down and analyze in detail the meaning behind each important aspect of your profile.

Instructions for Possible Self-Image Profile

1. Copy your Unified Self-Image Scores, from the Unified Self-Image Profile you completed in chapter 3, into the first row of color-coded boxes. Chart these scores on your Possible Self-Image Profile, using a "U" to signify your Unified Self-Image Score for each of the five

color-coded personality dimensions. Draw a line that connects all the "U's" that you marked.

2. Add together all the numbers from the orange lines that you marked on the Ideal Self-Image scorecard (Scorecard 4), then enter the total in the second box of the corresponding (orange) section for Expressive Style. Do the same for the green, yellow, red, and blue responses, entering the scores across the second row of boxes. These are your Ideal Self-Image Scores. Next, add together the color-coded numbers that you marked on your Feared Self-Image scorecard (Scorecard 5), exactly as you did for your Ideal Self-Image, and enter the total in the third row of boxes. These are your Feared Self-Image Scores.

3. Chart your Ideal and Feared Self-Image Scores on the Possible Self-Image Profile. First, write an "I" in the orange portion of the graph at the level of the number that corresponds to your Ideal Self-Image Score from the orange box. If your score is 35, you will mark an "I" at the very top of the graph. If your score is 7, you will mark an "I" at the very bottom. More moderate scores will be marked somewhere in between these two extremes. Do the same for the rest of your Ideal Self-Image Scores, writing an "I" at the correct level of each color-coded region of the graph. Now draw a line that connects all the "I's" you marked. This is your Ideal Self-Image Profile.

Chart your Feared Self-Image in the same way, using an "F" to signify your Feared Self-Image Score for the Big Five personality dimensions and drawing a line to connect all the "F's" that you marked.

4. Compare your Expressive Style (orange) scores for your Unified Self-Image and Ideal Self-Image. Mark a star next to the larger of these two scores. Then subtract the smaller from the larger score and write the result in the corresponding (orange) box in the fourth row. This is your Unified/Ideal Difference Score for Expressive Style. (If your Unified Self-Image and Ideal Self-Image Scores for Expressive Style are exactly the same, write a zero in the fourth

box and don't mark a star next to either score.) Follow the same procedure for each color-coded category to compute your Unified/Ideal Difference Scores for Interpersonal Style, Work Style, Emotional Style, and Intellectual Style. Record your results in the corresponding boxes in the fourth row. *(Don't plot your Unified/Ideal Difference scores on the graph. You'll be using these scores later on.)*

5. Compare your Expressive Style (orange) scores for your Unified Self-Image and Feared Self-Image. Mark two stars next to the larger of these two scores. Then subtract the smaller from the larger score and write the result in the corresponding (orange) box in the fifth row. This is your Unified/Feared Difference Score for Expressive Style. (If your Unified Self-Image and Feared Self-Image Scores for Expressive Style are exactly the same, write a zero in the fifth box and don't mark two stars next to either score.) Follow the same procedure for each color-coded category to compute your Unified/Feared Difference Scores for Interpersonal Style, Work Style, Emotional Style, and Intellectual Style. Record your results in the corresponding boxes in the fifth row. *(Don't plot your Unified/ Feared Difference scores on the graph. You'll be using these scores later on.)*

By looking at your Possible Self-Image Profile, you can see easily where your Unified, Ideal, and Feared Self-Image Scores differ dramatically, and where these scores are very close together. In addition, you can tell at a glance the Big Five personality dimensions for which you scored highest and lowest on each Self-Image. The interpretation guide in chapter 4 will help you analyze in detail the meaning of each important aspect of your profile.

Instructions for Role Identity Profile

1. Beginning with the Work Role Identity scorecard (Scorecard 6), add together all the numbers you marked from the orange-colored lines, then enter the total in the top box of the orange section for Expres-

sive Style. Do the same for green, yellow, red, and blue responses, entering the scores across the top row of boxes. These are your Work Role Identity Scores. Next, add together the color-coded numbers you marked for your Romantic Partner Role Identity scorecard (Scorecard 7), exactly as you did for the Work Role Identity Scores, and enter the totals in the second row of boxes. These are your Romantic Partner Role Identity Scores. Do the same for your Friend Role Identity scorecard (Scorecard 8), entering the totals in the third row of boxes, and your Other Role Identity scorecard (Scorecard 9), entering the totals in the fourth row of boxes. These are your Friend and Other Role Identity Scores.

2. Chart your scores on the Role Identity Profile. First, write a "W" in the orange portion of the graph at the level of the number that corresponds to your Work Role Identity Score from the orange box. For example, if your score is 35, you will mark a "W" at the very top of the orange region. If your score is 7, you will mark a "W" at the very bottom. More moderate scores will be marked somewhere in between these two extremes. Do the same for the rest of your Work Role Identity Scores, writing a "W" at the correct level of each color-coded region of the graph. Now draw a line that connects all the "W's" that you marked.

3. Chart your Romantic Partner Role Identity Scores in the same way. This time, write a "P" at the level of each color-coded region of the graph that corresponds to your Romantic Partner Role Identity Scores. Draw a line that connects all the "P's" that you marked.

4. Then chart your Friend Role Identity Scores, writing an "F" at the level of each color-coded region of the graph that corresponds to your Friend Role Identity Scores, and drawing a line connecting all the "F's" that you marked.

5. Finally, chart your Other Role Identity Scores, writing an "O" at the level of each color-coded region of the graph that corresponds to your Other Role Identity Scores, and drawing a line connecting all the "O's" that you marked.

6. Compare your Expressive Style (orange) scores for your Work Role Identity, Romantic Partner Role Identity, Friend Role Identity, and Other Role Identity. Subtract the smallest from the largest of these four scores, and write the result in the corresponding (orange) box in the fifth row. This is your Role Identity Difference Score for Expressive Style. (If all your Role Identity Scores for Expressive Style are the same, write a zero in the fifth orange box.) Follow the same procedure for each color-coded category to compute your Role Identity Difference Scores for Interpersonal Style, Work Style, Emotional Style, and Intellectual Style. Record your results in the corresponding boxes in the fifth row. *(Don't plot your Role Identity Difference Scores on the graph. You'll be using these scores later on.)*

By looking at your Role Identity Profile, you can see easily where your Work Role Identity, Romantic Partner Role Identity, Friend Role Identity, and Other Role Identity Scores differ dramatically, and where these scores are very close together. The interpretation guide in chapter 5 will help you break down and analyze in detail the meaning behind your scores and each important aspect of your chart.

Optional Scoring: As an optional method of scoring and interpreting the results of your Role Identity Profile, you may also add together the individual Role Identity Difference Scores you computed for each of the Big Five personality dimensions to determine your Total Role Identity Difference Score. Your total score will fall somewhere between 0 and 140. Record the result in the box shown on your Role Identity Profile. Then refer to chapter 5 to analyze the meaning behind your Total Role Identity Difference Score.

Instructions for Self/Partner Image Profile

1. Begin by copying your Unified Self-Image Scores, from the Unified Self-Image Profile you completed in chapter 3, into the first row of

colored boxes in your Self/Partner Image Profile. Chart these scores on your Self/Partner Image Profile, using a "UA" to signify your Unified Self-Image Score for each of the five color-coded personality dimensions. Draw a line that connects all the "UA's" that you marked.

2. Add together all the numbers from the orange lines that your partner or best friend marked to describe you on your Partner Image score-card (Scorecard 10), then enter the total in the second box of the corresponding (orange) section for Expressive Style. Do the same for the green, yellow, red, and blue responses, entering the scores across the second row of boxes. These are your Partner A: Partner Image Scores. Chart these scores on your Self/Partner Image Profile, using "PA" to signify your Partner Image Score for each of the five color-coded personality dimensions. Draw a line that connects all the "PA's" that you marked.

3. Compare the Expressive Style scores for your Partner A: Unified Self-Image and Partner A: Partner Image. Make a star next to the larger of these two scores. Then subtract the smaller from the larger score and write the result in the corresponding (orange) box in the third row. This is your Partner Difference Score for Expressive Style. (If your Unified and Partner Image Scores are exactly the same, write a zero in the third box and don't make a star next to either score.) Follow the same procedure for each color-coded category to compute your Partner Difference Scores for Interpersonal Style, Work Style, Emotional Style, and Intellectual Style. Record your results in the corresponding boxes in the third row. *(Don't plot your Partner Difference scores on this graph. You'll be using these later on.)*

4. Add together all the numbers from the orange lines that your partner or best friend marked to describe himself or herself on the Partner B: Unified Self-Image scorecard (Scorecard 11), then enter the total in the corresponding (orange) box in the fourth row. Do the same for the green, yellow, red, and blue responses, entering the scores across the fourth row of boxes. These are your Partner B: Unified Self-Image Scores. *(If your partner is also completing the full Berkeley*

Personality Profile, you may simply enter the Unified Self-Image Scores that he or she has already calculated in chapter 3.)

Using a different color ink than you used before to chart your own scores, chart your partner's or best friend's scores on your Self/ Partner Image Profile, using "UB" to signify his or her Unified Self-Image Scores for each of the five color-coded personality dimensions. Draw a line that connects all the "UB's" that you marked.

5. Add together all the numbers from the orange lines that you used to describe your partner or best friend on your Partner B: Partner Image scorecard (Scorecard 12), then enter the total in the fifth box of the corresponding (orange) row for Expressive Style. Do the same for the green, yellow, red, and blue responses, entering the scores across the fifth row of boxes. These are your Partner B: Partner Image Scores. Using the same color ink you used earlier for Partner B, plot these scores on your profile, using "PB" to signify your Partner Image Scores for Partner B.

6. Compare the Expressive Style scores for your Partner B: Unified Self-Image and Partner B: Partner Image. Make a star next to the larger of these two scores. Then subtract the smaller from the larger score and write the result in the corresponding (orange) box in the sixth row. This is Partner B's Partner Difference Score for Expressive Style. (If Partner B's Unified and Partner Image Scores are exactly the same, write a zero in the sixth box and don't make a star next to either score.) Follow the same procedure for each color-coded category to compute Partner B's Partner Difference Scores for Interpersonal Style, Work Style, Emotional Style, and Intellectual Style. *(Don't plot the Partner Difference Scores for Partner B on this graph. You'll be using these later on.)*

By looking at your Self/Partner Image Profile, you can see easily where your Unified Self-Image and Partner Image Scores differ dramatically, and where these scores are very close together. In addition, you can see the ways in which your partner's Unified Self-Image Scores do or do not relate to the Partner Image Scores you gave him or her. You may also visually compare your own and your partner's Unified Self-Image Scores. The interpretation guide in chapter 6 will help you to analyze in detail the meaning behind each important aspect of your Self/Partner Image Profile.

Instructions for Reflected Image Profile 1

1. Copy your Partner A: Partner Image Scores from the second row of boxes on the Self/Partner Image Profile you completed in chapter 6. Write these scores in the first row of boxes on Reflected Image Profile 1. These scores will now also serve as your Partner/Best Friend Reflected Image Scores.

2. Beginning with the Reflected Image scorecard for Coworker 1 (Scorecard 13), add together all the numbers that were marked from the orange-colored lines, then enter the total in the second box of the orange section for Expressive Style. Do the same for the green, yellow, red, and blue responses, entering the scores across the second row of boxes. These are your Coworker 1 Reflected Image Scores. Next, add together the color-coded numbers that were marked by Coworker 2 (Scorecard 14), exactly as you did for Coworker 1, and enter the total in the third row of boxes. Do the same for your Reflected Image scorecards for Friend 1 and Friend 2, and Family Member 1 and Family Member 2, entering the totals in the corresponding rows of boxes. These are your Reflected Image Scores.

3. Next, chart your scores on Reflected Image Profile 1. First, write a "P" in the orange portion of the graph at the level of the number that corresponds to your Partner/Best Friend Reflected Image Score from the orange box. If your score is 35, you will mark a "P" at the very top of the graph. If your score is 7, you will mark a "P" at the very bottom. More moderate scores will be marked somewhere in between these two extremes. Do the same for the rest of your Partner/Best Friend Reflected Image Scores, writing a "P" at the correct level of each color-coded region of the graph. Now draw a line that connects all the "P's" that you marked. Chart your other Reflected

Image Scores in the same way, using appropriate letters and numbers to signify your Reflected Image Scores for your Coworker 1 (C1), Coworker 2 (C2), Friend 1 (F1), Friend 2 (F2), Family Member 1 (FM1), and Family Member 2 (FM2).

4. Compare your Expressive Style (orange) scores for your Partner/Best Friend, Coworker 1, Coworker 2, Friend 1, Friend 2, Family Member 1, and Family Member 2 Reflected Image Scores. Subtract the smallest from the largest of these scores, and write the result in the corresponding (orange) box in the last row. This is your Reflected Image Difference Score for Expressive Style. (If all of your Reflected Image Difference Scores for Expressive Style are the same, write a zero in the last orange box.) Follow the same procedure for each color-coded category to compute your Reflected Image Difference Scores for Interpersonal Style, Work Style, Emotional Style, and Intellectual Style. Record your results in the corresponding boxes in the last row. *(Don't plot your Reflected Image Difference Scores on the graph. You'll be using these scores later on.)*

By looking at your Reflected Image Profile 1, you can see easily where your Reflected Self-Image Scores differ dramatically, and where these scores are very close together. In addition, you can identify at a glance the Big Five personality dimensions for which specific individuals drawn from different aspects of your life scored you highest and lowest. The interpretation guide in chapter 7 will help you to break down and analyze in detail the meaning behind each important aspect of your Reflected Image Profile 1.

Instructions for Reflected Image Profile 2

1. Begin by copying your Reflected Image Scores for your Partner/Best Friend, Coworker 1, Coworker 2, Friend 1, Friend 2, Family Member 1, and Family Member 2 from your Reflected Image Profile 1. Copy these scores into the corresponding boxes in the first seven rows so that they exactly match the first seven rows of boxes in Reflected Image Profile 1.

2. Next, add together all the Expressive Style (orange) boxes in the first column of Reflected Image Profile 2, and divide this number by 7 (or the number of people whose responses you have actually entered) to compute your Reflected Image Average Score for Expressive Style. Enter the result in the corresponding (orange) box for Expressive Style in the eighth row of boxes. Do the same for the green, yellow, red, and blue responses, entering your average score for each color across the eighth row of boxes. These are your Reflected Image Average Scores for Interpersonal Style, Work Style, Emotional Style, and Intellectual Style. Chart these scores on your Reflected Image Profile 2, using an "R" to signify your Reflected Image Average Score for each of the five color-coded personality dimensions. Draw a line that connects all the "R's" that you marked.

3. Copy your Unified Self-Image Scores, from the Unified Self-Image Profile you completed in chapter 3, into the color-coded boxes in the ninth row of boxes. Chart these scores on your Reflected Image Profile 2, using a "U" to signify your Unified Self-Image Score for each of the five color-coded personality dimensions. Draw a line that connects all the "U's" that you marked. You may now visually compare your Reflected Image Average Scores to your Unified Self-Image Scores and see easily where these scores differ dramatically, and where they are closest together.

4. Finally, compare your Reflected Image Average Score and your Unified Self-Image Score for Expressive Style, to be found in the orange boxes in the eighth and ninth rows. Mark a star next to the larger of these two scores. Then subtract the smaller from the larger score and write the result in the corresponding (orange) box in the tenth row. This is your Unified/Reflected Difference Score for Expressive Style. (If your Reflected Image Average Score and Unified Self-Image Score for Expressive Style are exactly the same, write a zero in the tenth box and don't make a star next to either score.) Follow the same procedure for each color-coded category above to compute your Unified/Reflected Difference Scores for Interpersonal Style, Work Style, Emotional Style, and Intellectual Style. Record your results in the corresponding boxes in the tenth row. *(Don't plot your*

Unified/Reflected Difference Scores on the graph. You'll be using these scores later on.)

The interpretation guide in chapter 7 will help you to break down and analyze in detail the meaning behind each important aspect of your Reflected Image Profile 2.

Instructions for Temporal Self-Image Profile

A reminder: We strongly recommend that you complete your Past Self-Image scorecard, chart your Past Self-Image Profile, and look up the meaning of your Unified/Past Difference Scores in the Temporal Self-Image Interpretation Guide (steps number 1 through 5, below) before beginning your Future Self-Image scorecard, profile, and interpretation (steps number 6 through 9). The insights gained from first completing all the Past Self-Image exercises may help you to project a more realistic Future Self-Image later on.

1. Copy your Unified Self-Image Scores, from the Unified Self-Image Profile you completed in chapter 3, into the first row of color-coded boxes. Chart these scores on your Temporal Self-Image Profile, using a "U" to signify your Unified Self-Image Score for each of the five color-coded personality dimensions. Draw a line that connects all the "U's" that you marked.

2. Add together all the numbers from the orange lines that you marked on the Past Self-Image scorecard (Scorecard 19), then enter the total in the second box of the corresponding (orange) section for Expressive Style. Do the same for the green, yellow, red, and blue responses, entering the scores across the second row of boxes. These are your Past Self-Image Scores.

3. Chart your Past Self-Image Scores on the Temporal Self-Image Profile. First, write a "P" in the orange portion of the graph at the level of the number that corresponds to your Past Self-Image Score from the orange box. If your score is 35, you will mark a "P" at the very

top of the graph. If your score is 7, you will mark a "P" at the very bottom. More moderate scores will be marked somewhere in between these two extremes. Do the same for the rest of your Past Self-Image Scores, writing a "P" at the correct level of each color-coded region of the graph. Now draw a line that connects all the "P's" you marked. This is your Past Self-Image Profile.

4. Compare your Expressive Style (orange) scores for your Unified Self-Image and Past Self-Image. Mark a star next to the larger of these two scores. Then subtract the smaller from the larger score and write the result in the corresponding (orange) box in the fourth row. This is your Unified/Past Difference Score for Expressive Style. (If your Unified Self-Image and Past Self-Image Scores for Expressive Style are exactly the same, write a zero in the fourth box and don't mark a star next to either score.) Follow the same procedure for each color-coded category to compute your Unified/Past Difference Scores for Interpersonal Style, Work Style, Emotional Style, and Intellectual Style. Record your results in the corresponding boxes in the fourth row. *(Don't plot your Unified/Past Difference Scores on the graph.)*

5. Examine the similarities and differences between your Past Self-Image and your Unified Self-Image as shown on your Temporal Self-Image Profile, paying special attention to the Big Five personality dimensions for which your self-image has changed the most, and those for which it has changed the least, from the time of your Past Self-Image to the present. Look up the meaning of all five of your Unified/Past Difference Scores in the Temporal Self-Image Interpretation Guide in chapter 8.

6. Return to the section of chapter 8 titled "Part II: A Glimpse into Your Future" and follow the instructions for selecting and characterizing your Future Self-Image, and for completing your Future Self-Image scorecard (Scorecard 20). Next, add together the color-coded numbers that you marked on your Future Self-Image scorecard, exactly as you did for your Past Self-Image, to obtain your Future Self-Image Scores. Write these scores in the third row of your Temporal Self-Image Profile.

7. Chart your Future Self-Image Scores on the Temporal Self-Image Profile. First, write an "F" in the orange portion of the graph at the level of the number that corresponds to your Future Self-Image Score from the orange box. Do the same for the rest of your Future Self-Image Scores, writing an "F" at the correct level of each color-coded region of the graph. Now draw a line that connects all the "F's" you marked. This is your Future Self-Image Profile.

8. Compare your Expressive Style (orange) scores for your Unified Self-Image and Future Self-Image. This time, mark a circle next to the larger of these two scores. Then subtract the smaller from the larger score and write the result in the corresponding (orange) box in the fifth row. This is your Unified/Future Difference Score for Expressive Style. (If your Unified Self-Image and Future Self-Image Scores for Expressive Style are exactly the same, write a zero in the fifth box and don't mark a circle next to either score.) Follow the same procedure for each color-coded category to compute your Unified/Future Difference Scores for Interpersonal Style, Work Style, Emotional Style, and Intellectual Style. Record your results in the corresponding boxes in the fifth row. *(Don't plot your Unified/ Future Difference Scores on the graph.)*

9. Your Temporal Self-Image Profile now reflects the similarities and differences you see in your personality from the past to the present, and from the present to the future. Examine your complete profile, paying special attention to the Big Five personality dimensions for which your self-image has changed the most, and those for which it has changed the least. Turn to the Temporal Self-Image Interpretation Guide in chapter 8 to find a precise description of your Unified/Future Difference Scores, just as you did for your Unified/Past Difference Scores.

Instructions for Alter Ego Profile

1. Copy your Unified Self-Image Scores, from the Unified Self-Image Profile you completed in chapter 3, into the first row of color-coded boxes. Chart these scores on your Alter Ego Profile, using a "U" to signify your Unified Self-Image Score for each of the five color-coded personality dimensions. Draw a line that connects all the "U's" that you marked.

2. Add together all the numbers from the orange lines that you marked on the Alter Ego scorecard (Scorecard 21), then enter the total in the second box of the corresponding (orange) section for Expressive Style. Do the same for the green, yellow, red, and blue responses, entering the scores across the second row of boxes. These are your Alter Ego Scores.

3. Chart your Alter Ego Scores on the Alter Ego Profile. First, write an "A" in the orange portion of the graph at the level of the number that corresponds to your Alter Ego Score from the orange box. If your score is 35, you will mark an "A" at the very top of the graph. If your score is 7, you will mark an "A" at the very bottom. More moderate scores will be marked somewhere in between these two extremes. Do the same for the rest of your Alter Ego Scores, writing an "A" at the correct level of each color-coded region of the graph. Now draw a line that connects all the "A's" you marked. This is your Alter Ego Profile.

4. Compare your Expressive Style (orange) scores for your Unified Self-Image and Alter Ego. Mark a star next to the larger of these two scores. Then subtract the smaller from the larger score and write the result in the corresponding (orange) box in the third row. This is your Unified/Alter Ego Difference Score for Expressive Style. (If your Unified Self-Image and Alter Ego Scores for Expressive Style are exactly the same, write a zero in the third box and don't mark a star next to either score.) Follow the same procedure for each color-coded category to compute your Unified/Alter Ego Difference Scores

for Interpersonal Style, Work Style, Emotional Style, and Intellectual Style. Record your results in the corresponding boxes in the third row. *(Don't plot your Unified/Alter Ego Difference Scores on the graph.)*

5. Examine the similarities and differences between your Alter Ego and your Unified Self-Image as shown on your Alter Ego Profile, paying special attention to the Big Five personality dimensions for which your Unified Self-Image and Alter Ego differ the most, and those for which they differ the least. Look up the meaning of all five of your Unified/Alter Ego Difference Scores in the Alter Ego Interpretation Guide in chapter 8.

THE BERKELEY PERSONALITY PROFILE

This personality test lists a series of thirty-five statements that broadly describe an individual's personality. On each scorecard, honestly indicate whether you agree or disagree that each statement applies to your personality, or to the personality of the person you are rating, when examined from a given point of view. For each item, circle the number in the left column of the scorecard if you strongly disagree with a statement, or the number in the right column if you strongly agree, or a number in between to indicate varying levels of agreement. For each item, simply circle your choice. Mark only one number per statement on each scorecard.

	Scorecard 1 *Inner Self-Image* — How you see yourself inside — Do you feel that you are someone who:					Scorecard 2 *Outer Self-Image* — How you think others see you — Do you believe others see you as someone who:				
	DISAGREE STRONGLY	DISAGREE A LITTLE	NEITHER AGREE NOR DISAGREE	AGREE A LITTLE	AGREE STRONGLY	DISAGREE STRONGLY	DISAGREE A LITTLE	NEITHER AGREE NOR DISAGREE	AGREE A LITTLE	AGREE STRONGLY
1. Is outgoing, sociable.	1	2	3	4	5	1	2	3	4	5
2. Tends to find fault with others.	5	4	3	2	1	5	4	3	2	1
3. Is a reliable worker.	1	2	3	4	5	1	2	3	4	5
4. Remains calm in tense situations.	5	4	3	2	1	5	4	3	2	1
5. Values artistic, aesthetic experiences.	1	2	3	4	5	1	2	3	4	5
6. Is reserved.	5	4	3	2	1	5	4	3	2	1
7. Is considerate and kind to almost everyone.	1	2	3	4	5	1	2	3	4	5
8. Can be somewhat careless.	5	4	3	2	1	5	4	3	2	1
9. Is relaxed, handles stress well.	5	4	3	2	1	5	4	3	2	1
10. Prefers work that is routine and simple.	5	4	3	2	1	5	4	3	2	1
11. Is full of energy.	1	2	3	4	5	1	2	3	4	5
12. Can be cold and aloof.	5	4	3	2	1	5	4	3	2	1
13. Does things efficiently.	1	2	3	4	5	1	2	3	4	5
14. Gets nervous easily.	1	2	3	4	5	1	2	3	4	5
15. Has an active imagination.	1	2	3	4	5	1	2	3	4	5
16. Is sometimes shy, inhibited.	5	4	3	2	1	5	4	3	2	1
17. Likes to cooperate with others.	1	2	3	4	5	1	2	3	4	5
18. Tends to be disorganized.	5	4	3	2	1	5	4	3	2	1
19. Is emotionally stable, not easily upset.	5	4	3	2	1	5	4	3	2	1
20. Has few artistic interests.	5	4	3	2	1	5	4	3	2	1
21. Is talkative.	1	2	3	4	5	1	2	3	4	5
22. Is sometimes rude to others.	5	4	3	2	1	5	4	3	2	1
23. Does a thorough job.	1	2	3	4	5	1	2	3	4	5
24. Is depressed, blue.	1	2	3	4	5	1	2	3	4	5
25. Is sophisticated in art, music, or literature.	1	2	3	4	5	1	2	3	4	5
26. Tends to be quiet.	5	4	3	2	1	5	4	3	2	1
27. Is generally trusting.	1	2	3	4	5	1	2	3	4	5
28. Is lazy at times.	5	4	3	2	1	5	4	3	2	1
29. Worries a lot.	1	2	3	4	5	1	2	3	4	5
30. Is ingenious, a deep thinker.	1	2	3	4	5	1	2	3	4	5
31. Generates a lot of enthusiasm.	1	2	3	4	5	1	2	3	4	5
32. Has a forgiving nature.	1	2	3	4	5	1	2	3	4	5
33. Is easily distracted.	5	4	3	2	1	5	4	3	2	1
34. Can be tense.	1	2	3	4	5	1	2	3	4	5
35. Is inventive.	1	2	3	4	5	1	2	3	4	5

Test 2

Scorecard 3 *Unified Self-Image*					Scorecard 4 *Ideal Self-Image*				
How you see yourself overall					*How you would ideally like to be*				
Do you agree that you are someone who:					The person you would ideally like to be is someone who:				
DISAGREE STRONGLY	DISAGREE A LITTLE	NEITHER AGREE NOR DISAGREE	AGREE A LITTLE	AGREE STRONGLY	DISAGREE STRONGLY	DISAGREE A LITTLE	NEITHER AGREE NOR DISAGREE	AGREE A LITTLE	AGREE STRONGLY
1	2	3	4	5	1	2	3	4	5
5	4	3	2	1	5	4	3	2	1
1	2	3	4	5	1	2	3	4	5
5	4	3	2	1	5	4	3	2	1
1	2	3	4	5	1	2	3	4	5
5	4	3	2	1	5	4	3	2	1
1	2	3	4	5	1	2	3	4	5
5	4	3	2	1	5	4	3	2	1
5	4	3	2	1	5	4	3	2	1
5	4	3	2	1	5	4	3	2	1
1	2	3	4	5	1	2	3	4	5
5	4	3	2	1	5	4	3	2	1
1	2	3	4	5	1	2	3	4	5
1	2	3	4	5	1	2	3	4	5
1	2	3	4	5	1	2	3	4	5
5	4	3	2	1	5	4	3	2	1
1	2	3	4	5	1	2	3	4	5
5	4	3	2	1	5	4	3	2	1
5	4	3	2	1	5	4	3	2	1
5	4	3	2	1	5	4	3	2	1
1	2	3	4	5	1	2	3	4	5
5	4	3	2	1	5	4	3	2	1
1	2	3	4	5	1	2	3	4	5
1	2	3	4	5	1	2	3	4	5
1	2	3	4	5	1	2	3	4	5
5	4	3	2	1	5	4	3	2	1
1	2	3	4	5	1	2	3	4	5
5	4	3	2	1	5	4	3	2	1
1	2	3	4	5	1	2	3	4	5
1	2	3	4	5	1	2	3	4	5
1	2	3	4	5	1	2	3	4	5
1	2	3	4	5	1	2	3	4	5
5	4	3	2	1	5	4	3	2	1
1	2	3	4	5	1	2	3	4	5
1	2	3	4	5	1	2	3	4	5

Scorecard 5
Feared Self-Image
How you fear being

The person you fear being is someone who:

Scorecard 6
Work Role Identity
How you see yourself at work

Do you agree that at work you are someone who:

Scorecard 7
Romantic Partner Role Identity
With your spouse/ a romantic partner

Do you agree that as a romantic partner you are someone who:

Scorecard 8
Friend Role Identity
With your friends

Do you agree that as a friend you are someone who:

Scorecard 9
Other Role Identity
Fill in role:

Do you agree that in this role you are someone who:

Column headers for each scorecard: DISAGREE STRONGLY | DISAGREE A LITTLE | NEITHER AGREE NOR DISAGREE | AGREE A LITTLE | AGREE STRONGLY

Scorecard 5					Scorecard 6					Scorecard 7					Scorecard 8					Scorecard 9				
1	2	3	4	5	1	2	3	4	5	1	2	3	4	5	1	2	3	4	5	1	2	3	4	5
5	4	3	2	1	5	4	3	2	1	5	4	3	2	1	5	4	3	2	1	5	4	3	2	1
1	2	3	4	5	1	2	3	4	5	1	2	3	4	5	1	2	3	4	5	1	2	3	4	5
5	4	3	2	1	5	4	3	2	1	5	4	3	2	1	5	4	3	2	1	5	4	3	2	1
1	2	3	4	5	1	2	3	4	5	1	2	3	4	5	1	2	3	4	5	1	2	3	4	5
5	4	3	2	1	5	4	3	2	1	5	4	3	2	1	5	4	3	2	1	5	4	3	2	1
1	2	3	4	5	1	2	3	4	5	1	2	3	4	5	1	2	3	4	5	1	2	3	4	5
5	4	3	2	1	5	4	3	2	1	5	4	3	2	1	5	4	3	2	1	5	4	3	2	1
5	4	3	2	1	5	4	3	2	1	5	4	3	2	1	5	4	3	2	1	5	4	3	2	1
5	4	3	2	1	5	4	3	2	1	5	4	3	2	1	5	4	3	2	1	5	4	3	2	1
1	2	3	4	5	1	2	3	4	5	1	2	3	4	5	1	2	3	4	5	1	2	3	4	5
5	4	3	2	1	5	4	3	2	1	5	4	3	2	1	5	4	3	2	1	5	4	3	2	1
1	2	3	4	5	1	2	3	4	5	1	2	3	4	5	1	2	3	4	5	1	2	3	4	5
1	2	3	4	5	1	2	3	4	5	1	2	3	4	5	1	2	3	4	5	1	2	3	4	5
1	2	3	4	5	1	2	3	4	5	1	2	3	4	5	1	2	3	4	5	1	2	3	4	5
5	4	3	2	1	5	4	3	2	1	5	4	3	2	1	5	4	3	2	1	5	4	3	2	1
1	2	3	4	5	1	2	3	4	5	1	2	3	4	5	1	2	3	4	5	1	2	3	4	5
5	4	3	2	1	5	4	3	2	1	5	4	3	2	1	5	4	3	2	1	5	4	3	2	1
5	4	3	2	1	5	4	3	2	1	5	4	3	2	1	5	4	3	2	1	5	4	3	2	1
5	4	3	2	1	5	4	3	2	1	5	4	3	2	1	5	4	3	2	1	5	4	3	2	1
1	2	3	4	5	1	2	3	4	5	1	2	3	4	5	1	2	3	4	5	1	2	3	4	5
5	4	3	2	1	5	4	3	2	1	5	4	3	2	1	5	4	3	2	1	5	4	3	2	1
1	2	3	4	5	1	2	3	4	5	1	2	3	4	5	1	2	3	4	5	1	2	3	4	5
1	2	3	4	5	1	2	3	4	5	1	2	3	4	5	1	2	3	4	5	1	2	3	4	5
1	2	3	4	5	1	2	3	4	5	1	2	3	4	5	1	2	3	4	5	1	2	3	4	5
5	4	3	2	1	5	4	3	2	1	5	4	3	2	1	5	4	3	2	1	5	4	3	2	1
1	2	3	4	5	1	2	3	4	5	1	2	3	4	5	1	2	3	4	5	1	2	3	4	5
5	4	3	2	1	5	4	3	2	1	5	4	3	2	1	5	4	3	2	1	5	4	3	2	1
1	2	3	4	5	1	2	3	4	5	1	2	3	4	5	1	2	3	4	5	1	2	3	4	5
1	2	3	4	5	1	2	3	4	5	1	2	3	4	5	1	2	3	4	5	1	2	3	4	5
1	2	3	4	5	1	2	3	4	5	1	2	3	4	5	1	2	3	4	5	1	2	3	4	5
1	2	3	4	5	1	2	3	4	5	1	2	3	4	5	1	2	3	4	5	1	2	3	4	55
5	4	3	2	1	5	4	3	2	1	5	4	3	2	1	5	4	3	2	1	5	4	3	2	1
1	2	3	4	5	1	2	3	4	5	1	2	3	4	5	1	2	3	4	5	1	2	3	4	5
1	2	3	4	5	1	2	3	4	5	1	2	3	4	5	1	2	3	4	5	1	2	3	4	5

Test 4

Scorecard 10 *Partner A: Partner Image* — How Partner A is seen by Partner B					Scorecard 11 *Partner B: Unified Self-Image* — How Partner B sees self					Scorecard 12 *Partner B: Partner Image* — How Partner B is seen by Partner A					Scorecard 13 *Reflected Image* — Rating by Coworker 1					Scorecard 14 *Reflected Image* — Rating by Coworker 2				
DS	DL	N	AL	AS	DS	DL	N	AL	AS	DS	DL	N	AL	AS	DS	DL	N	AL	AS	DS	DL	N	AL	AS
1	2	3	4	5	1	2	3	4	5	1	2	3	4	5	1	2	3	4	5	1	2	3	4	5
5	4	3	2	1	5	4	3	2	1	5	4	3	2	1	5	4	3	2	1	5	4	3	2	1
1	2	3	4	5	1	2	3	4	5	1	2	3	4	5	1	2	3	4	5	1	2	3	4	5
5	4	3	2	1	5	4	3	2	1	5	4	3	2	1	5	4	3	2	1	5	4	3	2	1
1	2	3	4	5	1	2	3	4	5	1	2	3	4	5	1	2	3	4	5	1	2	3	4	5
5	4	3	2	1	5	4	3	2	1	5	4	3	2	1	5	4	3	2	1	5	4	3	2	1
1	2	3	4	5	1	2	3	4	5	1	2	3	4	5	1	2	3	4	5	1	2	3	4	5
5	4	3	2	1	5	4	3	2	1	5	4	3	2	1	5	4	3	2	1	5	4	3	2	1
5	4	3	2	1	5	4	3	2	1	5	4	3	2	1	5	4	3	2	1	5	4	3	2	1
5	4	3	2	1	5	4	3	2	1	5	4	3	2	1	5	4	3	2	1	5	4	3	2	1
1	2	3	4	5	1	2	3	4	5	1	2	3	4	5	1	2	3	4	5	1	2	3	4	5
5	4	3	2	1	5	4	3	2	1	5	4	3	2	1	5	4	3	2	1	5	4	3	2	1
1	2	3	4	5	1	2	3	4	5	1	2	3	4	5	1	2	3	4	5	1	2	3	4	5
1	2	3	4	5	1	2	3	4	5	1	2	3	4	5	1	2	3	4	5	1	2	3	4	5
1	2	3	4	5	1	2	3	4	5	1	2	3	4	5	1	2	3	4	5	1	2	3	4	5
5	4	3	2	1	5	4	3	2	1	5	4	3	2	1	5	4	3	2	1	5	4	3	2	1
1	2	3	4	5	1	2	3	4	5	1	2	3	4	5	1	2	3	4	5	1	2	3	4	5
5	4	3	2	1	5	4	3	2	1	5	4	3	2	1	5	4	3	2	1	5	4	3	2	1
5	4	3	2	1	5	4	3	2	1	5	4	3	2	1	5	4	3	2	1	5	4	3	2	1
5	4	3	2	1	5	4	3	2	1	5	4	3	2	1	5	4	3	2	1	5	4	3	2	1
1	2	3	4	5	1	2	3	4	5	1	2	3	4	5	1	2	3	4	5	1	2	3	4	5
5	4	3	2	1	5	4	3	2	1	5	4	3	2	1	5	4	3	2	1	5	4	3	2	1
1	2	3	4	5	1	2	3	4	5	1	2	3	4	5	1	2	3	4	5	1	2	3	4	5
1	2	3	4	5	1	2	3	4	5	1	2	3	4	5	1	2	3	4	5	1	2	3	4	5
1	2	3	4	5	1	2	3	4	5	1	2	3	4	5	1	2	3	4	5	1	2	3	4	5
5	4	3	2	1	5	4	3	2	1	5	4	3	2	1	5	4	3	2	1	5	4	3	2	1
1	2	3	4	5	1	2	3	4	5	1	2	3	4	5	1	2	3	4	5	1	2	3	4	5
5	4	3	2	1	5	4	3	2	1	5	4	3	2	1	5	4	3	2	1	5	4	3	2	1
1	2	3	4	5	1	2	3	4	5	1	2	3	4	5	1	2	3	4	5	1	2	3	4	5
1	2	3	4	5	1	2	3	4	5	1	2	3	4	5	1	2	3	4	5	1	2	3	4	5
1	2	3	4	5	1	2	3	4	5	1	2	3	4	5	1	2	3	4	5	1	2	3	4	5
5	4	3	2	1	5	4	3	2	1	5	4	3	2	1	5	4	3	2	1	5	4	3	2	1
1	2	3	4	5	1	2	3	4	5	1	2	3	4	5	1	2	3	4	5	1	2	3	4	5
1	2	3	4	5	1	2	3	4	5	1	2	3	4	5	1	2	3	4	5	1	2	3	4	5

Scorecard 15 — *Reflected Image*
Rating by Friend 1

Do you agree that the person you are describing:

DISAGREE STRONGLY	DISAGREE A LITTLE	NEITHER AGREE NOR DISAGREE	AGREE A LITTLE	AGREE STRONGLY
1	2	3	4	5
5	4	3	2	1
1	2	3	4	5
5	4	3	2	1
1	2	3	4	5
5	4	3	2	1
1	2	3	4	5
5	4	3	2	1
5	4	3	2	1
5	4	3	2	1
1	2	3	4	5
5	4	3	2	1
1	2	3	4	5
1	2	3	4	5
1	2	3	4	5
5	4	3	2	1
1	2	3	4	5
5	4	3	2	1
5	4	3	2	1
5	4	3	2	1
1	2	3	4	5
5	4	3	2	1
1	2	3	4	5
1	2	3	4	5
1	2	3	4	5
5	4	3	2	1
1	2	3	4	5
5	4	3	2	1
1	2	3	4	5
1	2	3	4	5
1	2	3	4	5
1	2	3	4	5
5	4	3	2	1
1	2	3	4	5
1	2	3	4	5

Scorecard 16 — *Reflected Image*
Rating by Friend 2

Do you agree that the person you are describing:

DISAGREE STRONGLY	DISAGREE A LITTLE	NEITHER AGREE NOR DISAGREE	AGREE A LITTLE	AGREE STRONGLY
1	2	3	4	5
5	4	3	2	1
1	2	3	4	5
5	4	3	2	1
1	2	3	4	5
5	4	3	2	1
1	2	3	4	5
5	4	3	2	1
5	4	3	2	1
5	4	3	2	1
1	2	3	4	5
5	4	3	2	1
1	2	3	4	5
1	2	3	4	5
1	2	3	4	5
5	4	3	2	1
1	2	3	4	5
5	4	3	2	1
5	4	3	2	1
5	4	3	2	1
1	2	3	4	5
5	4	3	2	1
1	2	3	4	5
1	2	3	4	5
1	2	3	4	5
5	4	3	2	1
1	2	3	4	5
5	4	3	2	1
1	2	3	4	5
1	2	3	4	5
1	2	3	4	5
1	2	3	4	5
5	4	3	2	1
1	2	3	4	5
1	2	3	4	5

Scorecard 17 — *Reflected Image*
Family Member 1
Relationship:

Do you agree that the person you are describing:

DISAGREE STRONGLY	DISAGREE A LITTLE	NEITHER AGREE NOR DISAGREE	AGREE A LITTLE	AGREE STRONGLY
1	2	3	4	5
5	4	3	2	1
1	2	3	4	5
5	4	3	2	1
1	2	3	4	5
5	4	3	2	1
1	2	3	4	5
5	4	3	2	1
5	4	3	2	1
5	4	3	2	1
1	2	3	4	5
5	4	3	2	1
1	2	3	4	5
1	2	3	4	5
1	2	3	4	5
5	4	3	2	1
1	2	3	4	5
5	4	3	2	1
5	4	3	2	1
5	4	3	2	1
1	2	3	4	5
5	4	3	2	1
1	2	3	4	5
1	2	3	4	5
1	2	3	4	5
5	4	3	2	1
1	2	3	4	5
5	4	3	2	1
1	2	3	4	5
1	2	3	4	5
1	2	3	4	5
1	2	3	4	5
5	4	3	2	1
1	2	3	4	5
1	2	3	4	5

Scorecard 18 — *Reflected Image*
Family Member 2
Relationship:

Do you agree that the person you are describing:

DISAGREE STRONGLY	DISAGREE A LITTLE	NEITHER AGREE NOR DISAGREE	AGREE A LITTLE	AGREE STRONGLY
1	2	3	4	5
5	4	3	2	1
1	2	3	4	5
5	4	3	2	1
1	2	3	4	5
5	4	3	2	1
1	2	3	4	5
5	4	3	2	1
5	4	3	2	1
5	4	3	2	1
1	2	3	4	5
5	4	3	2	1
1	2	3	4	5
1	2	3	4	5
1	2	3	4	5
5	4	3	2	1
1	2	3	4	5
5	4	3	2	1
5	4	3	2	1
5	4	3	2	1
1	2	3	4	5
5	4	3	2	1
1	2	3	4	5
1	2	3	4	5
1	2	3	4	5
5	4	3	2	1
1	2	3	4	5
5	4	3	2	1
1	2	3	4	5
1	2	3	4	5
1	2	3	4	5
1	2	3	4	5
5	4	3	2	1
1	2	3	4	5
1	2	3	4	5

Scorecard 19 — *Past Self-Image*
Past Self Label:

Do you agree that your self past was:

DISAGREE STRONGLY	DISAGREE A LITTLE	NEITHER AGREE NOR DISAGREE	AGREE A LITTLE	AGREE STRONGLY
1	2	3	4	5
5	4	3	2	1
1	2	3	4	5
5	4	3	2	1
1	2	3	4	5
5	4	3	2	1
1	2	3	4	5
5	4	3	2	1
5	4	3	2	1
5	4	3	2	1
1	2	3	4	5
5	4	3	2	1
1	2	3	4	5
1	2	3	4	5
1	2	3	4	5
5	4	3	2	1
1	2	3	4	5
5	4	3	2	1
5	4	3	2	1
5	4	3	2	1
1	2	3	4	5
5	4	3	2	1
1	2	3	4	5
1	2	3	4	5
1	2	3	4	5
5	4	3	2	1
1	2	3	4	5
5	4	3	2	1
1	2	3	4	5
1	2	3	4	5
1	2	3	4	5
1	2	3	4	5
5	4	3	2	1
1	2	3	4	5
1	2	3	4	5

Test 6

Scorecard 20
Future Self-Image

Future Self Label:

_____

Do you agree that your future self will be:

DISAGREE STRONGLY	DISAGREE A LITTLE	NEITHER AGREE NOR DISAGREE	AGREE A LITTLE	AGREE STRONGLY
1	2	3	4	5
5	4	3	2	1
1	2	3	4	5
5	4	3	2	1
1	2	3	4	5
5	4	3	2	1
1	2	3	4	5
5	4	3	2	1
5	4	3	2	1
5	4	3	2	1
1	2	3	4	5
5	4	3	2	1
1	2	3	4	5
1	2	3	4	5
1	2	3	4	5
5	4	3	2	1
1	2	3	4	5
5	4	3	2	1
5	4	3	2	1
5	4	3	2	1
1	2	3	4	5
5	4	3	2	1
1	2	3	4	5
1	2	3	4	5
1	2	3	4	5
5	4	3	2	1
1	2	3	4	5
5	4	3	2	1
1	2	3	4	5
1	2	3	4	5
1	2	3	4	5
5	4	3	2	1
1	2	3	4	5
1	2	3	4	5

Scorecard 21
Alter Ego Image

Alter Ego Label:

_____

Do you agree that your alter ego is:

DISAGREE STRONGLY	DISAGREE A LITTLE	NEITHER AGREE NOR DISAGREE	AGREE A LITTLE	AGREE STRONGLY
1	2	3	4	5
5	4	3	2	1
1	2	3	4	5
5	4	3	2	1
1	2	3	4	5
5	4	3	2	1
1	2	3	4	5
5	4	3	2	1
5	4	3	2	1
5	4	3	2	1
1	2	3	4	5
5	4	3	2	1
1	2	3	4	5
1	2	3	4	5
1	2	3	4	5
5	4	3	2	1
1	2	3	4	5
5	4	3	2	1
5	4	3	2	1
5	4	3	2	1
1	2	3	4	5
5	4	3	2	1
1	2	3	4	5
1	2	3	4	5
1	2	3	4	5
5	4	3	2	1
1	2	3	4	5
5	4	3	2	1
1	2	3	4	5
1	2	3	4	5
1	2	3	4	5
5	4	3	2	1
1	2	3	4	5
1	2	3	4	5

Scorecard 22
Extra Scorecard

Fill in perspective:

_____

Do you agree that the person you are describing:

DISAGREE STRONGLY	DISAGREE A LITTLE	NEITHER AGREE NOR DISAGREE	AGREE A LITTLE	AGREE STRONGLY
1	2	3	4	5
5	4	3	2	1
1	2	3	4	5
5	4	3	2	1
1	2	3	4	5
5	4	3	2	1
1	2	3	4	5
5	4	3	2	1
5	4	3	2	1
5	4	3	2	1
1	2	3	4	5
5	4	3	2	1
1	2	3	4	5
1	2	3	4	5
1	2	3	4	5
5	4	3	2	1
1	2	3	4	5
5	4	3	2	1
5	4	3	2	1
5	4	3	2	1
1	2	3	4	5
5	4	3	2	1
1	2	3	4	5
1	2	3	4	5
1	2	3	4	5
5	4	3	2	1
1	2	3	4	5
5	4	3	2	1
1	2	3	4	5
1	2	3	4	5
1	2	3	4	5
5	4	3	2	1
1	2	3	4	5
1	2	3	4	5

Scorecard 23
Extra Scorecard

Fill in perspective:

_____

Do you agree that the person you are describing:

DISAGREE STRONGLY	DISAGREE A LITTLE	NEITHER AGREE NOR DISAGREE	AGREE A LITTLE	AGREE STRONGLY
1	2	3	4	5
5	4	3	2	1
1	2	3	4	5
5	4	3	2	1
1	2	3	4	5
5	4	3	2	1
1	2	3	4	5
5	4	3	2	1
5	4	3	2	1
5	4	3	2	1
1	2	3	4	5
5	4	3	2	1
1	2	3	4	5
1	2	3	4	5
1	2	3	4	5
5	4	3	2	1
1	2	3	4	5
5	4	3	2	1
5	4	3	2	1
5	4	3	2	1
1	2	3	4	5
5	4	3	2	1
1	2	3	4	5
1	2	3	4	5
1	2	3	4	5
5	4	3	2	1
1	2	3	4	5
5	4	3	2	1
1	2	3	4	5
1	2	3	4	5
1	2	3	4	5
5	4	3	2	1
1	2	3	4	5
1	2	3	4	5

Scorecard 24
Extra Scorecard

Fill in perspective:

_____

Do you agree that the person you are describing:

DISAGREE STRONGLY	DISAGREE A LITTLE	NEITHER AGREE NOR DISAGREE	AGREE A LITTLE	AGREE STRONGLY
1	2	3	4	5
5	4	3	2	1
1	2	3	4	5
5	4	3	2	1
1	2	3	4	5
5	4	3	2	1
1	2	3	4	5
5	4	3	2	1
5	4	3	2	1
5	4	3	2	1
1	2	3	4	5
5	4	3	2	1
1	2	3	4	5
1	2	3	4	5
1	2	3	4	5
5	4	3	2	1
1	2	3	4	5
5	4	3	2	1
5	4	3	2	1
5	4	3	2	1
1	2	3	4	5
5	4	3	2	1
1	2	3	4	5
1	2	3	4	5
1	2	3	4	5
5	4	3	2	1
1	2	3	4	5
5	4	3	2	1
1	2	3	4	5
1	2	3	4	5
1	2	3	4	5
5	4	3	2	1
1	2	3	4	5
1	2	3	4	5

Inner/Outer Self-Image Profile

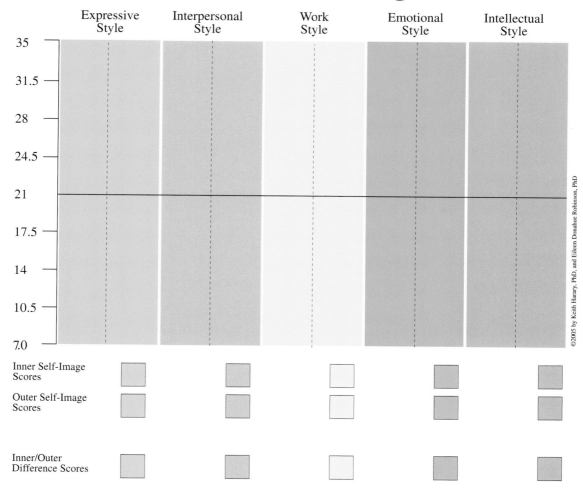

	Expressive Style	Interpersonal Style	Work Style	Emotional Style	Intellectual Style

Inner Self-Image Scores

Outer Self-Image Scores

Inner/Outer Difference Scores

©2005 by Keith Harary, PhD, and Eileen Donahue Robinson, PhD

Test 8

Unified Self-Image Profile

Possible Self-Image Profile

Role Identity Profile

	Expressive Style	Interpersonal Style	Work Style	Emotional Style	Intellectual Style
Work Role Identity					
Romantic Partner Role Identity					
Friend Role Identity					
Other Role Identity					
Role Identity Difference Scores					

Total Role Identity Difference Score

Self/Partner Image Profile

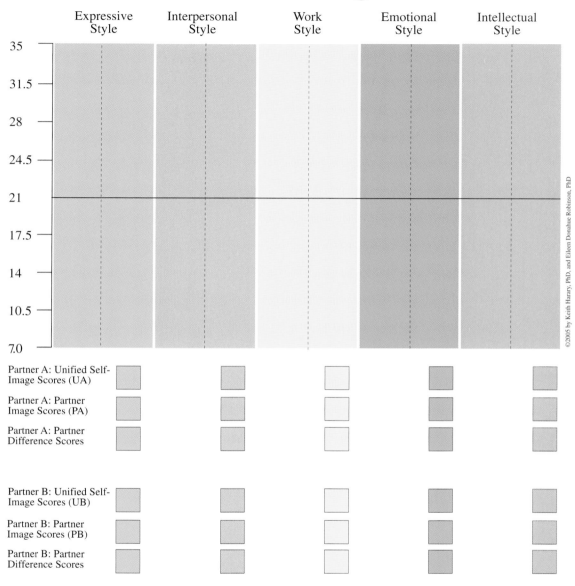

	Expressive Style	Interpersonal Style	Work Style	Emotional Style	Intellectual Style
Partner A: Unified Self-Image Scores (UA)					
Partner A: Partner Image Scores (PA)					
Partner A: Partner Difference Scores					
Partner B: Unified Self-Image Scores (UB)					
Partner B: Partner Image Scores (PB)					
Partner B: Partner Difference Scores					

Test 12

Reflected Image Profile 1

Reflected Image Profile 2

Test 14

Temporal Self-Image Profile

Alter Ego Profile

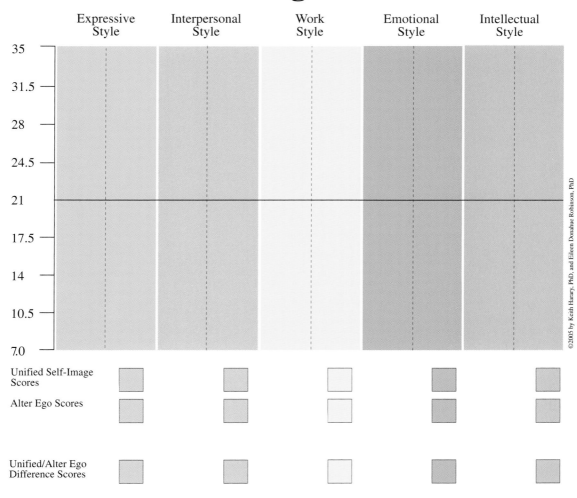

	Expressive Style	Interpersonal Style	Work Style	Emotional Style	Intellectual Style

Unified Self-Image Scores

Alter Ego Scores

Unified/Alter Ego Difference Scores

©2005 by Keith Harary, PhD, and Eileen Donahue Robinson, PhD

Berkeley Personality Profile
Self-Image Integrator Matrix

	Expressive Style	Interpersonal Style	Work Style	Emotional Style	Intellectual Style
Inner/Outer Difference Scores Check if 3 or greater	Circle larger score: Inner Outer	Circle larger score: Inner Outer	Circle larger score: Inner Outer	Circle larger score: Inner Outer	Circle larger score: Inner Outer
Unified/Ideal Difference Scores Check if 4 or greater	Circle larger score: Unified Ideal	Circle larger score: Unified Ideal	Circle larger score: Unified Ideal	Circle larger score: Unified Ideal	Circle larger score: Unified Ideal
Unified/Feared Difference Scores Check if 3 or LESS	Circle larger score: Unified Feared	Circle larger score: Unified Feared	Circle larger score: Unified Feared	Circle larger score: Unified Feared	Circle larger score: Unified Feared
Role Identity Difference Scores Check if 4 or greater	Circle larger score: Work Partner Friend Other	Circle larger score: Work Partner Friend Other	Circle larger score: Work Partner Friend Other	Circle larger score: Work Partner Friend Other	Circle larger score: Work Partner Friend Other
Unified/Past Difference Scores Check if 3 or greater	Circle larger score: Unified Past	Circle larger score: Unified Past	Circle larger score: Unified Past	Circle larger score: Unified Past	Circle larger score: Unified Past
Unified/Future Difference Scores Check if 3 or greater	Circle larger score: Unified Future	Circle larger score: Unified Future	Circle larger score: Unified Future	Circle larger score: Unified Future	Circle larger score: Unified Future
Unified/Alter Ego Difference Scores Check if 3 or greater	Circle larger score: Unified Alter Ego	Circle larger score: Unified Alter Ego	Circle larger score: Unified Alter Ego	Circle larger score: Unified Alter Ego	Circle larger score: Unified Alter Ego
Unified Self-Image Difference Scores Write your scores in the color-coded boxes					

Berkeley Personality Profile
Reflected Image Integrator Matrix

	Expressive Style	Interpersonal Style	Work Style	Emotional Style	Intellectual Style
Partner Difference Scores Check if 3 or greater	Circle larger score: Unified Partner	Circle larger score: Unified Partner	Circle larger score: Unified Partner	Circle larger score: Unified Partner	Circle larger score: Unified Partner
Reflected Image Difference Scores Check if 7 or greater	Circle larger score: Partner Coworker Friend Family	Circle larger score: Partner Coworker Friend Family	Circle larger score: Partner Coworker Friend Family	Circle larger score: Partner Coworker Friend Family	Circle larger score: Partner Coworker Friend Family
Unified/Reflected Difference Scores Check if 3 or greater	Circle larger score: Unified Reflected Average	Circle larger score: Unified Reflected Average	Circle larger score: Unified Reflected Average	Circle larger score: Unified Reflected Average	Circle larger score: Unified Reflected Average
Reflected Image Average Scores Write your scores in the color-coded boxes					

The Big Five Personality Dimensions

The Big Five dimensions describe the most basic differences in personality and social behavior. Although there are thousands of specific personality traits from which we each build our own unique personality, researchers have discovered that the Big Five effectively pull all these traits together into broad families of similar characteristics. As shown below, each of the five dimensions represents a range of behavior that stretches from one extreme to its opposite, with more moderate conduct in between.

Expressive Style

Extraversion vs. Introversion

Facets of Expressive Style Include:

Sociability
Ranging from talkative, animated and outgoing to quiet, shy and detached.

Energy Level
Ranging from lively, energetic and fast-paced to passive, subdued and retiring.

Positive Emotions
Ranging from eager, enthusiastic and upbeat to apathetic, reluctant and unexcitable.

Interpersonal Style

Agreeableness vs. Disagreeableness

Facets of Interpersonal Style Include:

Warmth
Ranging from kind, caring and affectionate to cruel, harsh and unforgiving.

Cooperativeness
Ranging from helpful, trusting and agreeable to stubborn, obstinate and antagonistic.

Generosity
Ranging from giving, charitable and unselfish to greedy, stingy and self-centered.

Work Style

Conscientiousness vs. Irresponsibility

Facets of Work Style Include:

Task Orientation
Ranging from diligent, hardworking and productive to aimless, distractible and lazy.

Order
Ranging from careful, systematic and precise to sloppy, disorganized and inefficient.

Dependability
Ranging from trustworthy, reliable and prompt to careless, fickle and irresponsible.

Emotional Style

Neuroticism vs. Emotional Stability

Facets of Emotional Style Include:

Negative Emotionality
Ranging from anxious, conflicted and despondent to calm, secure and well-adjusted.

Stability
Ranging from moody, erratic and temperamental to stable, balanced and even-tempered.

Intellectual Style

Openness to Experience vs. Conventionality

Facets of Intellectual Style Include:

Intellect
Ranging from clever, analytical and insightful to simplistic, illogical and naive.

Imagination
Ranging from creative, artistic and original to dull, predictable and commonplace.

Openness
Ranging from progressive, curious and well-rounded to rigid, conventional and narrow-minded.

THE BERKELEY PERSONALITY PROFILE

This personality test lists a series of thirty-five statements that broadly describe an individual's personality. On each scorecard, honestly indicate whether you agree or disagree that each statement applies to your personality, or to the personality of the person you are rating, when examined from a given point of view. For each item, circle the number in the left column of the scorecard if you strongly disagree with a statement, or the number in the right column if you strongly agree, or a number in between to indicate varying levels of agreement. For each item, simply circle your choice. Mark only one number per statement on each scorecard.

	Scorecard 1 — Inner Self-Image — How you see yourself inside — Do you feel that you are someone who:					Scorecard 2 — Outer Self-Image — How you think others see you — Do you believe others see you as someone who:				
	DISAGREE STRONGLY	DISAGREE A LITTLE	NEITHER AGREE NOR DISAGREE	AGREE A LITTLE	AGREE STRONGLY	DISAGREE STRONGLY	DISAGREE A LITTLE	NEITHER AGREE NOR DISAGREE	AGREE A LITTLE	AGREE STRONGLY
1. Is outgoing, sociable.	1	2	3	4	5	1	2	3	4	5
2. Tends to find fault with others.	5	4	3	2	1	5	4	3	2	1
3. Is a reliable worker.	1	2	3	4	5	1	2	3	4	5
4. Remains calm in tense situations.	5	4	3	2	1	5	4	3	2	1
5. Values artistic, aesthetic experiences.	1	2	3	4	5	1	2	3	4	5
6. Is reserved.	5	4	3	2	1	5	4	3	2	1
7. Is considerate and kind to almost everyone.	1	2	3	4	5	1	2	3	4	5
8. Can be somewhat careless.	5	4	3	2	1	5	4	3	2	1
9. Is relaxed, handles stress well.	5	4	3	2	1	5	4	3	2	1
10. Prefers work that is routine and simple.	5	4	3	2	1	5	4	3	2	1
11. Is full of energy.	1	2	3	4	5	1	2	3	4	5
12. Can be cold and aloof.	5	4	3	2	1	5	4	3	2	1
13. Does things efficiently.	1	2	3	4	5	1	2	3	4	5
14. Gets nervous easily.	1	2	3	4	5	1	2	3	4	5
15. Has an active imagination.	1	2	3	4	5	1	2	3	4	5
16. Is sometimes shy, inhibited.	5	4	3	2	1	5	4	3	2	1
17. Likes to cooperate with others.	1	2	3	4	5	1	2	3	4	5
18. Tends to be disorganized.	5	4	3	2	1	5	4	3	2	1
19. Is emotionally stable, not easily upset.	5	4	3	2	1	5	4	3	2	1
20. Has few artistic interests.	5	4	3	2	1	5	4	3	2	1
21. Is talkative.	1	2	3	4	5	1	2	3	4	5
22. Is sometimes rude to others.	5	4	3	2	1	5	4	3	2	1
23. Does a thorough job.	1	2	3	4	5	1	2	3	4	5
24. Is depressed, blue.	1	2	3	4	5	1	2	3	4	5
25. Is sophisticated in art, music, or literature.	1	2	3	4	5	1	2	3	4	5
26. Tends to be quiet.	5	4	3	2	1	5	4	3	2	1
27. Is generally trusting.	1	2	3	4	5	1	2	3	4	5
28. Is lazy at times.	5	4	3	2	1	5	4	3	2	1
29. Worries a lot.	1	2	3	4	5	1	2	3	4	5
30. Is ingenious, a deep thinker.	1	2	3	4	5	1	2	3	4	5
31. Generates a lot of enthusiasm.	1	2	3	4	5	1	2	3	4	5
32. Has a forgiving nature.	1	2	3	4	5	1	2	3	4	5
33. Is easily distracted.	5	4	3	2	1	5	4	3	2	1
34. Can be tense.	1	2	3	4	5	1	2	3	4	5
35. Is inventive.	1	2	3	4	5	1	2	3	4	5

Test 2

Scorecard 3
Unified Self-Image

How you see yourself overall

Do you agree that you are someone who:

Scorecard 4
Ideal Self-Image

How you would ideally like to be

The person you would ideally like to be is someone who:

DISAGREE STRONGLY	DISAGREE A LITTLE	NEITHER AGREE NOR DISAGREE	AGREE A LITTLE	AGREE STRONGLY	DISAGREE STRONGLY	DISAGREE A LITTLE	NEITHER AGREE NOR DISAGREE	AGREE A LITTLE	AGREE STRONGLY
1	2	3	4	5	1	2	3	4	5
5	4	3	2	1	5	4	3	2	1
1	2	3	4	5	1	2	3	4	5
5	4	3	2	1	5	4	3	2	1
1	2	3	4	5	1	2	3	4	5
5	4	3	2	1	5	4	3	2	1
1	2	3	4	5	1	2	3	4	5
5	4	3	2	1	5	4	3	2	1
5	4	3	2	1	5	4	3	2	1
5	4	3	2	1	5	4	3	2	1
1	2	3	4	5	1	2	3	4	5
5	4	3	2	1	5	4	3	2	1
1	2	3	4	5	1	2	3	4	5
1	2	3	4	5	1	2	3	4	5
1	2	3	4	5	1	2	3	4	5
5	4	3	2	1	5	4	3	2	1
1	2	3	4	5	1	2	3	4	5
5	4	3	2	1	5	4	3	2	1
5	4	3	2	1	5	4	3	2	1
5	4	3	2	1	5	4	3	2	1
1	2	3	4	5	1	2	3	4	5
5	4	3	2	1	5	4	3	2	1
1	2	3	4	5	1	2	3	4	5
1	2	3	4	5	1	2	3	4	5
1	2	3	4	5	1	2	3	4	5
5	4	3	2	1	5	4	3	2	1
1	2	3	4	5	1	2	3	4	5
5	4	3	2	1	5	4	3	2	1
1	2	3	4	5	1	2	3	4	5
1	2	3	4	5	1	2	3	4	5
1	2	3	4	5	1	2	3	4	5
1	2	3	4	5	1	2	3	4	5
5	4	3	2	1	5	4	3	2	1
1	2	3	4	5	1	2	3	4	5
1	2	3	4	5	1	2	3	4	5

Scorecard 5 *Feared Self-Image* — How you fear being — The person you fear being is someone who:						Scorecard 6 *Work Role Identity* — How you see yourself at work — Do you agree that at work you are someone who:						Scorecard 7 *Romantic Partner Role Identity* — With your spouse/a romantic partner — Do you agree that as a romantic partner you are someone who:						Scorecard 8 *Friend Role Identity* — With your friends — Do you agree that as a friend you are someone who:						Scorecard 9 *Other Role Identity* — Fill in role: — Do you agree that in this role you are someone who:				
DISAGREE STRONGLY	DISAGREE A LITTLE	NEITHER AGREE NOR DISAGREE	AGREE A LITTLE	AGREE STRONGLY		DISAGREE STRONGLY	DISAGREE A LITTLE	NEITHER AGREE NOR DISAGREE	AGREE A LITTLE	AGREE STRONGLY		DISAGREE STRONGLY	DISAGREE A LITTLE	NEITHER AGREE NOR DISAGREE	AGREE A LITTLE	AGREE STRONGLY		DISAGREE STRONGLY	DISAGREE A LITTLE	NEITHER AGREE NOR DISAGREE	AGREE A LITTLE	AGREE STRONGLY		DISAGREE STRONGLY	DISAGREE A LITTLE	NEITHER AGREE NOR DISAGREE	AGREE A LITTLE	AGREE STRONGLY
1	2	3	4	5		1	2	3	4	5		1	2	3	4	5		1	2	3	4	5		1	2	3	4	5
5	4	3	2	1		5	4	3	2	1		5	4	3	2	1		5	4	3	2	1		5	4	3	2	1
1	2	3	4	5		1	2	3	4	5		1	2	3	4	5		1	2	3	4	5		1	2	3	4	5
5	4	3	2	1		5	4	3	2	1		5	4	3	2	1		5	4	3	2	1		5	4	3	2	1
1	2	3	4	5		1	2	3	4	5		1	2	3	4	5		1	2	3	4	5		1	2	3	4	5
5	4	3	2	1		5	4	3	2	1		5	4	3	2	1		5	4	3	2	1		5	4	3	2	1
1	2	3	4	5		1	2	3	4	5		1	2	3	4	5		1	2	3	4	5		1	2	3	4	5
5	4	3	2	1		5	4	3	2	1		5	4	3	2	1		5	4	3	2	1		5	4	3	2	1
5	4	3	2	1		5	4	3	2	1		5	4	3	2	1		5	4	3	2	1		5	4	3	2	1
5	4	3	2	1		5	4	3	2	1		5	4	3	2	1		5	4	3	2	1		5	4	3	2	1
1	2	3	4	5		1	2	3	4	5		1	2	3	4	5		1	2	3	4	5		1	2	3	4	5
5	4	3	2	1		5	4	3	2	1		5	4	3	2	1		5	4	3	2	1		5	4	3	2	1
1	2	3	4	5		1	2	3	4	5		1	2	3	4	5		1	2	3	4	5		1	2	3	4	5
1	2	3	4	5		1	2	3	4	5		1	2	3	4	5		1	2	3	4	5		1	2	3	4	5
1	2	3	4	5		1	2	3	4	5		1	2	3	4	5		1	2	3	4	5		1	2	3	4	5
5	4	3	2	1		5	4	3	2	1		5	4	3	2	1		5	4	3	2	1		5	4	3	2	1
1	2	3	4	5		1	2	3	4	5		1	2	3	4	5		1	2	3	4	5		1	2	3	4	5
5	4	3	2	1		5	4	3	2	1		5	4	3	2	1		5	4	3	2	1		5	4	3	2	1
5	4	3	2	1		5	4	3	2	1		5	4	3	2	1		5	4	3	2	1		5	4	3	2	1
5	4	3	2	1		5	4	3	2	1		5	4	3	2	1		5	4	3	2	1		5	4	3	2	1
1	2	3	4	5		1	2	3	4	5		1	2	3	4	5		1	2	3	4	5		1	2	3	4	5
5	4	3	2	1		5	4	3	2	1		5	4	3	2	1		5	4	3	2	1		5	4	3	2	1
1	2	3	4	5		1	2	3	4	5		1	2	3	4	5		1	2	3	4	5		1	2	3	4	5
1	2	3	4	5		1	2	3	4	5		1	2	3	4	5		1	2	3	4	5		1	2	3	4	5
1	2	3	4	5		1	2	3	4	5		1	2	3	4	5		1	2	3	4	5		1	2	3	4	5
5	4	3	2	1		5	4	3	2	1		5	4	3	2	1		5	4	3	2	1		5	4	3	2	1
1	2	3	4	5		1	2	3	4	5		1	2	3	4	5		1	2	3	4	5		1	2	3	4	5
5	4	3	2	1		5	4	3	2	1		5	4	3	2	1		5	4	3	2	1		5	4	3	2	1
1	2	3	4	5		1	2	3	4	5		1	2	3	4	5		1	2	3	4	5		1	2	3	4	5
1	2	3	4	5		1	2	3	4	5		1	2	3	4	5		1	2	3	4	5		1	2	3	4	5
1	2	3	4	5		1	2	3	4	5		1	2	3	4	5		1	2	3	4	5		1	2	3	4	5
1	2	3	4	5		1	2	3	4	5		1	2	3	4	5		1	2	3	4	5		1	2	3	4	55
5	4	3	2	1		5	4	3	2	1		5	4	3	2	1		5	4	3	2	1		5	4	3	2	1
1	2	3	4	5		1	2	3	4	5		1	2	3	4	5		1	2	3	4	5		1	2	3	4	5
1	2	3	4	5		1	2	3	4	5		1	2	3	4	5		1	2	3	4	5		1	2	3	4	5

Test 4

Scorecard 10 *Partner A: Partner Image* — How Partner A is seen by Partner B — Do you agree that your partner is someone who:					Scorecard 11 *Partner B: Unified Self-Image* — How Partner B sees self — Do you agree that you are someone who:					Scorecard 12 *Partner B: Partner Image* — How Partner B is seen by Partner A — Do you agree that your partner is someone who:					Scorecard 13 *Reflected Image* — Rating by Coworker 1 — Do you agree that the person you are describing:					Scorecard 14 *Reflected Image* — Rating by Coworker 2 — Do you agree that the person you are describing:				
DISAGREE STRONGLY	DISAGREE A LITTLE	NEITHER AGREE NOR DISAGREE	AGREE A LITTLE	AGREE STRONGLY	DISAGREE STRONGLY	DISAGREE A LITTLE	NEITHER AGREE NOR DISAGREE	AGREE A LITTLE	AGREE STRONGLY	DISAGREE STRONGLY	DISAGREE A LITTLE	NEITHER AGREE NOR DISAGREE	AGREE A LITTLE	AGREE STRONGLY	DISAGREE STRONGLY	DISAGREE A LITTLE	NEITHER AGREE NOR DISAGREE	AGREE A LITTLE	AGREE STRONGLY	DISAGREE STRONGLY	DISAGREE A LITTLE	NEITHER AGREE NOR DISAGREE	AGREE A LITTLE	AGREE STRONGLY
1	2	3	4	5	1	2	3	4	5	1	2	3	4	5	1	2	3	4	5	1	2	3	4	5
5	4	3	2	1	5	4	3	2	1	5	4	3	2	1	5	4	3	2	1	5	4	3	2	1
1	2	3	4	5	1	2	3	4	5	1	2	3	4	5	1	2	3	4	5	1	2	3	4	5
5	4	3	2	1	5	4	3	2	1	5	4	3	2	1	5	4	3	2	1	5	4	3	2	1
1	2	3	4	5	1	2	3	4	5	1	2	3	4	5	1	2	3	4	5	1	2	3	4	5
5	4	3	2	1	5	4	3	2	1	5	4	3	2	1	5	4	3	2	1	5	4	3	2	1
1	2	3	4	5	1	2	3	4	5	1	2	3	4	5	1	2	3	4	5	1	2	3	4	5
5	4	3	2	1	5	4	3	2	1	5	4	3	2	1	5	4	3	2	1	5	4	3	2	1
5	4	3	2	1	5	4	3	2	1	5	4	3	2	1	5	4	3	2	1	5	4	3	2	1
5	4	3	2	1	5	4	3	2	1	5	4	3	2	1	5	4	3	2	1	5	4	3	2	1
1	2	3	4	5	1	2	3	4	5	1	2	3	4	5	1	2	3	4	5	1	2	3	4	5
5	4	3	2	1	5	4	3	2	1	5	4	3	2	1	5	4	3	2	1	5	4	3	2	1
1	2	3	4	5	1	2	3	4	5	1	2	3	4	5	1	2	3	4	5	1	2	3	4	5
1	2	3	4	5	1	2	3	4	5	1	2	3	4	5	1	2	3	4	5	1	2	3	4	5
1	2	3	4	5	1	2	3	4	5	1	2	3	4	5	1	2	3	4	5	1	2	3	4	5
5	4	3	2	1	5	4	3	2	1	5	4	3	2	1	5	4	3	2	1	5	4	3	2	1
1	2	3	4	5	1	2	3	4	5	1	2	3	4	5	1	2	3	4	5	1	2	3	4	5
5	4	3	2	1	5	4	3	2	1	5	4	3	2	1	5	4	3	2	1	5	4	3	2	1
5	4	3	2	1	5	4	3	2	1	5	4	3	2	1	5	4	3	2	1	5	4	3	2	1
5	4	3	2	1	5	4	3	2	1	5	4	3	2	1	5	4	3	2	1	5	4	3	2	1
1	2	3	4	5	1	2	3	4	5	1	2	3	4	5	1	2	3	4	5	1	2	3	4	5
5	4	3	2	1	5	4	3	2	1	5	4	3	2	1	5	4	3	2	1	5	4	3	2	1
1	2	3	4	5	1	2	3	4	5	1	2	3	4	5	1	2	3	4	5	1	2	3	4	5
1	2	3	4	5	1	2	3	4	5	1	2	3	4	5	1	2	3	4	5	1	2	3	4	5
1	2	3	4	5	1	2	3	4	5	1	2	3	4	5	1	2	3	4	5	1	2	3	4	5
5	4	3	2	1	5	4	3	2	1	5	4	3	2	1	5	4	3	2	1	5	4	3	2	1
1	2	3	4	5	1	2	3	4	5	1	2	3	4	5	1	2	3	4	5	1	2	3	4	5
5	4	3	2	1	5	4	3	2	1	5	4	3	2	1	5	4	3	2	1	5	4	3	2	1
1	2	3	4	5	1	2	3	4	5	1	2	3	4	5	1	2	3	4	5	1	2	3	4	5
1	2	3	4	5	1	2	3	4	5	1	2	3	4	5	1	2	3	4	5	1	2	3	4	5
1	2	3	4	5	1	2	3	4	5	1	2	3	4	5	1	2	3	4	5	1	2	3	4	5
1	2	3	4	5	1	2	3	4	5	1	2	3	4	5	1	2	3	4	5	1	2	3	4	5
5	4	3	2	1	5	4	3	2	1	5	4	3	2	1	5	4	3	2	1	5	4	3	2	1
1	2	3	4	5	1	2	3	4	5	1	2	3	4	5	1	2	3	4	5	1	2	3	4	5
1	2	3	4	5	1	2	3	4	5	1	2	3	4	5	1	2	3	4	5	1	2	3	4	5

Scorecard 15 *Reflected Image*					Scorecard 16 *Reflected Image*					Scorecard 17 *Reflected Image*					Scorecard 18 *Reflected Image*					Scorecard 19 *Past Self-Image*				
Rating by Friend 1					Rating by Friend 2					Family Member 1 Relationship:					Family Member 2 Relationship:					Past Self Label:				
Do you agree that the person you are describing:					Do you agree that the person you are describing:					Do you agree that the person you are describing:					Do you agree that the person you are describing:					Do you agree that your self past was:				
DISAGREE STRONGLY	DISAGREE A LITTLE	NEITHER AGREE NOR DISAGREE	AGREE A LITTLE	AGREE STRONGLY	DISAGREE STRONGLY	DISAGREE A LITTLE	NEITHER AGREE NOR DISAGREE	AGREE A LITTLE	AGREE STRONGLY	DISAGREE STRONGLY	DISAGREE A LITTLE	NEITHER AGREE NOR DISAGREE	AGREE A LITTLE	AGREE STRONGLY	DISAGREE STRONGLY	DISAGREE A LITTLE	NEITHER AGREE NOR DISAGREE	AGREE A LITTLE	AGREE STRONGLY	DISAGREE STRONGLY	DISAGREE A LITTLE	NEITHER AGREE NOR DISAGREE	AGREE A LITTLE	AGREE STRONGLY
1	2	3	4	5	1	2	3	4	5	1	2	3	4	5	1	2	3	4	5	1	2	3	4	5
5	4	3	2	1	5	4	3	2	1	5	4	3	2	1	5	4	3	2	1	5	4	3	2	1
1	2	3	4	5	1	2	3	4	5	1	2	3	4	5	1	2	3	4	5	1	2	3	4	5
5	4	3	2	1	5	4	3	2	1	5	4	3	2	1	5	4	3	2	1	5	4	3	2	1
1	2	3	4	5	1	2	3	4	5	1	2	3	4	5	1	2	3	4	5	1	2	3	4	5
5	4	3	2	1	5	4	3	2	1	5	4	3	2	1	5	4	3	2	1	5	4	3	2	1
1	2	3	4	5	1	2	3	4	5	1	2	3	4	5	1	2	3	4	5	1	2	3	4	5
5	4	3	2	1	5	4	3	2	1	5	4	3	2	1	5	4	3	2	1	5	4	3	2	1
5	4	3	2	1	5	4	3	2	1	5	4	3	2	1	5	4	3	2	1	5	4	3	2	1
5	4	3	2	1	5	4	3	2	1	5	4	3	2	1	5	4	3	2	1	5	4	3	2	1
1	2	3	4	5	1	2	3	4	5	1	2	3	4	5	1	2	3	4	5	1	2	3	4	5
5	4	3	2	1	5	4	3	2	1	5	4	3	2	1	5	4	3	2	1	5	4	3	2	1
1	2	3	4	5	1	2	3	4	5	1	2	3	4	5	1	2	3	4	5	1	2	3	4	5
1	2	3	4	5	1	2	3	4	5	1	2	3	4	5	1	2	3	4	5	1	2	3	4	5
1	2	3	4	5	1	2	3	4	5	1	2	3	4	5	1	2	3	4	5	1	2	3	4	5
5	4	3	2	1	5	4	3	2	1	5	4	3	2	1	5	4	3	2	1	5	4	3	2	1
1	2	3	4	5	1	2	3	4	5	1	2	3	4	5	1	2	3	4	5	1	2	3	4	5
5	4	3	2	1	5	4	3	2	1	5	4	3	2	1	5	4	3	2	1	5	4	3	2	1
5	4	3	2	1	5	4	3	2	1	5	4	3	2	1	5	4	3	2	1	5	4	3	2	1
5	4	3	2	1	5	4	3	2	1	5	4	3	2	1	5	4	3	2	1	5	4	3	2	1
1	2	3	4	5	1	2	3	4	5	1	2	3	4	5	1	2	3	4	5	1	2	3	4	5
5	4	3	2	1	5	4	3	2	1	5	4	3	2	1	5	4	3	2	1	5	4	3	2	1
1	2	3	4	5	1	2	3	4	5	1	2	3	4	5	1	2	3	4	5	1	2	3	4	5
1	2	3	4	5	1	2	3	4	5	1	2	3	4	5	1	2	3	4	5	1	2	3	4	5
1	2	3	4	5	1	2	3	4	5	1	2	3	4	5	1	2	3	4	5	1	2	3	4	5
5	4	3	2	1	5	4	3	2	1	5	4	3	2	1	5	4	3	2	1	5	4	3	2	1
1	2	3	4	5	1	2	3	4	5	1	2	3	4	5	1	2	3	4	5	1	2	3	4	5
5	4	3	2	1	5	4	3	2	1	5	4	3	2	1	5	4	3	2	1	5	4	3	2	1
1	2	3	4	5	1	2	3	4	5	1	2	3	4	5	1	2	3	4	5	1	2	3	4	5
1	2	3	4	5	1	2	3	4	5	1	2	3	4	5	1	2	3	4	5	1	2	3	4	5
1	2	3	4	5	1	2	3	4	5	1	2	3	4	5	1	2	3	4	5	1	2	3	4	5
1	2	3	4	5	1	2	3	4	5	1	2	3	4	5	1	2	3	4	5	1	2	3	4	5
5	4	3	2	1	5	4	3	2	1	5	4	3	2	1	5	4	3	2	1	5	4	3	2	1
1	2	3	4	5	1	2	3	4	5	1	2	3	4	5	1	2	3	4	5	1	2	3	4	5
1	2	3	4	5	1	2	3	4	5	1	2	3	4	5	1	2	3	4	5	1	2	3	4	5

Test 6

©2005 by Keith Harary, PhD, and Eileen Donahue Robinson, PhD

Scorecard 20 *Future Self-Image*					Scorecard 21 *Alter Ego Image*					Scorecard 22 *Extra Scorecard*					Scorecard 23 *Extra Scorecard*					Scorecard 24 *Extra Scorecard*				

Future Self Label: _____ Alter Ego Label: _____ Fill in perspective: _____ Fill in perspective: _____ Fill in perspective: _____

Do you agree that your future self will be: / Do you agree that your alter ego is: / Do you agree that the person you are describing: / Do you agree that the person you are describing: / Do you agree that the person you are describing:

Column headers (each scorecard): DISAGREE STRONGLY / DISAGREE A LITTLE / NEITHER AGREE NOR DISAGREE / AGREE A LITTLE / AGREE STRONGLY

20					21					22					23					24				
1	2	3	4	5	1	2	3	4	5	1	2	3	4	5	1	2	3	4	5	1	2	3	4	5
5	4	3	2	1	5	4	3	2	1	5	4	3	2	1	5	4	3	2	1	5	4	3	2	1
1	2	3	4	5	1	2	3	4	5	1	2	3	4	5	1	2	3	4	5	1	2	3	4	5
5	4	3	2	1	5	4	3	2	1	5	4	3	2	1	5	4	3	2	1	5	4	3	2	1
1	2	3	4	5	1	2	3	4	5	1	2	3	4	5	1	2	3	4	5	1	2	3	4	5
1	2	3	4	5	1	2	3	4	5	1	2	3	4	5	1	2	3	4	5	1	2	3	4	5
5	4	3	2	1	5	4	3	2	1	5	4	3	2	1	5	4	3	2	1	5	4	3	2	1
5	4	3	2	1	5	4	3	2	1	5	4	3	2	1	5	4	3	2	1	5	4	3	2	1
1	2	3	4	5	1	2	3	4	5	1	2	3	4	5	1	2	3	4	5	1	2	3	4	5
5	4	3	2	1	5	4	3	2	1	5	4	3	2	1	5	4	3	2	1	5	4	3	2	1
1	2	3	4	5	1	2	3	4	5	1	2	3	4	5	1	2	3	4	5	1	2	3	4	5
1	2	3	4	5	1	2	3	4	5	1	2	3	4	5	1	2	3	4	5	1	2	3	4	5
1	2	3	4	5	1	2	3	4	5	1	2	3	4	5	1	2	3	4	5	1	2	3	4	5
5	4	3	2	1	5	4	3	2	1	5	4	3	2	1	5	4	3	2	1	5	4	3	2	1
1	2	3	4	5	1	2	3	4	5	1	2	3	4	5	1	2	3	4	5	1	2	3	4	5
5	4	3	2	1	5	4	3	2	1	5	4	3	2	1	5	4	3	2	1	5	4	3	2	1
5	4	3	2	1	5	4	3	2	1	5	4	3	2	1	5	4	3	2	1	5	4	3	2	1
5	4	3	2	1	5	4	3	2	1	5	4	3	2	1	5	4	3	2	1	5	4	3	2	1
1	2	3	4	5	1	2	3	4	5	1	2	3	4	5	1	2	3	4	5	1	2	3	4	5
5	4	3	2	1	5	4	3	2	1	5	4	3	2	1	5	4	3	2	1	5	4	3	2	1
1	2	3	4	5	1	2	3	4	5	1	2	3	4	5	1	2	3	4	5	1	2	3	4	5
1	2	3	4	5	1	2	3	4	5	1	2	3	4	5	1	2	3	4	5	1	2	3	4	5
1	2	3	4	5	1	2	3	4	5	1	2	3	4	5	1	2	3	4	5	1	2	3	4	5
5	4	3	2	1	5	4	3	2	1	5	4	3	2	1	5	4	3	2	1	5	4	3	2	1
1	2	3	4	5	1	2	3	4	5	1	2	3	4	5	1	2	3	4	5	1	2	3	4	5
5	4	3	2	1	5	4	3	2	1	5	4	3	2	1	5	4	3	2	1	5	4	3	2	1
1	2	3	4	5	1	2	3	4	5	1	2	3	4	5	1	2	3	4	5	1	2	3	4	5
1	2	3	4	5	1	2	3	4	5	1	2	3	4	5	1	2	3	4	5	1	2	3	4	5
1	2	3	4	5	1	2	3	4	5	1	2	3	4	5	1	2	3	4	5	1	2	3	4	5
5	4	3	2	1	5	4	3	2	1	5	4	3	2	1	5	4	3	2	1	5	4	3	2	1
1	2	3	4	5	1	2	3	4	5	1	2	3	4	5	1	2	3	4	5	1	2	3	4	5
1	2	3	4	5	1	2	3	4	5	1	2	3	4	5	1	2	3	4	5	1	2	3	4	5

Inner/Outer Self-Image Profile

Unified Self-Image Profile

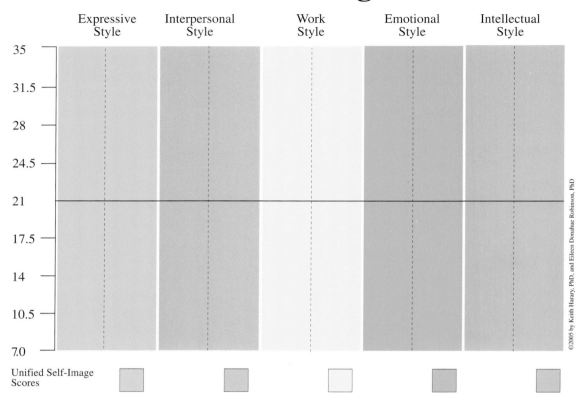

	Expressive Style	Interpersonal Style	Work Style	Emotional Style	Intellectual Style

Unified Self-Image Scores